petals, emblems

Lynn Behrendt

Lunar Chandelier

ISBN: 978-0-9846076-1-7

Lunar Chandelier Press
323 Atlantic Avenue, Brooklyn NY 11201
lunarchandelier@gmail.com

Cover photo © Lynn Behrendt
Design & typesetting by HR Hegnauer | hrhegnauer.com
Interior text typeset in Helvetica and Cochin.
Colophon designed by David Borchart.

I want to thank my dearest and most wonderful poet friends, whose
insights, feedback, talents, patience, and good cheer sustain me, and
without whom this book would not be: Vyt Bakaitis, Anne Gorrick,
Geof & Nancy Huth, Robert Kelly, Kimberly Lyons, Ron Silliman,
and Lorna Smedman.

Lunar Chandelier Press
Brooklyn, NY

Delirious Avenues
lit
with the chandelier souls
of infusoria
– Mina Loy

For Jake,

the bright spot

in all my days

Foreword

Thee thine hat is a ship called Ruth.
What is & what is & what isn't a that?
Epiphany, if any, is not lens, less not than
what the slender is broad form then seen.

What are our whos?
Where are our whats?
How exp/a/end
if not by sibyl of self?

It used to depend on red define it map—
a faux history, part prep part roach,
how the hook plex
re matters the so next now into such

exact pleural writhing—
love's contextual It.

petals, emblems

.

If This

If this were room-temperature silk, slid over cheekbone or temple. If it were gauze with which to dress wounds. If it wound itself around and around. If you found it clawed at noon in the shade, grown out of moist rock. If it burned blue & became charcoal. If it could carry your keys. Protect you from thieves. Call you Dove or Snake or Comet. If this weren't an algae-covered barge, but rather pleasantly beige, besieged by ants, without the urge to spurn decay. If this were a palsied arcane conspiracy, if it sparked a sparse heresy, and you turned to face the wall. If suddenly a yellow car appeared in the driveway, out of which stepped a small blond boy.

Marcasite

I'm nothing & can therefore never be locked up or even captured really
since I'm the absence that lies in the center of a lake
and you are a boat in bloody water.

I'm the clouds—I just coagulated—did you see that?
You're the retrograde hail that starts to fall
a mathematical migration, boyscout carrying a canteen.

You're a bridge with a flag on it, obstruction in the rock salt road
a crucified rune or rock carving—after the third or fourth sedative
I'm something small & spin-dried, a bull in a labyrinth.

I'm a cretin with icing smeared all over my face.
You're a pre-Colombian hieroglyph, your cogent arpeggio intellect still intact.
I'm marcasite, quicklime, saffron, timothy.

Om Before Daylight

It
is here
here is your
chance your
soft leather pleasure
shiver a revolving interlaced
attraction collision
like garnets
on water
the wet
fur of
a red
fox
it's
here
thunder
in the pear
shaped recess
of an ear where honey
collects and sound pools it's got
pearl-diver hands and a mouth with which
to chew this strip of pink pulp that

becomes a throbbing percussive
double-jointed serpent in the
vines that climbs its own
torrid rutting self in
equal rhythm it
spawns you
then turns
inside
out
an
ess
a snake
or euphoric
eel its spiked
heat tempered then
melting into rings and ions
that thicken the air as violet walls
become hushed and its *Om* before daylight
and your pun-pollinated brain tastes of divination
flower in full bloom moves over it like
milk in water in reverse order
parts of it sprung one into
the other a stone cast
skitters ripples
transports us
like reeds

that we

blow

in

t

o

f

l

a

m

e

The Ulna Slash Uvula
Laid Bare Lingual Age

I am a language vole too.
I got glue
in my vagina.

It's me & thee & analog glee —
lingo vogue
in isotope tetrameters.

A gal who lags is like the sun:
burned out
about a billion years ago.

But you always Gnu
who you whir,
didn't you, jellied iguana?

All gaga over ovules
a lunge lizard,
ego bun in the oven.

Why so guava spoiled?
And why me,
an innocent eel ogler?

You're one alluvial egg
you lover of lingo slag
a lovely oval lung

all agog on the avenue
with a lei draped over your stodgy navel
and lava lava everywhere.

We're slouching toward
loin of veal, darling—
It's the agile edge of lugnuts,

the ulna slash uvula laid bare Lingual Age.
So lean toward élan,
you old handsoap goalie.

Strike a velcro gavel get
to it, sticky vegetable guy
cause I'm still lost in vague village

seeking one lost glove from an alien gang
slugging Euripides syrup—
the juice of living

how long, lonely little Anglo?
I'm venial Eve hitting a gong
in a dollar store lounge

you give good gull and I'm
strung out on a gag line
with strict orders to unveil

Logic

static signal is to robe
as inlay is to rock

stork is to swamp
as is penance to spasm to tendril

upper eyelid to ashes
ashes to artifice

Slats

tree stripped of bark
moss miasma
coastal stain

lotus bowl
rope derision
forceps

chemical slipper
osmotic paste
rattle

slats
larval socket

Genre Tongs

Yet
this is
what it's
derived from:

Ten gig news tort
Genre tongs tongue-twister

Character as collage:
uber scooper pup
pydog arts fuck
ed-up version
recognizable
social aims
this is no
t it th
is is n
ot it
this
is

I'm Ugly I Love You America

I'm ugly I love you America inside its voice quivers
old allegory acetone spill April sprung

don't swallow gasoline
bury the chatter in your chest

pull up your skin
there's a car fire over there

your source is showing again
say what's what & what just juts

don't cotton to prayer swear instead
to both & bite the unread book

tucked away in murder dream
scrap of ice under the mattress

ascetic doubt so costly to remove animal
hovers the fringed rim

husband in a 2 acre kitchen fire at eleven
locust in the apple tree, rolled sleeves, ravaged ears

leave beauty for the self-conscious acrobats among us
pigs don't fly but pork can fry

because pardon my feathers I gave birth
in this patriotic absurd falcon of a hurricane

Diffraction

Was I not born in spittle? Were my parents not of this country of spotted cheetahs? From whom shall I steal unto a gripping torridity? What irrigated acres have yet to go from yellow to green on this decade's futile corner so that I should be freed from needless scraping?

Was I cutting stone or not on that dung heap I radiantly withstood until diffraction on the day my black-lung spine flowed down and cubit-braced sham overturned?

You may think yourself into a city-state of ambulatory remorse but would you do so in a burning ship such as this? Or might you instead just run like hell?

Have you yet cornered your wandering appaloosa foal in order to spice your zigzag bunting?

Worm holes dent the big orb but did you say elder? Nothing is oval until we decide it is. Was it you, Pink Pussycat?

Why do you continually ask me why I fuck or barf on the so-called infrastructure?

Nothing ever bothers you! All you care about is your own measure! Suppose you wake up some morning and find sister rat cut our veins at night, leaving only a note: "If you cut off my reproductive choice, can I cut off yours?"

Your Way Back

This knot
of trees.

Koan demo
erosion.

A squirrel skitters
cross an attic beam.

There — the scent of fresh blacktop
& orange juice.

A little hand
reaches up:

Can you find
your way back?

Hibiscus

Your lips are hibiscus sugar on a frilly lizard's wing. Your form's lovely, like frog spit in a dry season: an edible root, scrub hen, round yam, ibis, paperbark, or white berries eaten by a blind magpie goose. Everything about you is a night orchid.

I've got one arm in the cold creek up to my elbow and my foot sinks into the sand composed of centipedes, semen, & guts. So it is only right that you should listen.

In the gum tree with your name carved in it there's a bluetongue lizard that stares out at us, & peers also into my sleep, as if he *knows* this idea of you, permanently housed now inside my glass liver like a whistling duck, Old Man, as if he *knows* the secret black fruit and words that Little Sister taught you, who in turn, taught me.

Often I Am Permitted to Return to a Ghetto

What is it that you cannot bear?
Is it beauty? Something in bed?
To do with beetles?
A beehive, or embryo?

Perhaps pictures of tadpoles & apricots
on an aqua tablecloth in Rockland—
a talisman, no doubt:
talk tall & carry a turtle.

Often I am permitted to return to a ghetto
where nauseous geese bray & swarm
above a herniated ganglia of jagged streets

and I think of Shelley on that last boat.

Next to Nothing

Reflexive nebulous arbitrary molecules
made ugly through use or misuse

baryonic marginalia suspended
then reasonably rounded off
as next to nothing we're

a repetitive collection of
tiny gadgets doled out,
interchangeable
bones, spleens
nostril hairs
a swathe
of air
be
t
w
e
e
n

Wrong Bed Jaw Red

wrong
bed

jaw
red

mechanomorphic opium in a jar of foul-smelling mind revelling in the
unmixed mercurial dung-eating ballroom dance of it all

florid bees
hive the swarm

personal
or animal?

parts of a whole wall narrow embrace segmented unsuitable factions
where unlikely immersion seems a moderate crop woven & feudal

an I, an organism
an error, an event

small city vivisection of a shop-girl named Lent such dainty migraine
the timid fish mimicry and splintered dogma dedicated to effluvium of
Baroque possibility

molt from animate matter
to dwarfed tissue

this my yoke
panel & frame

This my vertical body

ALL

Do you feel a blue metal bucket with the word ALL printed in yellow letters inside you? Can you enter the hologram of a barn with carpenter bees just as you start to fall asleep? Do you perhaps have small diagrams deeply embossed onto telephone poles, then miniaturized, and plunged deep into the muscles of your neck and shoulder?

Do animals bite from the inside out near the bottom of your left breast? Is there the hissing sound of steam heat all along the back corridor of your skull?

Are there endlessly complex buildings connected by walkways and halls with closets, trap-doors, and built-ins? Is there a pantry in you, as well, big enough to sleep in?

Do you recognize that magnet inside your ribcage? Is it shaped like a checker with a King's carved crown on top?

Building in the Background

You always say that, and in the background a building. A building.
There's a building in the background. A brick building in the
background and a building in the back. There's a building in the
background. A building. You build a building in the background and
in the foreground a walkway. In the foreground in back. You build a
walkway out of stone in the foreground in front of the house and in back
of the building. You remember. A building. There's a building in the
background. There. In the back. There's a building. There's a building in
the background and in the building a building and behind that building
another building in the background behind that. There's a building in
the background. Insouciant climbing vines. Slate roof.

Idioms 1 & 2

1.

I hereby give notice of my intention:
we'll cross that road when I eat my hat.
Meanwhile got a bone to pick a number any number with.
So if at first you don't have a nickel for every time it ain't broke
get out of the kitchen & and take your lemons with you.
If you fly with crows (pardon my French) —
you'll be in a fog-fixed heartbeat
before you know it tight spot
in all honesty a jam or jiffy,
pickle in a rut in an instant cold blood
like Flynn or error message
in one ear and over your head
in so many words in stitches tandem black
cards the way it crumbles if you walk through a ballpark at night
something's bound to occur in a not doghouse-bound way.
A hole in the face of a hot lap long run, first
you'll lurch the pink pipeline bank account
running on same empty bowl of soup.
Just keep swimming.

In the twinkling of two minds
DNA's no longer a question,
just a velvet fist with fingers in the fire.
It's not over until the fat lady asks,
"how much do I owe you?"
an arm and a leg, amputated,
the earth *pours*.
It takes a tango, Jane Doe
crying over spilt Jekyll & Mr. Hydes
as if memory were executioner
mere jury of frog jugglers
so we jump in with both feet
down a shark's shadowy throat,
desert silence just around the corner
& it's nine o'clock any second now.

2.

This chain link short dollar is a bit much.
A fool at 40 parts his giddy-up on a lick and promise compromise
but I'll tell you what a little bird learned:
a little electronics is a dangerous thing.
It's a long row of weeds to hoe in order to find that lost call.
Here's a penny for your I'm A-okay You're A-okay thoughtless sentiments anyway.
A picture poor man's quite something other than perfect
slice off the old stern
abject lesson that never boils
seems to abide as if by absence makes the tumor grow fonder.
Aces fall out of holes in your sleeves
like acid poured on Achilles' heel
to fuel the fire against clock
but before you know it beauty
becomes cock agony
the dirty laundry that later you'll wear
like an albatross alive and kicking in a pod with no bite.
Do you hear that barking?
It's all in your head—
modified pros and cons,
an I for an I in 20th century trousers.
All roads lead to skin and bone, dear.

It's time for tea in China
so get ready, get set—shop!
Hey are those ants in your pants
or are you just happy to be my port in a storm?
Any rule is cold as stone and as you sow
so shall you fall asleep at the switch.
At the drop of a dime your ends loosen
you comply at arms length with God knows what
kind of snail's pace cross-purpose
and at the end of the day you're the rope they tether
shouting at the top of your back-to-back salt mine babe in arms.

Door

He will absorb and appear in atmospheric windows—a single
bandwidth of coherent, temperate, sound. You will recognize the dialect
when you hear it, a doppler effect emission of what was once his voice,
in its infrared return. It will even look like him—gray outline of a
body against jittery, irradiated light. And since he loved you so, some
quantum radiance might escape his veins, and you can follow that light
on your way home, hear its white noise nearing like a siren as you wait
in your scattered oblique attenuated arc of a doorway.

Obey Each Prism

Obey each
seasonal trap
its sure street in situ
orgasmic scintilla switch
swollen delta lintel
vertical pissoire
sigmund vichyssoise
molten convection
tectonic & gear-shaped
incredulous cranial
Belgian-like hoity toit
indelible Dupont fondu
in expericode kink
with furzy granite pompoms
strum tripe flu churn
stinky clot burr
intermittent oozer
shoot-meter turned tangible
lap-sit breaker slant
blow scent faucet
every prism portal
to shudder
glisten
cull

Dreams

A turtle bites your ear. Huge tree falls between two houses, neither damaged. Cat in a sunlit painting becomes a crow, flies out of the painting, lands on your shoulder. Tire tracks. White cat. Baby that didn't grow. Glass in a field. A red birthday box with yellow bow. Child's face full of blood. Machinery. Deer. Dust & ink. Wet suitcases & snow. Lawn ornaments. Ordinary Lhasa Apso dog that lives in the hospital. Library with nothing in it but a miniature shadow box in which tiny silver people wash tiny silver clothes. Several Edward Hopper figures on a porch, not looking at one another, all facing the same direction. Strangely large rooms occupied by spiders that burrow under the skin. You're running with him, running & running, & then he's gone. A screwdriver drags deep across the perfect red finish of a sports car. You find Father Kafka, his long lost helmet, while Keebler elves grow corn inside your body.

14th Blackbird

Suffer pure

&

form follows.

This yearning's not shelter,
loyal only to calamity,
or colloidal underspirits
mood, a salve, tyrannical rosin,
bivalve dragged into morning
then pried open.

Not a Russian doll in a loaner limo
entropic code unraveled
by an enamored oarsman
snared raving soiled
trapped in a tiny little room
& mired in really lame rhyme

rubbed raw in vines
lesions nails roe lilies ore
a road rash map
or slab of meat rinsed clean

public collision the glittery
narrow well-dressed machine.

There are two of you:
one soft-boiled
the other annihilates
deeply concave
& torn to shreds —
the insistent, unbound
hard, thorny need
of a seamstress, say,
or monkfish
some fisherman snagged.

❖

You've a problem with "perhaps,"
a place dwarfed by gnawing.
You've petals, emblems,
an arbitrary bank of snow
and white blood cell latticework,
just ulcerated copycat.

❖

It occurs in accidental black —
the rancid skeleton of a whale

ribs caved in
where someday birds nest

❖

It happens in spore
flute sweater sewer
overhead doors
under a streetlamp
covalent mange
in turnstiles static & wet
vibrates at first then blurs.

Should one sit zazen near a wide open window?

❖

Here is a diagram:
inward arch of nostalgic ocean
tick-infested calla
torpor-girded stave
in A-flat minor.

❖

You dream an egret,
half-dead, lands
on a peak of rock
& algae in a shivering fit
becomes resin from turpentine trees,
a pudding out of which acrobats leap
silt bodies
just fortune telling slits
clove-scented compartments.
You crave form like alms
an animal with both lungs & gills
you sense shadow breathe light
bees swarm in your lungs
and you say things
by stating
that you will not say them.

❖

You're incorporeal also
in sibilant pursuit
a deranged passenger
ragged edge of paper
unleavened & lost

you sift through the debris
still you can't see
where you're going
kernel of anarchy
in each esoteric event
a somehow removed she-psalm statue
with stung thorn blue diction
coniferous stench
glandular nozzle
a shadow pressed & hung on a hook
or late singsong doorbell
summer fever
garnets, barley
spontaneous generation
after generation
air sensate gamete
coral cyanide tissue hallucination
hysterical jaundice
jigsaw-cut ore myth
transverse narwhal
division by sperm
abnormal heat spike
how hairs must feel
as they grow.

❖

Things scatter —
let them.

Gray branches
geese
incipient yellow sky.

Have pity on your brain that keeps you company.

❖

This object anarchy
textbook vaccine
gold fillet of dawn

is formed from below
name not given
fossil of a human hand.

Goodbye, sweet sycamore
my non-reactive baby
smile, smile, at the source of acute leaving.

❖

Am I or am I not
autotelic
trumpetvine slack hem
coiled knobby tempest
raised ridge of skin
where the pin once dragged?

Is this low tide antithesis
fixed flock
threshed landscape
or just thirty second swoon?

Dip into a more scattered pitch
Lookie there yonder, you sob
the deep anguish an opulent
uninhabited chasm.

❖

Be lapse without discord
bare-faced rapture
merciless sincerity
without tools
vigilant & idiotic
bitter lust experiment
of a test moth

Run, little flower, run!

Be a culture burden
fixed counterfeit veil
accidental innovation occurrence
choice dust
spoiled & obscene
a withered redemptive error

Help me, small lamp!

Be the egotistic sun
wretched prick of anxiety,
perpetually almost-exposed pussy

archaic tumor welkin extract

saddle-brown pear

swiveled rim

textured we

pink cardigan

Be innate

the daily sublime walk uphill

tongue-wound time tress

genre-woven

pliant & bound

carved pattern on a door

swollen joint ass winch

squall of willow

twilled augur

C-sharp hammer

scarlet bale

sprained storm-sack

machine rot pipe rune

innocent fallacious timber

seeped quarrelsome river

a cog in a column of not knowing

Be unseeded hood indigo keel pretense rib
heavy gyn grief cress
barbed star
feathery vein
stone tongue liver
lingu lang lith liber
memor meter measured morph
form mort fool
nym onym
pneu polis
port psych
sol scrib sens
reg rupt
spect
spond
temp
terr
vert
via
keen pitch
or lethal catalepsy
wear sloth like a bandage
wound round the 14th blackbird
that never should have flown anyway.

Luminous Flux

I irrigate.
my musk lasts forty days.
I'm a curve by which a circle may be squared.
I've arches, columns
artillery split into four leaves
a wood-burned eccentricity
tranquil quince on forehead
oiled extinct lock of hair
crosspiece mnemonic device
salient cornerstone
scarred Madagascar
edge molten iron
stalk anecdote
root-like organ
sensitive to radiation
with chaffed froggy hind legs
what kind of pony am I anyway
do you like rapture erasure buttercups
& what's with the drumming
confused mastery
meal in a monastery
tidal reflexes that refract to withstand fire

salt-bearing waterproof stucco or weak twig

made of silk not naïve not shroud

it's sobbing then hiccups

bandaged spleen & spiral breathing

planks, sponges, sea-onion at dusk squints

an iced over heraldic animal profile

with head toward river

seized a bunch of stalwart grapes

family tree with spots

hypnotic sculpture of a life-size orifice you can walk through

spare wheel excremental vision

fee levied like a hymn

me no sing me no sing

ship moves backward

pick up a book at random

it's one drop of stigma and a whole lot of caste

the mine in the folktale

street that runs full round the earth

constricted haughty mewling of kittens

militarily strategic aversion to

noisy mirror disorder

template of sound scraping cross an owl-streaked sky

I've got my scythe and I'm not afraid to use it

put this in your choke weed persuasion pipe

and smoke the somber pubic sudden

shift to tropical city, sound of hooves

bass soloist finishes a note
sap-producing suckling pig turned on a spit
black and blue sheep jump over a fence
yellow silt at the edge
strapped to propagation ritual
& up to ankles in mud
depressed meadow provisions low
then flannel-like rustling and whispers
Look what I found—it looks
just like an eyeball
with a perfect eyelid over it
seek symmetry not symbiotic
measure not mortar
symptom of emancipation
sudden diphthongal impulses
two flowers emitting vowels
nouns sewn all along the edge
ecclesiastic syphilitic citizens
melted tabernacle
apron wrapped around
silent link to survey points
nascent tachometer
splattered spoken element
buried not crested
stiff upper lip don't fib
trial and error yew trees for sale

in a black tarry underworld
stone tool structural torch
earthquake in the semaphore system
seismic ripples
roiled quandary
winged, on all fours
god the donkey in a coated capsule
3x a day with water
don't forget your headgear
an all-purpose telepathy
just temporarily sheathed
a face for everything
and everything in your face
so lick my nipples
I believe in skin
not marriage
in savage love

❖

I am no accidental person or thing
I separate diaphanous from syndrome
inflate lungs
in the corner of your eye
an aerial fixed sum
with divine need

to divide

hunted from hunter

eagle-eyed ethics

from consonant baptism

coquettish after-effect of water on forehead

I fear and long for

open spaces

zero gravity

disfigured animals in fields

rows and rows of corn and surnames

in a stringy barbed pasture

jeweled spray of water

a wing for balance

lost in membranous vision

funereal sour ale in a leather bag

it's cold here cold remember

the violet shoreline's

reddish honeycomb glow

like a dead mouse left on an altar

or aluminum dust nestled in a pulpit

cupboard or niche of being

here now yet gone it burns

a spawned anesthetized

sundial in bas-relief

the convalescent science of cannibals

extreme unction pitch system

belligerent seizure
censured unequal
blind inscription on a thickening wall
& the measured sentence that leads us
there. Who'll take my hand
and lead me when I don't
know who I am anymore
& start craving sweets
linseed oil chattering
scent of human entrails
omega horseshoe
tossed into the allness
and my how they howl
the legally competent then dead
their wavy memories rise like heat
a tedious milky-white iridescence
an urban liniment
stormy mouth pawn
orchid ordeal
liturgical headline
if you don't wake up if you don't
watch things circle
learn to spell, learn to spell
practice cockroach-like survival against all odds
observe osprey then slip into the ozone
I a spangle a jury a spade-shaped gymnasium

wanly vibrate am winking at you
give pussy some milk
prepare an all-night vigil near my vagina
I'm not minor I'm not minor I'm not nothing
drugged in the back room
papilla drawn on paper
verily my dried buffalo skin
performs coitus with just the thought of you
a tingling sensation doctrine
lump of something in the throat
it's dangerous, isn't it sister, dangerous
but I want to eat strange foods
and not even ask what they are
perform pathopoeia on what used to be
lumbered, embezzling
your gallows lousy with verbs

❖

Am I coarse linen?
Harangued form?
Harpoon or sharp dog?
Am I to plunder?
Do you cook words like animal entrails
then serve them, kneeling, on a cushion in church?
Are you spear-shaped & plunged?

Does a long chain mail coat clang around your ankles?
Why is everything covered in petty Socratic white questions?
Why hang a series of vertical cords, ethical decorations, ulcerous doubt?
Do you think pleasure just a coincidence?
A little toy plane circling?
A twisted branch scratching at your window?
Could anyone wade through this thought-infested marsh?
Can you? Am I supposed to screw
whatever it is you worship & fear?
Is this an instrument for counting or something?
What calendar is one supposed to use or be, anyway?
Don't you know everything about me grows like a weed and always has?
Can you hear the self-pollination?
Am I mold? Do I creep?
An amphibian sloping into a swamp
with yesterday's news printed on its head in 3 point type?
Why do you bristle?
Don't you love my tomb
I mean temple
my variable body inflected torso
wave frequency of undaunted desire?
Is this hip-thrust hierogram
hinged on everything that's happened?
Do you not love my corruption and scheming?
Do you not find my peevish pink nipples pleasing?
Do you not yearn to lick my stinky armpits

stroke my coarse shaggy hair

and swallow the pus of my scarred vagina?

Are you totally clamped shut?

Irrevocably soldered?

Are your eyes on a text or a ceiling?

How much longer is this question?

Is it even shaped like a human?

Is it hobbled in a field?

Did you bring a saw?

What have you seen?

Should we bury something?

Did you bring your urn?

Have I earned this somehow?

Why this glass in my chest?

Will you touch me now, even as I cry?

Will you touch me now?

❖

Some inherent

need to swallow

to drink in

I've got an ache between my ribs

between my legs

I flow

in two directions

an endless conversation
walled between skin & branches
What penetrates? Is it the truth?
Is it to cast shade upon?
To rub a loved thing with ointment
doesn't seem wrong
I want some peace inside
the place that can't be pried open
by crowbar or corkscrew
I want something irrigated after all
some soothing water & sky
a not derisive equality
blind to interval
point of radiation dip
or magnetic reasoning.
Privilege isn't geographic
nor lust source-annotated.
Say I'm wearing a loud orange dress
say I am sluggish and armed.
Could I be like dark sugar?
Shutter with slats?
Say you are a wheel
a wave emission
jazz on a hill or horse of a different lamentation
then ordinary and exhausted
you taste this early pear

half in, half out and sort of hoisted,
pinned maybe, unlucky, not sure really
could be shuffling behind in bound feet or burka
but instead take 2 Tylenol PM tablets
wait to feel them placed on tongue
like a thin sweet cake
one can chew until morning
starts in the chest
like an old scar
empty space beneath a pillow
it starts with this ache to tell you something
and the purpose of telling is to connect
and it seems to me—not sure why—
that to connect I need you closer.
so I kind of sink the letter *L*
into the concrete of your ever-changing memory
though I would rather put something on your plate
that you like to eat
and speak
in a clear, calm tone.
Can you see through into the storage space
between neck and belly?
Will it always feel this full?
Gulls, larva, tired larynx
I am trying to tell you something
but can't get my lens right,

gray smoky words you don't really see
a *K* for karmic disaster
or *A* for you know what
or is it just the *L*
I've always known—
verbal turtle in luminous flux
to and fro fraught and tumbled
a ship passes under a bridge.

petals, emblems

Afterword

wheel of
unconstruable
beginning.

spoke

not a place
not a process
that I am

just this,
these words —
that *anything* is

barrage
of having been
born at all.

my body's *here* —
I didn't leave it
on a hill somewhere

it's right
here
?

then gone
thus
going

(your hand in me
when you aren't
even here)

thus gone
such
as it

petals, emblems

is

always
changing
(such as

the way
you look
right before

you fall
asleep)
that *thatness*,

what I
wanted to say,
instead of this

WHISKEY ISLAND

WHISKEY ISLAND

A MILAN JACOVICH MYSTERY

LES ROBERTS

GRAY & COMPANY, PUBLISHERS
CLEVELAND

Gray & Company, Publishers
www.grayco.com

Library of Congress Cataloging-in-Publication Data
Roberts, Les
Whiskey island : a Milan Jacovich mystery / Les Roberts.
p. cm.
1. Jacovich, Milan (Fictitious character)—Fiction. 2. Pri-
vate investigators—Ohio—Cleveland—Fiction. I. Title.
PS3568.O23894W49 2012
813'.54—dc23
2012023011

ISBN 978-1-938441-39-4

Printed in the United States of America

1

To the Memory of Figaro Albin.
And to Holly and Irene Albin,
who loved him so much.

WHISKEY
ISLAND

PROLOGUE

MILAN

I think I've lived long enough to figure it out: Everybody is in one way or another corrupt.

Maybe they got a little too much change back from a supermarket cashier and quietly pocketed it without comment. Maybe in school they copied answers from another kid's paper—or shoplifted a comic book or a candy bar from the local store. Maybe they cheated on their income tax. Perhaps they took sexual advantage of someone, leading them on while knowing all along it would only be a one-night stand. And they've all driven faster than the speed limit just to save a little time. (Oh, come on—you *know* this one, at least, is you.)

It gets worse, of course. Take bribery, for example. That can start small, too, but it can wind up big—in the thousands or even millions. Burglary. Picking pockets. Armed robbery. Rape. Abuse. Cruelty to animals. Cruelty to women. Cruelty to children.

And then, of course, there's murder.

The small-timers—the ones who smoke too much weed, eat too many Big Macs with cheese and fries, the ones who speak out against those closed minds who truly believe their opinions are the only opinions and everyone else is criminal—those are the ones who get nailed. Those who commit bigger crimes are more likely to skate because they're rich or powerful or important. They get away with it.

Does that sound cynical? I don't know. Do you ever read anything in the newspapers besides sports scores?

I prefer to hang out with the people who give back their too-much change, but that's not easy for a private investigator. While I built my business some thirty years ago as an industrial security specialist—it says *Milan Security* on my business card—too often I've wound up chasing down and punishing real criminals. I've been hurt doing that—too many times. I'm tired of pain, tired of crime and criminals, and I wish I could quit. But I'm too old to get a regular job, and I don't know how to do anything else.

Cleveland, where I've lived all my life, is a blue-collar town, and I'm a blue-collar guy. My parents were born in Ljubljana, Slovenia, and I grew up in the Saint Clair–Superior corridor on the east side. I attended Kent State for both a bachelor's and a master's degree, but it was too long ago for me to do anything with those diplomas now. I was a Cleveland cop, but I never liked the regimen and the rules, so I quit and went private.

Corrupt people just seem to find me, as they did recently— only days after I barely escaped with my life solving the last stink bomb escapade. An indicted and practically convicted crooked politician asked me for help. By the time I finished, I was up to my neck in government corruption at both the city and the county levels. The city government was mad at me, the county govern- ment wanted my head on a pole, and the federal government, which I've tried to avoid, was once more very put out with me.

And, oh yes—there's murder in the mix.

What follows, then, is pretty much how it happened . . .

CHAPTER ONE

MILAN

Waiting for a new client who's half an hour late arriving for his first appointment gets on my last nerve.

That's because the wait-ee believes he's a hell of a lot more important than everyone else and thinks he must be waited for. It doesn't matter what type of business one conducts, but it's especially exasperating for me because, as a private investigator, I make my money on the clock.

On this particular morning I was expecting my tardy visitor, Berton K. Loftus. He's a long-time Cleveland city councilman from the 22nd ward, and I can't even count how many times he's been re-elected. He'd promised to be in my office at eleven o'clock—but he was a no-show at eleven twenty-five, and the clock resolutely ticked away.

I hadn't bought a desk and chair yet for my new employee, Kevin O'Bannion, although there was a phone connection in the corner he would eventually occupy. I'd only known him for a few weeks and had actually hired him less than twenty-four hours earlier, so now he was hanging out by the floor-to-ceiling windows in my office, open to catch the summer breeze. He looked out at the Cuyahoga River flowing past the building toward Lake Erie, and across to the two back-to-back venues midtown where the Cleveland Indians and Cleveland Cavaliers play. The Indians were on a western road trip, and the Cavs don't play basketball in August, but it was a great view nonetheless. Kevin—he prefers being called K.O., which has nothing to do with his impressive fighting ability—had been working part-time for a colleague and good friend, Suzanne Davis, a P.I. in Lake County, who suggested I employ him and teach him the ropes. It had taken me awhile to decide.

I'm getting older, as are we all, and an assistant could help me out when my cases get complicated—and they usually do. Also, I get headaches often, having been hit in the head a few times too many. K.O. turned up at the right time, wandering into my most recent investigation to save my ass. So Suzanne Davis talked me into putting him on full-time, at least until he earns enough working hours to secure his own private investigator license. He's just a kid, but he's very smart and tougher than hell. On this morning he'd dressed up a little—sports jacket and pressed slacks—to mark his first meeting with a client—but Loftus was late and the day was beginning badly.

"Are we going to spend forever waiting for this dick?" K.O. groused. "I thought you were running a business."

I shrugged. "He'll spend money with us, so we wait politely until he shows up. Bert Loftus isn't someone to be jerked around, even if he deserves it."

Those who know Bert Loftus—anyone who lives in Greater Cleveland—recognize him immediately. A bluff man with short, gunmetal-gray hair, Hugo Boss suits, and a huge selection of out-of-date bow ties, he walks ramrod straight, nodding royally to his constituents but rarely acting cordial to them, his personal magnetism convincing them how important he is. When you're a Cleveland councilman, people tend to take you seriously. I had to the day before, when he phoned and said someone was trying to kill him.

The local press had already murdered his reputation. After a long, drawn out investigation—the usual M.O. for the Federal Bureau of Investigation, which crosses every *T* and takes forever—he was indicted in federal court on thirty-one counts of accepting bribes and kickbacks from local businessmen who courted him for contracts to make them all richer, and the *Plain Dealer* and the local radio and TV newscasters reported his every malfeasance with relish. Even those fiercely loyal to his political party—approximately three-quarters of city voters—screwed up their noses when anyone mentioned his name now because his repute stank to high heaven. But no one deserves to die violently, so when he asked for my help, I set up his appointment for eleven o'clock. His tardiness might be a clue that he wasn't in as much danger as he professed.

He finally arrived without his usual driver, who, along with his secretary, his aide, his cadre of lickspittles, and anyone else who jumped when he told them to, earned his salary from us tax-payers. He entered Milan Security alone, egotistical as usual, but he'd chucked the bow tie somewhere, today sporting a dress shirt with an open collar beneath his almost-gold suit. The last time I saw anyone wearing sunglasses as enormous as his, they rested on the nose of Jackie Kennedy Onassis.

Either he'd spent time at the beach or basked in a suntan par-lor, because he glowed golden, blending into his suit. The skin around his neck was loose and wobbly, nearly a wattle. He took off his sunglasses to reveal a web of wrinkles at the corners of his eyes, matching the creases on his lips. Bert Loftus was growing old, whether he admitted it or not.

Me too.

He skulked in like a bad actor in a melodrama, tendering me a dead-fish handshake and bestowing on K.O. somewhat less than that when I introduced them. Then he perched on the edge of a chair as if the smallest sound would send him flying away—like a bird on a power wire. My first-floor tenants ran a busy shop in which they constructed wrought-iron gates and screens and window guards that were really decorative bars, like in an upscale jail, and their banging seemed to bother Bert Loftus.

"Milan, I appreciate your seeing me on such short notice," he said, nodding his head for no discernible reason. His fingers dug into his pants legs, nervously kneading bread dough on his lap. He said my first name correctly—it's *MY*-lan, but his use of my surname sounded too familiar, considering we'd never had a con-versation before. It's pronounced *YOCK*-o-vitch but spelled the Slovenian way, *Jacovich*.

"Not so short," I said, looking at my watch and making no ef-fort to disguise my annoyance. "You're late, Councilman."

"Bert," he corrected me as he'd done on the phone the day be-fore. "Call me Bert. I couldn't just drive here openly. I might be followed. I've been tailed for two weeks now." He seemed fearful, as though monsters of his nightmares lurked in every shadowy corner. "So I drove around, turning where I shouldn't have, going down twisty streets—and I eluded my tail, because here I am."

"No one's driving around out there," K.O. said, jerking a finger toward the window. "You're okay."

"Whew," Loftus said. Maybe he learned that word from a dialogue balloon in a comic book. He settled into his chair, breathing deeply. "Where should I start?"

"You asked for this meeting. We're listening."

He cleared his throat as though about to deliver a speech in council chambers. Then he frowned, listening to the noise from downstairs. "What the hell are they doing down there, anyway?"

"Making a living," I said, "like I'm trying to do up here."

Loftus frowned, then shifted in his chair. "Oh, well . . . Listen, Milan, I guess you know what's been going on with me and the federal government."

K.O. said, "Why don't you start with that?"

Loftus looked at him, annoyed. "Don't you read the newspapers?"

K.O.'s eyes got small and squinty. I but could already recognize a squint as a dead giveaway that he was pissed off. "I live in Lake County."

"Jesus!" Loftus caught K.O.'s sarcasm and glared at him. Now we were *all* mad for various reasons. But Loftus had been across the street a few times and knew when to blow his top and when to calm down. Finally he said, "I've been indicted for accepting bribes." Loftus wriggled in his chair, unused to being questioned. "Oh—different things. Campaign contributions, remodeling work on my homes, business people looking for government contracts."

K.O.'s eyes opened wide when he heard the plural of "home." Loftus lived in one of Cleveland's better sections, and he kept a Florida vacation home on Sanibel Island—a very expensive piece of real estate—and a condo in the Short North in Columbus.

"Also, gifts from friends," Loftus admitted. "Football tickets, free dinners, that kind of thing. And trips. Plane tickets, hotel rooms, to New York sometimes—or Florida or Vegas."

"Does that include the Las Vegas hookers?" K.O. said, moving from the window over to where Loftus sat. He was more aggressive than I'd expected, and he *did* follow the news—he knew about the councilman's extramarital activities. I assumed K.O. was more of a puncher than an inquisitor. "Or just the ones you spend time with in an apartment in the Warehouse District?"

That was one jab too many, and Loftus drew himself as tall as he could, ridiculous considering he was sitting down. "How *dare* you say that to me? Who do you think you are?"

"I'm like everyone else," K.O. said, "who watches the local news."

"Well, fuck you!"

"Hey," I said, trying to soothe. "Let's not get pissy."

Loftus pointed what he presumed to be the finger of God at K.O. "Tell him to watch his mouth."

K.O. backed off a few steps and jammed his hands into his pockets.

"Bert," I said, "you can turn blue trying to deny what you've done already, but nobody believes you. Your lawyers can take the sting away, but that's not my job. You're here because somebody's trying to kill you?"

"Of *course* that's why I'm here. I've never been threatened before. Everybody loves me, everybody kisses my ass," He said, lifting his head proudly. "They treat me like I'm Jesus of Nazareth."

"Well, it's almost time for the crucifixion."

"Huh?"

"Everybody *used* to kiss your ass, Bert. Now they just want a piece of it."

Now he looked sad. "You disapprove of me, don't you?"

"Not really. I just don't live in your world."

"I do favors for people who do favors for me—and you run around shooting people or beating them up. No, you don't live in my world, and I sure as hell couldn't live in yours."

I leaned forward, elbows on the desk. "That remains to be seen. Why haven't you told your lawyer to hire me? That way we'd have attorney-client privilege, and I won't have to answer to anybody."

"My lawyer? Fuck him in the ass—he let me get indicted and hardly lifted a goddamn finger! So now he only knows what I want to tell him—and I don't want him spreading all this around."

"That's your call, Bert. Tell your lawyer whatever you want. But if you want us to work for you, we have to know everything. And I mean *everything!* So now—about these murder attempts . . ."

Loftus crossed his arms in front of him, defensive, almost sulky, and breathed hard for about twenty seconds.

"How do you know someone's trying to kill you?" I said.

"Things have been happening, and I'm getting scared. It causes me—uh—undefinable tension."

Undefinable tension. Holy crap. I took out a yellow pad. "What kinds of things?"

"The first time," Loftus said, "was about three weeks ago. I'd met a friend out at Bass Lake Tavern in Chardon for dinner. We stayed for quite some time, as it was dark by the time we left."

"You were drinking?"

"Not excessively. A few drinks—I didn't really count them."

K.O. said, "Who was the friend?"

"Excuse me?"

"You said you met a friend for dinner. Who was the friend?"

Loftus sniffed angrily. "That's hardly pertinent."

"We'll decide what's pertinent," I said.

"Oh. Um—her name is Dolores Deluke. She lives in Chardon, so it was convenient to meet at the Bass Lake Tavern."

K.O. stifled a snicker, but not very well. "Dolores Deluke. You have that written down, Milan?"

I waved the pen at him. "She was in the car with you?"

Loftus said, "No, we each arrived in our own car."

"And after dinner—and drinks—you were heading back to her place?"

"For a nightcap?" K.O.'s eyes were innocently wide.

"What the fuck's the difference where I was heading?" Loftus snapped.

I was weary of calming things down. "Get to what happened."

Reluctantly: "So all of a sudden there's some kind of pickup truck coming up behind me, fast as hell. It banged my rear bumper hard enough to jar my brain. Then it zoomed over next to me on the driver's side—and nudged me hard. I fought the wheel but I lost control, and I went off the side of the road and into a ditch."

I nodded. I'd been the victim in a very similar Lake County

road assault only a few days earlier, and I was currently driving a rented car—a Kia—while my Honda was being repaired. "You look okay," I said. "Were you hurt?"

"Just shook up. Bruised my elbow and my thigh—on the steering wheel." He gently tapped where he was talking about. "It scared the crap out of me."

"Did the truck stop or slow down?"

"I was too concerned about my own ass to even look."

"What did the police have to say about it?"

Loftus reached up to his throat to straighten the bow tie that wasn't there. Feeling foolish, he scratched his neck instead and then let his fluttering hand fall back into his lap. "I didn't report it to the police."

"Why not?"

Loftus studied his well-shined shoes. "I didn't want this getting out, y' know? Because of—my current problems."

"Bert," I said, "everyone knows about your problems. Why keep this a secret?"

He half-closed his eyes. "Personal reasons."

"If you're going to keep secrets from us, we won't take your case. I don't like working blindfolded."

"It'll stir up more shit than there is already, and I can't take much more of it."

I considered it. "Okay—for now. What about your car? Is it totaled?"

Loftus shook his head definitively. "A friend of mine owns a body shop—Deuce Auto Body. He fixed the damage for me— quietly."

"What kind of car do you drive?"

"A Lincoln Town Car. Leased."

"Did you see the truck's license plate?"

"No," Loftus said. "I was more worried about *me* than checking license plates."

"Not even two or three numbers or letters?"

"No."

K.O. jumped in. "What make was the truck?"

"Make?"

"Ford? GMC? Dodge Ram?"

"I don't know." The councilman's eyelids serial-blinked.

"What color was it?"

Now he lost his temper altogether. "It was the middle of the goddamn night!" he shouted at K.O. "All I saw was bright lights in the rearview mirror, and then *boom!* By the time I got my ass together, it was gone down the road." He whipped his head around at me and demanded, "Who is this fucking kid, anyway?"

"I introduced you," I said quietly. "Kevin O'Bannion. My associate."

"Now here's what I'm wondering, *Bert*," K.O. said. If Dolores Deluke was driving behind you, she'd have seen the entire thing. And if she was in front of you, she must've noticed the truck barreling by her. Is that right?"

Loftus looked as if he'd been struck by lightning. "I'm not sure; it was a dark night. Besides, I didn't see her afterwards. I gave it a few minutes and then called her home to tell her I wasn't coming. Uh, it's better if we don't mention Ms. Deluke's name."

"You don't want that 'getting out' either?"

Loftus took half a minute wrestling with his problem before nearly collapsing in his chair. "You know how things are. I mean, I'm married."

I had other questions, but I'd save them for awhile. "You said that was the first time—the first attempt on your life. What were the others?"

"I have to be careful what I put in my mouth. I could be poisoned," he said *à la* Cardinal Richelieu.

"In a downtown restaurant?"

"You never know."

"So there *wasn't* a second attempt on your life?"

"Oh, there was! The last one was three days ago. I was having a drink at the Tiny Bar. You know where that is?"

"Sure," I said. "It's just off West Sixth. Small, quiet little street."

Loftus nodded. "I was leaving sometime after midnight—heading back to my car. Then this big black sedan cruised by, and somebody took a shot at me. Took a little piece out of the brick wall it hit. Thank God somebody was a lousy shot."

"A handgun or a rifle?"

"How the hell do I know? It was probably a handgun, but I couldn't tell. They were driving fast and I didn't bother looking at them until after the shot." He looked grim. "I hit the sidewalk pretty fast, I can tell you. Ripped my pants!"

"And the police didn't show up?"

Humiliated, Loftus forced himself to admit it. "I didn't report it. I couldn't hang around waiting for the police. It would have sounded like a car backfiring to anyone else. Besides, there were no witnesses." He coughed nervously.

I'd scribbled notes, but I put my pen down and pushed the legal pad away. "You keep lots of secrets. That makes it hard to do our job."

"What? To be my bodyguard?"

"We're not bodyguards. Other people can provide private security if you want it. What's important is finding who's out to get you—and stopping them cold."

Loftus looked awestruck. "You can *do* that?"

"I thought you knew about me, Bert. You must have checked me out before you even called me."

"Yeah, I know you're good, but I didn't think—I mean, can you help me?"

"That's what the job will be."

"And what about the federal indictments? Can you fix those?"

"Fix the federal government? What are you smoking? I'm no lawyer; I won't touch that. But if your life is in danger, *that* we can find out about—and fix."

That made him surly again. "Whaddya mean, *if?* Are you calling me a liar?"

"Nobody called you anything," K.O. observed.

"If things played out the way you say they did, we'll find out."

"*We*, huh?" His mouth became a nearly disappeared straight line. He jerked a thumb at K.O. "What about him?"

K.O. wandered over slowly to stand over Loftus. He was only about five foot nine or so, but there's something about him—*gravitas*, they used to say when talking about a possible presidential candidate—that rendered him intimidating. "If you don't talk about me as if I'm not in the room, we'll get along fine. You can call me K.O."

Loftus got angry again. His frequent outbursts wore on my nerves. "K.O.? What is that? Like in boxing? A knockout?"

"*K* and *O* are my initials. Kevin O'Bannion." He made a fist with his right hand and massaged it with his left. "But if you want to think 'knockout,' be my guest."

I jumped in again. "K.O. is my outside guy—researching. You'll spend more time with me—but you won't like me much better." I pulled a contract out of my drawer and slid it across the desk.

Loftus perused each word as if it were written in Lithuanian. "Your rates are sky-high! This is a hell of a lot of money."

"My rates are what any private investigator charges."

He ran his fingers over the contract as though speed-reading. I didn't think anyone did that anymore. "Yeah, but you're a Clevelander—and *my* business is solving *your* problems. Maybe we can work a little discount here—like I'll just pick up your expenses."

"You want me to save your life *and* give you a discount?"

The scorn reappeared around his eyes. "Everyone gives me a break."

"That's why you've been indicted. Only the government calls the breaks something else. Don't play games with our heads. Don't make shit up or only tell us half. Tell everything—the whole truth—or hire somebody else."

"That's a pretty big order," Loftus said.

"And you're a pretty big pain in the ass. So sign the contract, Councilman—or take a hike."

Loftus thought it over. Finally he took a pen from his inside pocket—a silver Mark Cross he probably hadn't paid for; one of those "gifts" from someone who wants him to do something for them.

"You people," he muttered as he slashed his name across the bottom like a crazed rebel with a machete, "will drive me fucking crazy!"

I suppose if I were African American, the use of "you people" would have offended me. Since I'm not, I chose to let it go.

When Loftus left, he offered neither of us a handshake, probably enraged that he'd written me a sizable check. K.O. and I listened to him clatter down the stairs, then heard his car engine kick over in the parking lot. I made out a bank deposit envelope as K.O. watched.

Finally I said, "You were pretty rough with our client."

"He's an asshole."

"He's a scared asshole who's hired us to save his ass."

"What would you bet that Dolores Deluke—or whatever her name is—is a hooker?"

"No bet."

"Loftus is arrogant, too."

"Can you think of anyone elected to public office who isn't arrogant?"

K.O. laughed. "If they had sense they wouldn't *act* arrogant."

"It's part of their job. Now, here's what comes with your job, K.O. Sit down."

He frowned slightly. "I'm just fine standing up."

"I don't like people looming over me. Sit down."

Sulking, he unwound his body into the chair Loftus had recently vacated. "Will this be Lecture 101?"

"You're being almost as obnoxious as he is. I suppose acting like a jerk worked for you in juvie—or in the army. It's a shitty way to be in business—any sort of business. So start thinking like a P.I. in this job—not like we're good cop/bad cop."

"Loftus throws his weight around like he's got brass balls."

"Brass balls and an Achilles heel," I said. "But if he really is in danger, he deserves to be protected like anybody else. And if he's not in danger, he'd love everyone to think so, just to work up public sympathy."

"Why didn't he tell the police about the shooting? He's a city councilman—the cops work for him."

"Cleveland's tough," I said. "If word gets out he's hiding behind police skirts, he'll get known as a wuss—and become history."

"*If* he's telling the truth—and not inventing stories like the Brothers Grimm."

"Did you like Grimm's Fairy Tales when you were little?"

"Only the one about that king who turned everything he touched to gold."

"Midas."

"More like Loftus. So we take his money even if he's faking?"

"We already took it. He might be making it all up. But if we blow him off and he's *not* lying—and somebody shoots his head off—we'll feel like shits. Can you take that chance?"

K.O. made a face. "I'll still feel like I'm stealing money for nothing."

It was past noon. I suggested we have lunch together before we set out on our separate assignments. That felt strange; I'd always worked alone, but K.O. was bright and aggressive, and I hoped he'd handle himself, and my business, in the right way.

We drove in separate cars to The Harp, an Irish restaurant nearby on Detroit Road overlooking Lake Erie, and chose to eat inside. They have an outdoor patio, but the lake is on the other side of a freeway and it gets noisy out there. Besides, I hate eating right next to heavy traffic and watching my food get dirty.

Harp's menu offers excellent meals, especially the too-fattening boxty cakes; the bad reputation about Irish food is a mean-spirited myth. And the paintings high on the wall, along with quotes from Yeats and Oscar Wilde, contribute to the Celtic experience. I rarely miss Harp's dessert—ice cream flavored with Guinness Stout! On this particular day, though, I foreswore it. I've learned that at my age I can't indulge myself in the foods that have kept me smiling all my life, or else I'd rapidly gain weight and become a type 2 diabetic.

"Will you be okay?" I asked K.O. as we made our way back out to the parking lot.

"I promise to look both ways when I cross the street."

"I didn't mean that."

His look was sour. "I'm all grown up. I didn't get killed in Iraq, so I'll survive in Cleveland."

"I want you comfortable in this job. The other stuff was part-time. This is—well, you're really an employee."

"Is that another word for wage slave?"

"It is until you open your own firm and be your own boss, and you have to put in a certain amount of legwork before they let you have the license. Until then, you're stuck with me."

"And unfortunately," K.O. said, opening his car door and sliding behind the steering wheel, "you're stuck with me, too."

CHAPTER TWO

K.O.

Working actively to digest his lunch of Irish chicken boxty and too much coffee, Kevin O'Bannion drove away from The Harp to snoop on his own. It felt strange to him—working for a private investigations firm—and even stranger answering to Milan Jacovich. He hated answering to anyone.

He'd done some part-time stuff for Suzanne Davis and more for Milan before he was put on Milan's regular payroll. He still had a few bruises from his first case, but they were fading. Now, though, he was really an employee, with an honest-to-God paycheck every two weeks, and every hour he worked would be credited toward his eligibility for a P.I. license of his own.

He really wanted to be a police officer, but three of his teen years were spent in a juvenile facility, and that might not be something the police department would accept. The charge had been felonious assault, a fancy way of saying he hurt someone who deserved it. If he had a chance to live his life over again, he'd do the same damn thing. Bullies who abuse animals—or kids or women—deserve the same punishments they'd dished out—and K.O. would have no problem delivering them.

He checked his to-do list. Deuce Auto Body Works wasn't far from The Harp; it took him less than five minutes to get there. Inside the front office, the man behind the counter wore a well-pressed blue shirt with his first name—Tyler—on his breast pocket. K.O. thought he didn't do much auto repair himself because his squeaky-clean hands looked more like those of a sur-

geon than a mechanic. But the work bay behind him was noisy—
hammering, drilling, the whine of machinery, male talk back and
forth—so someone was getting his hands dirty. He introduced
himself as being new with Milan Security and said that Bert Lof-
tus had sent him.

It was just a little lie.

Tyler was in his forties, his hair dark brown and curly. He
was about K.O.'s size and weight, but he had twenty years on
the younger man. His genuine smile showed off his teeth, which
needed some work. "Oh, yeah," he said. "Bert Loftus—he's a great
guy. I'm lucky I live and work in his ward."

"He's a prince," K.O. said.

"You better believe it. A councilman like him sends city work-
ers here for body repair—and that's how I pay my mortgage." He
craned to see K.O.'s car parked right outside his window. It's a five-
year-old Ford Fiesta, but it looks older and a little tired because
it had been driven ever since K.O. got back from Afghanistan.
"So—you had a fender-bender? Or something more serious?"

"No, I'm checking up on the councilman's Lincoln you fixed."

Tyler frowned. "Checking up? It's already fixed, good as new."

"I know. Could I take a look at the bill?"

"The bill? Why?"

"As I said, just making sure everything checks out."

Tyler's welcoming smile was disappearing over the hill faster
than a passing flock of geese. "I don't understand. Did Bert ask
you to look at the bill?"

"No. I'm just making sure the I's are dotted and the T's are
crossed."

Tyler looked for a quick exit, but none existed. "Uh, well—
there is no bill." K.O.'s raised eyebrows upset him more. "Council-
man Loftus is a friend of mine. He's done me lots of favors over
the years, so I do him favors right back."

"Tit for tat."

"Yeah, exactly."

"So, if I have a minor accident, like someone backs into me
in a parking lot, I can bring my car to you and you'll fix it for no
charge?"

Tyler looked blank for a moment too long. "I wouldn't say that."

"You only give freebies to rich people? Or important people? The rest of us poor bastards have to cough up the full price? That doesn't seem fair."

Tyler finally caught on that his chain was being jerked, which made him point his jutting chin in the general direction of the North Pole. "Look, how I run my business is my—uh—my own business. It's none of yours, mister."

"Mr. O'Bannion," K.O. said, leaning on his own surname. "Tell me, Tyler—do you have a customer named Dolores Deluke?"

"I don't have to give you that information."

"Why? Dolores Deluke isn't rich, famous, or powerful. Do you charge her full price when she has a bent rear bumper?"

"I don't know who you're talking about," he said. "I never heard of her. And I never heard of you, either. So I'll have to ask you to leave."

K.O. considered making a fuss about being thrown out, but it wasn't really worth it—especially on his first day of work. Tyler didn't come from behind the counter to try backing up his demand, so K.O. just said good-bye and went out to his car at a leisurely pace, Tyler watching every step. Before he kicked on the ignition he scrawled a few things in the pocket notebook Milan had given him, and then headed back downtown, crossing eastbound over the Detroit–Superior Bridge.

He'd never been to the main branch of the Cleveland Public Library on Superior Avenue, bordering the northeastern edge of Public Square. The two buildings, one many decades older than the other, are connected by a pleasant fenced-in garden, and on this summer midafternoon it had drawn busy downtowners who wanted to spend a few quiet moments relaxing by the fountain before the homeless gathered there closer to dusk.

The main hall is like a palace court, its ceiling as if it had been painted by Michelangelo lying flat on his back. K.O. couldn't stop looking at it. He kicked himself for never coming to this library before, but more people would visit if they didn't have to pay a small fortune to park at the garage across the street.

When he finally settled in front of a computer, he dug a larger notebook and three pens from his briefcase and set to work looking up everything written about Bert Loftus within the past eighteen months. There were thirty-one federal indictments against him.

Bert's "leased" Lincoln Town Car had cost him nothing, just like his body work, and both of those perks were viewed as illegal by the federal prosecutors.

Approximately $170,000 in repairs and improvements had been made to his home on the west side of Cleveland within the last five years, making it into more of a mini-mansion than just a house. His elegant condominium in Columbus enjoyed about $40,000 worth of remodeling in 2006. Bills were sent to him by the same contractor in Cleveland—one was for $2,600 for the rehab, and one for $535. Apparently he never paid them, either.

A luxury box at the Q—the Quicken Loans Arena in which the Cavs play—was made available at no charge to Loftus on four separate occasions, back in the day when LeBron James was still Cleveland's "king," when the games were sold out every night and King James was not yet the perceived perpetrator of Cleveland high treason. Records state Loftus had invited ten other people on one evening and twelve on the other three, and those parties and whatever food they stuffed in their mouths were paid for by the same company that owned the executive box, a real estate investment firm that developed and built high-end homes in Cuyahoga County.

The CEO of that investment company was also under indictment.

A few of the other Loftus complaints list all the personal errands he demanded of his aides and other city workers, such as picking up his dry cleaning, shopping for gifts for his wife and/or girlfriends, and showing up at his home on weekends to mow the lawn or shovel the winter driveway. Furthermore, all the people on his staff were expected—read "commanded"—to donate approximately 10 percent of their salaries, paid by Cleveland's taxpayers, toward the Berton Loftus Reelection Campaign. The federal authorities categorized that last expectation as racketeering.

The Loftus trips to Las Vegas or Atlantic City casinos were all "comped," paid for by someone else—and his indictments name all of those someones. Several of his gift assignations were with young hookers. Cleveland's an understanding town when it comes to the political hacks who run it, but old farts like Loftus with teen prostitutes rang a few off-key public bells.

What got the most media notoriety was that Councilman Loftus had at least seven times contacted a Common Pleas judge, Lawrence McTeague, to "treat well and kindly" some of his best friends—including many who gave him gifts and freebies. The judge had baldly lied to the FBI when questioned, was indicted, and now awaited trial from the federal bench. He'd probably have to trade his flowing black robes for an orange jumpsuit—but one never knows.

K.O. nearly filled his notebook with Councilman Loftus's once-private and now very public problems, including some he hadn't read about before. No wonder Bert quivered in his boots; K.O. would, too, if the FBI walked into his house waving a warrant, and packed up and took away everything he owned except his clean socks folded and put in a drawer.

Loftus was a schmuck; K.O. knew that the minute he'd walked into the office as if he owned it. From the local dogcatcher to the city and statewide politicians right up through the House of Representatives and the United States Congress, they all thought they were better than everyone else, that they were entitled to everything and responsible for nothing at all. And those douche bags made laws and told others, including K.O., what to do and how to think!

No wonder Kevin O'Bannion didn't vote.

He ransomed his car and headed home toward Mentor, about twenty minutes from downtown Cleveland. Last week's sizzling temperature had tamed itself down into the high seventies, so K.O. cranked all his windows open as he drove north along Lake Erie on I-90, thinking how odd it was that Northeast Ohio gets warmer at 5 p.m. than at noon.

He lived in an apartment complex on Mentor Avenue, not far from the Great Lakes Mall and two blocks from the historic home of President James A. Garfield, one of Ohio's eight who became president. Garfield was one of the unluckier ones; he, along with William McKinley, was assassinated. Two other Ohio-based presidents didn't make it through their first terms, either. William Henry Harrison caught cold at his inauguration and died of it, and Warren G. Harding, probably the most inept crook who ever sat in the White House, died under mysterious circumstances.

K.O.'s one-bedroom apartment was on the second floor, and when he opened the door, Rodney was waiting to greet him.

Rodney was a tiger-striped gray cat K.O. rescued from a shelter forty-eight hours before he was scheduled to be euthanized. He was about four years old at the time and had been given a froufrou name by an attendant. K.O. hated to think about what might have happened if he'd waited until the following week to visit the shelter. The little cat was a tough, no-nonsense guy, but when K.O. was home, he never roamed more than five feet away. He cuddled on his owner's lap and slept on his pillow, liked to hang over his shoulder, and often rubbed his head gently but firmly against K.O.'s nose when he wanted attention. He was an indoor cat; if he were let out he'd bring home a half-eaten bird or squirrel every day for praise and approval, and K.O. would hate scooping the remains off the floor and into the garbage.

K.O.'s love for animals had gotten him slammed into juvie jail for taking his rage out on two teen punks who'd actually cooked a dog alive in a Weber kettle, just for the fun of it. He still got enraged every time he allowed himself to think of it.

Rodney was the best friend K.O. had ever had.

He picked the purring cat up and buried his nose in the soft fur around his neck, telling Rodney all about his day until the cat started wriggling, anxious to be fed. K.O. filled one of his bowls with water, then dished out his food in the other one and watched Rodney eat while he munched on a bologna sandwich with some pickle chips and a few slices of American cheese.

For some reason he'd bought the loaf of bread at a nearby convenience store instead of the supermarket, and hadn't noticed until he got it home that it was called "Bimbo Bread." A ridiculous name for something with which to make a sandwich, a word still used sometimes to describe a loose, immoral woman. Maybe they should have just called it "Slut Bread" or just "Skanky."

It wasn't a great meal, but a bologna sandwich beat hell out of the K-rations the infantry subsisted on in Afghanistan—and being with Rodney was even better than having dinner with a human.

Except he didn't have many two-legged friends.

He was working on getting one, though. During his first stint with Milan Jacovich, while he was running around talking to witnesses and suspects, K.O. had met the prettiest girl in the world, or at least he thought she was, and that's what counts. Carli Wysocki worked in a makeup store in the Beachwood Place Mall, and right off the bat, even before questioning her about Milan's case, K.O. found himself crazy about her. They'd been out a couple of times since but hadn't gone much past the kissing stage. Most women K.O. had slept with before had been one-night stands. He'd never really had a girlfriend. When he went away to juvie he'd been fifteen years old, and when they finally cut him loose, he had joined the army and spent three tours hauling eighty pounds of protective gear around, getting shot at, eluding landmines and IEDs, and spitting sand.

He'd learned in jail to get strong and tough or else be used up by bigger, stronger inmates and thrown away before he was old enough to vote. Now he went to the gym early to work out on the treadmill, the cross-trainer, and the stationary bike. If he had enough time some mornings, he'd lift weights.

He had no real feelings about his apartment. The refrigerator and dishwasher worked, and the john flushed, although the shower dripped. He'd furnished the rest of the place with thrift shop merchandise from Mentor or Painesville—like a sofa with a yellow, blue, and green checkerboard upholstery that gave him a headache if he stared at it too long. His easy chair was comfortable enough, but his battered dining table had rickety chairs that didn't quite match. He even went to a "starving artist" sale at which pictures were painted by number—and bought several to hang on the wall and give his place some personality, mostly landscapes depicting Spain or Italy or a seacoast. Boring, but the colors are pretty.

There were no photographs. He had no family; his mother had disappeared when he was a small boy. His father moved to

Richmond Township while he was in Iraq, and they hadn't seen each other for more than two years. Their phone conversations occurred every nine or ten months. Neither had much to say after about thirty seconds. K.O. counted the awkward moments of silence.

His closest thing to a friend was Sergeant Jake Foote of the Mentor police, who'd busted K.O. in the first place and then pled for K.O. in court. It didn't work, at least not with that judge—but when K.O. finally got out, he looked up Jake Foote again. They kept in touch during K.O.'s army tours and met again when K.O. returned stateside, civilian and looking for a job.

Foote introduced him to another acquaintance of his—Suzanne Davis. She and Foote had once dated, but they'd recalibrated their relationship to being good pals. She was in her fifties, a real-life private eye in Lake County—funny, sexy, and a woman you wouldn't want to mess with. And of course, she put K.O. together with Milan Jacovich.

As for Milan—they were feeling each other out. Milan was gruff—a guy who only knew black and white and had no idea that most of the world was gray. Sometimes K.O. bit his tongue before lashing back at him, and sometimes he just let fly. They'd butt heads. As for being friends, they'd just have to wait and see.

The phone rang—relatively unusual, because K.O. was not a social butterfly people call all the time. He picked it up and said hello.

"Well," Carli said, "how was your first real day at the office, dear?"

He smiled and chuckled at the same time his heart found its way into his throat. The chuckle was inspired by Carli's humorous use of the very dated word "dear" in a sentence. His smile came from just hearing her voice—she sounded older on the phone than she was.

"It was interesting—and thanks for asking." Everything in him wanted to add "honey" or "sweetheart," but their relationship was nowhere near that point yet.

"Can you tell me about it?" Carli said.

"I probably shouldn't. It involves somebody pretty well known, and we're not supposed to talk about it."

"You talked to me a lot about your last case."

"That's because you were a witness."

"Ah."

"All you're witnessing now is me."

"It's a dirty job, but someone has to do it."

He leaned down to kiss Rodney on the top of his head and then gently scratched him under the chin. The cat closed his eyes in pleasure and purred so loudly that Carli could hear him.

"Aww," she said, and just listened to him for a moment. "Your kitty sounds very happy. So—when do we celebrate this new adventure in your life?"

Someone actually wanted to *celebrate* something with him? That was new—brand new. "You mean go out to dinner? Uh—yeah, sure. When?"

"How about tomorrow? Tomorrow evening, I mean."

He tried stifling a gulp. "Where should we meet?" They'd been on two dates so far, meeting at a preordained place each time. Their after-dinner makeouts—what little there was of them—had been in his car or hers.

"What if I come out to your place?" suggested Carli. "We can figure out what to do from there. I don't get out to Lake County much."

"I'll make sure you see every inch of it. Seven o'clock?"

"I can't wait."

When they hung up he was on Cloud Eighteen—the traditional Cloud Nine wasn't anywhere near high enough. He wondered where he should take Carli for dinner. He didn't hang out in nice restaurants; to him, Subway was elegant. Bass Lake Tavern was nice, but after listening to Bert Loftus's disastrous experience after leaving there, K.O. wanted to choose something else. He didn't want a Lake County pickup truck running *him* off the road into a ditch.

That got him thinking about Loftus again. Bert was a politician, and even the most pure in heart got swept away by power, money, sex, and people lining up around the block just waiting for the chance to kiss their asses. They did whatever they wanted, figuring nobody else would find out, and if someone did—and they always do—they were shocked to be called out for it.

The name Dolores Deluke was itching at K.O. somewhere behind his eyes. Loftus had made it clear he didn't want her used or mentioned. Hoping to find out more about her, as Loftus was not forthcoming, K.O. sat at his dining table and googled her on his laptop.

There were names listed that he could click on, one Delores Deluke, with an *e*, and three more who fashioned their surnames Deluke. After a few tries, he found the one he was looking for. She lived in Chardon—not too far from him. He couldn't find her address or phone number, but she maintained a site on Facebook—along with 900 million other people. K.O. rarely visited Facebook; in fact, 90 percent of his Facebook "friends" were people he'd never met. He had no idea who they really were. It took him several days to decide which photograph of himself to post. Finally he chose none at all. His face, like his name, was shanty Irish, and there wasn't a damn thing he could do about it.

He went to the profile page of Dolores Deluke from Ohio.

Most mature Facebook members don't admit too much about themselves, but Deluke was open and obvious, or else she just didn't give a damn. In her profile picture, she wore a white T-shirt with print on its front, looking as if she'd just awakened and hadn't combed her hair in awhile. K.O. couldn't make out the words on her chest, though. She'd graduated from Holy Name High School in Parma Heights and had gone on to college at Cleveland State. She was somewhere in her middle thirties. She listed herself as "Single" and declared that her interests were rock concerts and "MEN." She wrote that she loved romantic movies, *The Bachelor* and a couple of other TV reality shows, and she announced to everyone that she worked at Meacham, Bestwick and Wardwell, one of Cleveland's major conservative law firms downtown.

He thought about it for awhile, then decided to request being a "friend" of hers on Facebook so he could view her full profile and see all of her friends. He wondered if she and Bert Loftus had been careless, as many social media junkies are, to be each other's "friends."

Dolores Deluke confirmed him as a friend within about an hour. The alacrity didn't surprise him—some people on FB are desperate for friends, even ones who are completely unknown to them.

He wrote down her law office phone number and address after googling it. Milan Jacovich still looked up numbers in his Cleveland Yellow Pages, but K.O. didn't own a directory. He'd learned to use a computer when incarcerated and acquired further skills during his military service. He'd also gotten deeply hooked on movies and watched several films on DVD a week. He had almost memorized all of the scenes from *The Hurt Locker;* he closely identified with that one.

Since he wasn't sleepy yet, he decided to check out Carli to see if she were a Facebook member, too.

She was.

She'd gone through Kent State—just like Milan. She'd listed the name of the cosmetics store where she worked, where K.O. had first met her. Most of her "Favorite" things were political causes. The left side of her profile said that she'd posted more than four hundred photographs for the world to see.

It took him an hour and a half to get through all of them.

There were several of her alone, usually dressed casually because she was outside somewhere like at a lake—not Lake Erie but a smaller one that looked more fun—or a park. There were many photos of her with other women, almost all her age and almost all pretty; not as pretty as she was, though, in his humble opinion. She smiled in every picture—but then she smiled all the time when she was with him, even when he had quizzed her about Milan's last missing-persons case.

Some photos he didn't enjoy—snapshots of Carli with other men. He couldn't tell if they were on a date together in those pictures or just buds. Past lovers? Maybe. A few were good-looking, smiling as broadly as she was. Did it bother him? No, if the operative word was "past." If not, if she currently had a boyfriend—or boyfriends—well . . .

He logged off the computer, went over notes to share with Milan in the morning, and tried not to think about Carli Wysocki. He forced himself to concentrate on Councilman Bert Loftus. Was someone actually trying to kill him? His federal indictments would take a lot of influential people over the side with him, so he must have few friends left. But murder? His report of the two attempts sounded like fanciful made-up crap to K.O., possibly to Milan, too.

Even grumbling to himself, K.O. almost wished Loftus really was telling the truth. Then the assignment to make sure no one came along and cut him off at the knees would sound like a job worth doing.

CHAPTER THREE

MILAN

Sometimes—not always, but once in a while—I felt about Kevin O'Bannion the way most people feel when they've just bought a house they couldn't afford and locked themselves into buyer's remorse. Watching him drive away from our lunch at The Harp, I couldn't help wondering: Does he dislike me the way he dislikes everyone else, himself included—except the Lake County cop who busted him when he was fifteen, and his new girlfriend Carli? Or does he actually think, deep in his gut, that I just might be okay?

He'd helped me in my last case—saved my life, actually—and I hoped he'd remain as helpful, providing he curbed his hair-trigger temper. But I reminded myself that I'm not his mentor.

As for Bert Loftus, I find myself watching over him—and if he's on the level about the attempts on his life, we might be in for some rough sledding. If he's lying—if this is a scheme of his to garner public sympathy—I'll kick his ass all the way to the city border.

I drove eastward, into the Slovenian-Croatian neighborhood off Saint Clair Avenue, to deposit Loftus's check. I have a personal account at a larger bank in Cleveland Heights, but I keep my business accounts at this one, not far from the home where I grew up. Not surprising, at least to me. The patron saint of Cleveland Slovenians is the Saint Clair Savings and Loan.

Once the check was safely stored in my bank—or as safe as it

could be until it bounced—I drove back downtown, lucky enough
to find a parking place on East 9th Street, saving myself eight
bucks in a nearby lot, and strolled over to the Tiny Bar. I didn't go
in at first but put in some time outside in comfortable sunshine,
carefully examining the sidewalk and the bricks.

There wasn't much to see. Downtown Cleveland, especially
this section of it, the Warehouse District, was relatively clean. I'm
sure the bartender came out with a broom and cleaned off the
sidewalk, maybe sweeping all the crap into the gutter, so I looked
there, too. I couldn't see a spent cartridge, but Loftus claimed
someone had taken a shot at him three days ago, and if the bullet
hadn't bounced off the bricks to be swept away, perhaps someone
had removed it. The shooter, perhaps, returning after the bars
had closed? A passerby picking it up as a souvenir or keepsake?
Or had someone mindlessly kicked it to wherever it might be
now?

One of the bricks, just to the right of the door, as high as my
own shoulder, had been half-chipped away, leaving a gash a dif-
ferent color than the other bricks. Whatever caused it had been
recent—and violent. So some drive-by gun-toter probably *had*
taken a shot at Bert Loftus. At least he hadn't lied to us about
that.

The marksman—or markswoman—might have missed him
because the car was moving. Or maybe the shooter couldn't hit
water if he fell out of a boat.

Or—they might have deliberately missed, the shot fired close
to Bert's ear as a warning.

About what, I wondered. He was in such trouble with the feds
that they'd probably lock him up and forget where they put the
key. The bribe-taking might be overlooked, as brazen as it had
been—but government prosecutors will hang him high on the
RICO charges, and most Clevelanders will hate him forever for
his fun times with high-priced teenaged call girls.

I walked inside—dark as always. It's now illegal to smoke ciga-
rettes in a public place in Cleveland, but the air was still redo-
lent with the years-old stink of burning tobacco that had never
been blown away. Squinting, I recognized a few newspaper men
at the bar who nodded at me, some blue-collar county workers

who'd knocked off their jobs early, two lawyers huddled over a table discussing their next courtroom moves, and a middle-aged couple holding hands and looking fearfully at the door in case their actual spouses walked in on their tryst and surprised them. Two middle-aged women dressed for the office except for their sneakers sat alone at either end of the bar, staring into the back-bar mirror and getting a jumpstart buzz on the evening.

Over in the corner at his usual table was a well-known Common Pleas judge well past his halfway-drunk state, his eyes closed and his head nodding. Within an hour his upper body would be sprawled across the table among his empty glasses.

The Tiny is *that* kind of bar.

The bartender—I recalled his name as Rich but I wasn't sure enough to use it—greeted me and said, "Haven't seen you around for awhile." From my earlier times in this establishment, I know he used to be a redhead, but what hair he had left was now steel gray, and grandpa-style glasses were perched on the end of his nose. I guessed him on the other side of sixty.

"Almost," I said, "but I could handle a Stroh's today. No glass." I didn't really want a beer, but I always feel like a jerk asking questions in a bar without spending a dime. I'd write off the price of a Stroh's to my client.

"You working nights now?" I said when he put the beer in front of me.

"Days, nights, Christmas, Rosh Hashanah—whenever they need me."

"Were you on three nights ago when Bert Loftus was in here late?"

"Maybe." Rich thought it over. "Yeah—having a nightcap after whatever he spent the evening doing." He regarded me quizzically. "Are you investigating him, too? Jesus, he's got more people squealing on him than a barn full of pigs."

"Confidential—sorry."

He threw up his hands. "No skin off my ass."

"When he left—what was that, about one o'clock?"

"I didn't look at the clock—but it was late."

"Was he talking to anybody?"

"Loftus, he doesn't talk to nobody if they're not important—or sexy. But he was chumming it up with two people that night—a couple, if you could call 'em that, because they were the two ugliest people I ever saw in my life." He closed his eyes and shook his head as if distressed by the memory.

"Did they come in with Loftus?"

He shook his head. "They were here first. Loftus headed right for their table and not for where he usually sits at the bar. They did most of the talking, and Loftus listened."

"Do you know who they were?"

"I'm no social director. They been in here a few times before, but I'd never have forgotten people who look like that." He made a monster face.

"Do you know what they were talking about?"

"I didn't pay attention because I was rooting for them to haul ass and go home. But I couldn't of heard anyway because the music was blaring. The broad kept feeding the box money to play some of that hop hop shit."

"Hip hop," I corrected him.

"Huh?"

"It's hip hop—not hop hop. Did they leave together?"

Rich swished his rag across the top of the bar. "No. Bert hadda finish his drink. He hung around another ten minutes or so."

"When he went outside, did you hear anything sounding like a shot?"

"I wouldn'ta heard a nuclear bomb dropping out there. Why? Did Bert get shot? I didn't know nothing about that."

"No, Bert's healthy as a horse—at least he was this morning."

Rich sucked in a relieved sigh. "Good—cuz he got a tab running here."

"I didn't think anybody ran bar tabs anymore."

"Cleveland councilmen? Are you kidding me? I could retire on the unpaid tabs of the councilmen and county commissioners and judges who run up tabs they're never gonna pay." He shook his head almost angrily. "They do anything they goddamn please—or else the next day some asshole inspector from the health department or safety department or some other goddamn department will show up here with a list of errors in this place a mile long—compliments of one of my non-paying-up customers."

One blue collar waved his beer glass, hollering for another drink, and Rich moved off down the bar to serve him. I'd gotten all the information from him I was going to, and it didn't amount to much.

I wanted to talk to Loftus again before I wrapped up my workday. Businessmen get indicted for bribery of one sort or another almost every week, but apparently the feds hadn't gotten around to the Tiny Bar. Loftus might open up to me if K.O. wasn't looming over him. I think he was more afraid of K.O. at our first meeting than he was of anyone really out for his scalp.

I managed to pass through the security check downstairs at City Hall; the guards working the metal detector arch knew who I was. When I got to Bert Loftus's office, the enormous photograph of the president of the United States loomed over the woman assigned to keep everyone not invited out of Bert's inner sanctum.

Pam Marek—that's what the nameplate on her desk said—was forty-five or so, big brown eyes behind black-framed glasses, and all business, but when I told her my name and gave her my business card, she warmed up slightly.

"I've read your name in the papers," she said. "Councilman Loftus called you this week."

"I was passing by and thought I'd drop in to say hello."

"To say hello? You pay a hefty parking fee and argue your way past security downstairs to say hello?"

"I was lonely," I said, smiling to make sure she knew I was joking.

"No wife to go home and talk to?"

"No wife, girlfriend, significant other, or roommate—not even a dog."

"Well, Bert Loftus left for the day," Pam Marek said, pointedly looking at her wristwatch. "I'm about to do the same. So if you'll excuse me . . ."

"I'd be happy talking to you instead," I said.

She switched off her computer and cocked her head, studying me. "Is this going to be a date?"

"No, just looking for conversation. Can I buy you a beer? Or do *you* have a husband or boyfriend waiting for you at home?"

She sighed. "Nobody's there except my mother—and if I don't

go home right away she'll have an extra hour to perfect her whin-
ing."

"But over a beer, you'll have an extra hour to prepare your de-
fense."

She thought about that for a moment. "I like that. But let me
warn you, I'm not looking for a relationship."

That took me unawares. "Me, neither."

"Or a one-night stand."

"It never occurred to me," I said. "You're a city employee."

"Yeah, who'd sleep with a city employee anyway?" She looked
at my card again. "Milan, right?" She incorrectly emphasized the
second syllable.

"MY-lan," I said. "Guilty."

She finally gave in. "Okay—one beer."

I waited while she closed up the office, and we walked a few
blocks down Lakeside Avenue to The Blind Pig on West Sixth
Street. It attracts a younger, noisier crowd, but it was still early
and the inside was cool and quiet.

"So," Pam Marek said, clinking her beer glass against my bot-
tle, "you aren't coming on to me—and I know Bert contacted you
recently—so my guess is you're on a case, and you want to ask me
questions. Am I right? What do I win?"

"You're drinking your winner, Pam."

She tasted her beer and smacked her lips loudly. "If I'm al-
ready winning, I want another one."

"When you finish that one," I said.

"So—what are you private-eyeing? I don't tell secrets—not
mine and not Bert's, either."

"You and he are good friends?"

"No, because he's an asshole. But I work for him and if I blab
his secrets, I'd be pond scum. You know the trouble he's in. The
feds are warming up the hot seat for him."

I laughed. "Number one, they don't use electric chairs any-
more, and they never fried anyone for accepting bribes. Number
two, that 'warming up the hot seat' line is from a movie called *On
the Waterfront*, which you're not old enough to have seen."

"Oh, yeah? Well, number one back at you: They still use electric
chairs for executions in six states—I can name them if you want.

And number two: I wasn't born when they made that movie, but I've seen it on DVD—and I loved that line about the hot seat." Her smile disguised her pugnacious attitude. "Anything else?"

"Who does Loftus know that I don't? Who does he hang out with?"

"He's a politician, he knows everybody—most of them are indicted right along with him."

"I'm more interested in the ones that aren't indicted."

"Yet," she added, narrowing her eyes at me. "Are you trying to get Bert into even *more* trouble? If you are, buy me another beer so I can throw it in your face and walk out of here."

"Just the opposite," I said. "I'm trying to help him."

"So you're working for him?"

"I'm self-employed."

"Excuse me for living. I mean, is he your client?"

I just looked at her, hard, and after a moment she nodded. That way I didn't have to betray a business relationship by telling her so.

"All right, then," Pam said. She drummed a nonexistent piano on the bar top with her fingers. "He knows all the judges, but they haven't hung around with him, hoping the prosecutors won't even look at them. I guess he knows Paddy O'Malley best; they used to have lunch a couple of times a month."

"Used to?"

"He hasn't been around for a while, and I don't think Loftus called him from the office. Can't blame O'Malley, can you?"

"Is there anybody mad at Bert? Really mad?"

Her shrug was elaborate. "Everybody."

"Everybody who's been indicted?"

She nodded vigorously. "Or who's *about* to be indicted. Everybody in town has dealt with him in one way or another. They're all scared shitless, and I don't blame them. Like company people who'd suck around him so he'd throw more city business their way. Real estate, manufacturing—everybody who needs a favor they don't deserve. Landlords, too."

"Landlords? How does that work?"

She held her hands out, palms up. "Some poor tenants who can barely make their rent report their landlords because they don't have heat in their apartments. You know what it's like in Cleveland without heat in January? Or maybe the roof leaks, the walls are moldy—the usual stuff."

"And Bert Loftus fixes it for them?"

She frowned at me. "What he fixes is that nobody ever sees those complaints, so the landlords aren't fined or made to do the repairs—and Loftus gets to throw a party in one of the private suites at the ballpark or at the Q, and somebody else buys all of it for him."

I took out my notebook. "Who are these landlords, Pam?"

"I can't remember names; there are too damn many. They're not regulars in the office. Probably Reverend Whitby—Clarence Whitby—from one of those Baptist churches on the near west side. I can't recall which one."

"Heard of him," I said. "Anybody else?"

"When I go home at night, I block out my work so I don't have to think about it." She frowned, trying to recall. "I guess the only ones hanging around a lot in the last month or so are Mr. and Mrs. Ogre."

"Ogre? Big and green and ugly, like Shrek?"

Pam giggled. "You're not far off, except for the green part. Their name is Ogrin—Jeff and Vicki Ogrin. They're on the phone at least three times a week to Loftus. But everyone in our office calls them Ogre, cuz that's how they look."

"Can you describe them?"

"Let's see," she said. "Jeff Ogre is probably in his fifties, almost as tall as you are—but he must weigh more than four hundred pounds." She grinned. "I'm guessing about that. And he has a face like a monster in a cheap Hollywood gore movie—one who eats people!" She pushed her bangs out of her face. "Honest to Jesus, it's hard looking at him. He walks with a cane, and I worry he might fall over on me and crush me flat! As for Vicki—she's about the same age, and she keeps dyeing her hair differently. When I first saw her, it was jet black. Then she dyed it orange for a while—with gray roots showing. Now it's an almost scarlet red— one of those do-it-yourself dye jobs from the drug store. She's not gruesome-looking, but she's got one of those mean, nasty faces that are pure poison! She doesn't just look at you, she glares."

"Glares?"

"They came by the office one day, with no appointment, wanting Bert. When I told them he had meetings all day long and couldn't see them, she looked daggers at me like she wished I was dead." She shuddered, and at least part of it was real. "I swear she's worse than he is."

"Are they landlords?"

"Yes—except they live in a shitty little apartment just off West 28th Street—at least that's where Loftus sends their mail."

"How do you know it's a shitty little apartment?"

"I lived in that neighborhood myself when I first got out of college," she said, rolling her eyes. "That was a while ago. Anyway, they own that building, and some others, too—because every time they talk to Bert Loftus, within minutes he's on the phone to Metro Housing, trying to keep them from landing on the Ogres."

I scratched away at my notes. "If Bert's convicted, he'll lose his job, right?"

"Probably—but in this town, you never know."

"What happens to your job, then?"

She sighed. "I couldn't guess. I'll land somewhere else at City Hall—or at another city department. I hope not at Water—they're in as much trouble as Bert."

"And if you don't?"

"If I don't," Pam Marek said, "then you'll have to come around more often and buy me a beer."

CHAPTER FOUR

K.O.

Do you want a metal desk or a wooden one?" Milan asked. It was 9:30 a.m. K.O. had spent the previous night thinking about a lot of other things. He'd shared with Milan the notes he took from his labors the day before; now he shrugged, not having considered what kind of desk he wanted.

"Mine's wooden," Milan went on, "so if we got one kind of like it, the office will look better."

"Whatever. I can sit anywhere. Don't spend a lot of money on my desk."

"A used one—and pick out a laptop for yourself at Best Buy."

"I own a laptop."

"That's your personal laptop. Set up the new one for business. You can do that, right?" He took a blue-and-yellow Best Buy gift card from his wallet and gave it to K.O.

K.O. tried not to laugh. "I'm a hell of a lot better on computers than you are. It's the age difference, old timer."

"Old timer? *That* stings so early in the morning. Are you going to talk with this Deluke woman face-to-face?"

"That's my plan."

"How will you swing that?"

"I haven't figured it out yet. Don't worry."

"I'm not a worrier. I believe in you."

"Don't make me cry." Compliments discomfited K.O.; he wasn't used to them.

He spent the next two hours in a used office furniture warehouse on East Superior Avenue, looking at desks. He'd never worked behind a desk before; in Afghanistan, desks weren't issued to combat-enlisted men. There were a few hundred desks in the warehouse, most too big for Milan's office and too big for him. Finally he spotted one he thought he could handle—tired and beaten up, with several scratches and cigarette burns on its surface, but it'd probably fit in the corner Milan would dedicate to his new assistant, or intern, or whatever K.O. thought he was. He chose a desk chair to go with it, knowing he'd feel dumb sitting in it like an important executive. He was twenty-four years old—still a kid!

He paid for everything with the business credit card Milan had loaned him, jotting down what time they'd be delivered. He still carried notebooks, not an iPad—and was certain Milan wouldn't pop for one.

Once back downtown, K.O. found his way into the lobby of the Tower at Erieview, one of Cleveland's more prestigious buildings, connected to the Galleria. The Galleria used to be an elegant shopping and restaurant destination, but that was nearly two decades ago. Now most of the shops are empty, or they've become pricey art galleries that only open by appointment. There's always the Food Court, of course, with fast-food stands endemic to every other mall in the world, and a higher-end restaurant on the second level, the Café Sausalito, mostly catering to the business lunch crowd.

He checked the directory to see on what floor Dolores Deluke worked, but the law firm fooled him—they occupied three stories, near the top of the Tower. Switching to Plan B, K.O. moved to a position from which he could see the elevator that serviced those floors and checked his watch. It was a few minutes before noon. He waited—just to see what would happen.

At 12:07 Dolores Deluke stepped out of the elevator, looking better than her Facebook profile pic. She'd combed her mouse-brown hair and traded in her wrinkled T-shirt for a businesslike blouse and a skirt ending just above the knee. She didn't have bad legs at all. Her face, better made up than in the photograph, wavered for K.O. anywhere between a five and a seven.

As she crossed the lobby, he began his move, timing it so he'd almost run into her.

"Hey—you're Dolores Deluke, aren't you?"

She looked startled. "Hi," she stammered. "Do we know each other?"

"Sort of. I just friended you on Facebook last night and you accepted. I'm Kevin O'Bannion—but most people call me K.O."

For a moment or two Deluke was at sea. Finally the name clicked, and she offered a reluctant smile. "Oh. Oh yeah. How did you see my Facebook pic in the first place?"

"I don't even remember. We probably have one or more friends in common. Are you on your lunch hour?"

She checked her watch and nodded.

"Let me take you to lunch."

"Oh, that's okay."

"No, really. I can't just ignore lunch with a pretty lady. We can run upstairs to Café Sausalito. They have great salads there."

"Um," she said, casting hopeful looks around her for a savior. "I'm sorry, uh—Kevin, is it?"

"K.O.," he corrected her.

"K.O. Look, that's nice of you, but—" She giggled, more at herself than at him. "Frankly, you're a little young for me."

He oozed all the innocence he could muster. "I'm not hitting on you. I'm just back from Afghanistan, and I don't know many people in Cleveland. But I wasn't looking for you today; I was down here on business, and I ran into you by accident." Dolores still looked nervous.

"Look, you have to eat, right?" K.O. said.

"Well . . ."

"I'm buying."

That was the closer.

Café Sausalito is a pleasant-enough restaurant that unfortunately overlooks the Galleria's food court, noisy by design for two midday hours. It's hardly a "date" restaurant, but this was nowhere near a date. Dolores Deluke refused a glass of wine—she had to return to work later—but chose a salad. K.O. ordered a plain cheeseburger with hash browns. He knew salads were better for one's health, but he was still young enough to risk a heart attack on a plate.

"So," he said, clinking his iced tea glass against hers, "tell me all about yourself, Dolores. I read your profile last night, but I want to hear more."

"There's not much to tell. I'm an office assistant. I work upstairs."

"At Meacham, et cetera, et cetera?"

"Meacham, Bestwick and Wardwell, yes. I live in Chardon— alone. I have a cat . . ."

"No kidding! I have one, too. His name's Rodney."

She smiled. "Aw."

"A rescue cat—when I found him at the pound, he only had two days left."

She smiled. "Nice. My cat is Barbara."

K.O. burst out laughing.

"What?"

"I never heard of a cat named Barbara."

"It's a name!"

"Yeah—a person's name."

"So is Rodney. Why is it okay to name a cat Rodney but not Barbara?"

That stopped K.O. She had him cold—and was boring him senseless. "Okay, sorry. Barbara it is."

She grew quiet. She had little more to say, so her gaze wandered. She poked at her salad, enjoying it less than enduring it. He didn't want to press too hard, but a lunch hour is just that— and time was ticking away.

"I read about your law firm in the paper," K.O. said. "You're famous."

That got a smile out of her. "*I'm* not famous. The firm isn't all that famous, either—but some of our clients are."

"Movie stars?"

"In Cleveland? Not likely."

"Ballplayers, then—Indians and Browns. Or isn't it that kind of law firm?"

"We don't have athletes. We represent big industrial companies—and several local politicians, too."

"Like who?"

She found a mushroom slice, speared it, and chewed it thoughtfully. "I guess our biggest client is Jim Hundley—the most important one, anyway."

K.O. tried not to show too much interest. "Hundley. Isn't he the county prosecutor?"

She nodded. "He's on the phone with one of our lawyers at least three times a week. He comes up to the office once in a while, too—although mostly our lawyer has to go to *his* office."

"You don't know him personally?"

"God, no—he never even bothers saying hello to me. I'm just one of the 'little people.'" She used the expression bitterly, and K.O. couldn't blame her. Big shots, politicians, and celebrities—and those who *think* they are—rubbed him the wrong way when they referred to the rest of the world as "little people."

He tried making his next step a careful one. "Isn't Mr. Hundley one of the political guys in trouble with the feds?"

That made her laugh. "He's just about the only one who isn't."

"Not like, say, Councilman Loftus."

Dolores Deluke's forkful of lettuce was halfway up to her mouth, but it never arrived. "Bert Loftus isn't one of our clients," she almost whispered.

"But you know him—personally."

"Yes."

"I'm sorry, Dolores. Did I upset you?"

"No." Hesitant—lying.

"Are you dating Bert Loftus?"

"No!" More forceful. Probably truthful. "My God, no. I've—gone to dinner with him. But it wasn't a date. I mean, he never laid a hand on me—or acted like he wanted to."

"Why would Councilman Loftus invite you to dinner and not hit on you? Did it have something to do with your boss?"

She put her fork down and angrily pushed her plate away. "Say, who the hell are you, anyway? You didn't just happen to friend me on Facebook; you *knew* who I was—and you made it your business to be here when I took my lunch hour. You're *stalking* me. What's the deal anyway, Mr.—uh—?"

"K.O.," he corrected her, trying to make light of all of it.

"I don't give a shit what your initials are," she hollered, standing up so rapidly that silverware toppled off the table. Other customers glanced over, thinking it was a romantic spat.

"Stay the hell away from me!" she snarled. "Don't call me, don't e-mail me, don't Facebook me, and don't ever come near me again or I'll call the cops on you! I swear to God."

She didn't exactly flounce out. "Flouncing" is an angry girlfriend making a point with her temporarily eighty-sixed lover. Dolores Deluke's exit didn't disguise her fright.

K.O. stayed making notes that he didn't want to write down while Dolores Deluke was present. He hadn't told her he was a private eye.

Then again, he wasn't a private eye, exactly. Not yet.

He'd been so busy talking that he'd only taken a few bites of the cheeseburger and had hardly touched his french fries. Now they were cold. Besides, he wasn't hungry anymore, too anxious to find the last piece to complete the jigsaw puzzle that was Dolores Deluke. He waved to the waiter and pantomimed writing something on his hand that let him know he wanted a check.

The waiter strolled over; it *was* a stroll, accompanied by a contemptuous smirk—amused by Deluke's dramatic exit. He looked down at what was left of K.O.'s lunch. "You want a doggy bag for that, *sir*?" he said.

That cost him about one-third of his tip.

K.O. took the long escalator ride downstairs and killed another fifteen minutes on the first floor, looking through plate glass windows at the paintings and sculptures on display at the appointment-only art gallery. Then he wandered into the food court, only half-full at twenty minutes past one, sat down, and pulled out his cell phone.

"Meacham, Bestwick and Wardwell," a not-very-cheery female voice answered. "How may I direct your call?"

K.O. lowered his voice as much as possible. He was twenty-four and sounded like it, so he wanted to seem older, more solid, and more important. "I'm trying to reach whichever attorney represents County Prosecutor Hundley."

"One moment," she said, and typed something on her computer. Then: "That would be Mr. Wardwell's office. Hold on, sir, I'll connect you."

After about fifteen seconds, another voice said, "Curt Ward-well's office. May I help you?"

K.O. took a few seconds more to smile and then hung up. Curtis Wardwell was one of the managing partners of the law firm, the personal attorney of the powerful county prosecutor—and the voice of the office assistant answering his phone belonged to Dolores Deluke.

CHAPTER FIVE

MILAN

I stopped by my office after my meeting with Pam Marek and deciphered with difficulty my notebook jottings because I can barely read my own handwriting. Bert Loftus had been a councilman for so long he'd forgotten what a leader was supposed to be. I'd probably cheer when he got packed off to Club Fed—but he didn't deserve to be murdered. Anybody could be after him, even someone who had read about all of Loftus's shenanigans, bribes, and kickbacks and decided to wreak their own vengeance.

But I didn't think so. There were nutcases out there wanting to assassinate the president or some movie star who made a film they didn't like, or even a local writer who unwittingly pissed them off by using the wrong name in a novel. Maybe even a Cleveland politician. One way I could find out the bad guy's name is by bothering people close to Loftus for answers. And that sent me back on the Internet—to Google.

"Reverend Clarence Whitby Baptist Cleveland" got me to his name and parish—Baptist Enlightenment Church in the Ohio City area. Ohio City, by the way, is not really a city—at least not anymore. During the nineteenth century it was Cleveland's rival on the west side of the Cuyahoga River until feuding, economy, and bragging rights allowed Cleveland to take it over as its own. The good news is that it was no more than a ten-minute drive from my office—one reason I count myself fortunate to have moved my business to the Flats more than a decade ago.

Jeff and Vicki Ogrin didn't live that far from me, either, and the Internet taught me that they owned seven different apartment buildings, some in Tremont and some in Ohio City. One of those buildings, built right on the riverbank, was relatively new and a lot more expensive than its closest neighbors. The rest of them were very near to collapsing and falling in on themselves.

The Baptist Enlightenment Church was in a ramshackle old house north of Clark Street, on Fulton Avenue. The sidewalk had been swept clean, but otherwise it didn't look well taken care of. The sign announced the church's name and that of its pastor. The building's reddish-brown paint job had flaked off in several places. A bare 100-watt bulb burned over the front door; some-one, at least, was inside.

Another lower-wattage bulb burned in the tiny vestibule, barely illuminating the church. The inner walls had been knocked down to form one large room. At one end was a raised platform, like a stage; in its middle was a lectern. Behind it a large, plain cross was mounted on the wall. There was no music playing at five-thirty on a weekday afternoon. I called out a tentative hello.

I heard movement above me—footsteps on the uncarpeted floor—and a late-middle-aged woman appeared at the top of the stairs. I'm no judge of fashion, but the dark green suit she wore looked upscale for this part of Ohio City. So did the diamond-encrusted wedding ring. "Hello," she said cheerily as she started down. "May I help you with something?"

"Thank you," I said. "I hope I didn't disturb you."

She smiled. "Not at all." When she got down to my level she extended her hand. "I'm Mrs. Whitby—the pastor's wife."

I introduced myself and gave her one of my business cards. Her eyes lit up with recognition. "I've read about you, I think. You're pretty famous."

"Not so famous—but thanks anyway."

Her smile was subtle. "I'm guessing, knowing your back-ground—your name *is* Catholic, isn't it?—and your profession, that you're not here to talk about Jesus."

"Good guess," I said. "I wonder if Reverend Whitby can spare me a moment."

"He's working on a sermon."

"I won't take up much of his time."

Her shrug was nearly unnoticeable. "All I can do is ask," she said. "Make yourself comfortable." She turned and floated up the stairs. The only chairs on the first floor were folding metal chairs—three different kinds and colors that didn't match. I sat close to the staircase and waited, hearing murmuring from above.

After about five minutes I wondered if they'd decided to pretend I didn't exist and hope I'd go away. Not the case, as finally Reverend Clarence Whitby descended—dignified and dramatic. Slim and Lincoln-tall, perhaps as tall as I am, his well-barbered curly white hair set off his dark brown skin, looking good in the soft pink illumination of the weak light bulb. He had no jacket, as it was too warm and the church had no air conditioner. His shirt was light lavender silk, and his tie a Jerry Garcia creation. "Mr. Jacovich," he said majestically. He must have worked on his voice for years to make it sound like James Earl Jones's.

"Reverend Whitby," I said, rising and shaking his hand. "Sorry to bother you, sir, but I have a few questions—if you don't mind."

His frown was slight. "I *hope* I don't mind." He gestured for me to sit back down. He sat in the row ahead of me and turned his body toward me. "What can I tell you?"

"You're acquainted with Bert Loftus."

"Of course. He's my councilman."

"Are you friends?"

"I would say so. We lunch every month or so—or have dinner with our wives."

"Then you know about his current legal—difficulties?"

His brown eyes narrowed to an irritated squint. "I don't spend all my time with my nose buried in the Bible. Every so often I actually read a newspaper."

I thought that was snarky, so I didn't waste time on polite conversation. "You're a landlord."

"I own a few properties."

"In Councilman Loftus's district?"

"That shouldn't surprise you."

"It doesn't."

Whitby shrugged. "I own my own home, naturally, and I own this property—the church." His genial smile missed by several miles. "Well, I don't own the church, exactly—God owns the church." He looked up in the direction of that particular landlord. "But I own the building and the land—bought it eighteen years ago. It's in the 22nd Ward—Loftus's ward—as I'm sure you know."

"Are there other residential buildings you own?"

It took him a while to answer in the affirmative. Then he said, "I know your name, that you're a private detective—"

"Investigator," I said. "'Detective' is a police rank, and 'private' means I don't carry a badge."

"If you aren't wearing a badge, then why do I have to talk to you?"

"You don't *have to* do anything, Reverend."

"I'd prefer knowing who your client is."

"That's—confidential."

He grew a little taller, ready to score a palpable hit. "Then the other buildings under my name are confidential, too."

"Not at all, sir. They're right there on the Internet."

That seemed to tickle him. "Why ask me if you already know?"

"Because I want to know more about your relationship with Councilman Loftus—and whether you two exchanged—favors."

"Favors?"

"Call it whatever you want."

"Then," Whitby said, "I call it insulting. Everyone does favors for people they care about, and they do favors for you. That's how the world works." He rose to his full height and snarled at me like God himself rumbling from His secure perch on a cloud. "You have a nerve waltzing in here, disturbing my work and accusing me—*me*, an accredited minister, a man of the cloth—of doing, or helping Councilman Loftus do, anything illegal."

A man of the cloth? I hadn't heard that expression in forty years—and this coming from someone wearing a Jerry Garcia tie. Was some lousy ventriloquist supplying the tired clichés while Whitby just moved his mouth? For whatever reason, he wasn't about to tell me anything about what he did or didn't do, businesswise, with Bert Loftus. I stood, too. "I see."

"Do you? *Do* you see? Do you understand?"

"I understand, Parson, that those were an awful lot of words— considering a simple 'no' would have been sufficient." I started for the door, then turned to fire one last broadside at him. I noticed

Mrs. Whitby—or at least her legs—at the top of the staircase, listening. "Unless," I said, "that simple 'no' would've been a lie."

As I walked out to my car, I waited uncertainly for a lightning bolt from on high to strike me down, but it didn't happen, making me believe Clarence Whitby is *not* God. He just thinks he is.

My next stop wasn't far away. The apartment building, probably ninety years old, was located in the west fifties north of Detroit Avenue, a few blocks from Lake Erie. It was a lower-middle-class neighborhood—or was it an upper-lower-class neighborhood? I've never been able to figure out those upper-lower-middle categories. In any event, the building was short and squat, red brick you might see in every section of Cleveland—a multiple residence on the nickel end of a dollar street. I wasn't sure, but it seemed one of those subsidized housing places, mostly supported by the government. In the vestibule it was easy finding a buzzer for "J. and V. Ogrin," their names scrawled on white fabric tape with a thick black Sharpie. I pushed it for about five seconds and then put my hand on the knob of the inner door, waiting for the answering buzz. The door was jerked open instead, fast, the knob almost coming off in my hand.

The woman blocking the doorway had hair dyed an improbable bright red, her eyes a blue so faded they almost disappeared, her stance angry and challenging, and her cheeks burning scarlet, contrasting with the white lines around her lips. Her appearance was less a fashion choice than something she couldn't control. Her facial expression reminded me of a furious wolverine.

"What's the matter with you?" she demanded. No "hello," no "can I help you"—she must be one of those people who are enraged all the time. She made up in aggressiveness what she lacked in attractiveness. "Can't you read?" She pointed triumphantly to a sign over the mailboxes: NO SOLICITORS ALLOWED.

"I'm not selling anything—or asking for donations, either. Are you Ms. Ogrin?"

Fists on hips. *Fists.* "What's it to you?"

I produced one of my business cards. "I'm Milan Jacovich— I'm a security specialist. I'm hoping I might speak with you and Mr. Ogrin for a few minutes."

She looked at my card for so long, I thought she might memorize it to recite verbatim at a later date. Finally she said, "He doesn't feel well."

"I'm sorry to hear that. Shall I come back tomorrow?"

"He's always not feeling well."

She began closing the door, but I stopped it with a hand. "You don't know what I want yet."

"I don't give a damn what you want."

"Probably not—but you'd better talk to me before the guy with the subpoena comes knocking on your door."

The red in her face disappeared, leaving her cheeks and lips a taut white, her angry look not replaced, but joined by a frightened one. "What are you talking about? What subpoena?"

"You know perfectly well what subpoena," I said, my job forcing me to lie too often for comfort. "Shall we go inside?"

The fearsome glare was back again, as though I'd stolen her identity on the Internet and bought a luxury car with it, or set fire to her underwear drawer, or poisoned a litter of puppies. I wondered if she practiced that coruscating glower in front of a mirror every day or whether she'd been born with it. Still, she didn't slam the door in my face—or on my foot, which I'd extended over the sill just in case—but spun around and marched down the hall to her apartment at the rear. She didn't invite me in, but I chose to pretend she had.

The living room had no personality; everything had been purchased in second-hand furniture shops. Two windows looked out onto a dismal backyard needing a lawnmower. On the opposite wall hung an ugly print of an eighteenth-century painting featuring dead pheasants and geese stretched out on a butcher block kitchen table, waiting for plucking and beheading. Cheery.

On every flat surface, however—tables, shelves, even the top of the TV set—were articles I'd never seen before. When I discreetly looked closer, I saw they were all Buddha heads. Not Buddhas, mind you—I've seen plenty of those. Just Buddha *heads*. It looked as though at least fifty Buddhas had been beheaded.

"Jeff!" the woman barked, like a command, and almost at once the bedroom door opened and Jeff Ogrin came in to answer her summons.

It was as if a large building had walked through the door. Ogrin was nearly a quarter ton of humanity—the size and shape of a full-grown hog. He was almost as tall as I but weighed more than twice as much. I sympathize with people suffering from morbid obesity, but Jeff Ogrin took my breath away. He tottered, leaning on a cane to keep himself from toppling over, weaving from side to side and waving his arms for balance as he walked. Most men pack their weight in their bellies, arms, and chests, but Ogrin carried most of his in his wide womanly hips and lumpish legs. It didn't help that he was dressed in an old white XXXXL T-shirt stretched out of shape at the neck, gray sweatpants from a Big and Tall Men's Shop that cruelly cut into his lower mid-section, and white socks and dirty white sneakers. His reddish, squinty eyes looked as if he'd been fast asleep if he hadn't come through the door so quickly—and a strange odor hovered over him. I'd noticed it when I first walked in, but his presence in the room made it worse. I couldn't quite identify the smell. Maybe as if he'd died three days ago and was decaying.

As for his face—well, what could I say about that face? It was almost identical to that of the grotesquely octopussian intergalactic villain that gets blown away into space by the Green Lantern at the end of that terrible movie.

It's no wonder everyone at Bert Loftus's office referred to them as "The Ogres."

"Good evening," he mumbled like he didn't mean it. For such a huge man, he had an unusually high voice.

I introduced myself again and said I had a few questions, which made Jeff Ogrin uncomfortable. My surprise visit was upsetting him, or maybe he was just in physical discomfort—probably a bit of both. He didn't want to shake my hand but finally did so as if I'd been cleaning up after my dog and had forgotten a plastic bag to take on our walk.

Nobody suggested taking a seat, so we stood in that relatively small living room, filling up all the space. I'm a fairly big guy—around two-thirty if I weigh myself first thing in the morning—but Jeff made me feel like Mini-Me.

Initially my questions were answered by Vicki Ogrin's repetitive "None of your damn business!" She was more than a foot shorter than I, which saved me from her wrathful face thrusting inches from my own.

Finally Jeff broke in—I guess it took him that long to muster his breath. "Naturally we know Bert Loftus," he wheezed. "He's our councilman."

"Good friends?"

"*We* think so." Vicki again; she wouldn't let Jeff take more than two sentences away from her.

"You know he's under federal indictment?"

"Of *course* we know. We're not stupid."

"Do you care?"

Her angry chin jutted out like Bill Cowher's when he coached the Pittsburgh Steelers. "It's none of your business."

"Have those charges anything to do with you personally?"

"We haven't been charged with anything," Jeff offered.

"We haven't *done* anything," Vicki edited.

"I've looked you up on the Internet, Ms. Ogrin. I know how many buildings you own in this district. Mostly low-income residences—like this one."

"You're snooping! That's what you do, isn't it? You snoop on other people." She brandished my business card like a *West Side Story* dancer waving a switchblade. "Don't try bullying us. We can look *you* up, too!"

That gave me pause. It never occurred to me that I could be googled—but almost everyone could be, especially those who've done things they'd prefer not be exposed to the world with one computer click.

"Google away," I said.

"Don't worry, I will! I don't trust you." She wrinkled her nose as if uttering an obscenity. "You don't look honest."

She doth protest too much, I thought. "Who else knows you're in business with Bert Loftus?"

"Nobody said we're in business with Loftus!"

"Nobody had to," I said. "You've got an interesting business going in real estate, don't you? With all the money you're making, I wonder why you live in a building like this."

"What's wrong with this building?" she demanded, her face

upturned and angry. The distance between my height and hers didn't help her breath any.

"If I made the money you do, I'd live someplace that was a bit more homey."

"Homey?" Her brain was on boil now, her eyes glowing red, her words screamed instead of spoken. "Well, where is my home, then? Where *is* my home? And what the hell are you doing *in* it?"

I glanced at my watch. It was well into the evening, and I'd grown weary of her. "I can't even answer that," I said.

The door slammed violently behind me, and not a moment too soon. I started back down the hall when another apartment door opened and a woman poked her head out and said, "Psst!"

I tried not to smile. I've never really heard anyone actually *say* "Psst!" before. She looked furtively at the Ogrin apartment and then silently motioned me to come inside. When I did so, she closed the door behind me.

"Well, hello there," I said.

"Shh!" she whispered, jerking her thumb toward the wall. "You can hear right through these walls. I heard everything you said to them."

I began apologizing but she waved me quiet again. "They're such terrible people! They talk so loud! They argue all the time, or else he yells at her and calls her a stupid b-i-t-c-h—or a fag."

That threw me. Men call women many different names, some of them obscene—but I never heard one refer to a woman as a fag.

"That high voice cuts right through the walls and it's like he's sitting in *my* apartment instead of his." She ran a hand through her curly, recently permed white hair. "Their phone and computer are in their bedroom, right on the other side of the wall, and they keep me up all night long. He's always looking somebody up on the Internet and then whining and moaning about them to her. And when he's on the phone—oh, Lord! The other night he was talking to somebody—I think the name he called him was Henry or Harvey or something—and he told him at the top of his voice that Vicki is constipated all the time and has to take Miralax." She stuck her fingers in her ears, accompanied by a grimace. "I don't want to hear things like that!"

I didn't, either. Vicki Ogrin takes Miralax—pass it on. "Can't you complain about them?"

"Who can I complain to? They're the management! The Ogrins don't play loud music or have loud parties or anything—they hardly ever talk to anyone else except to bitch at them. They're just loud! And when he's in bed, well, I guess his bed is right next to the wall, so every time he turns over, the side of the bed scratches the wall and wakes me up. And if he doesn't do that, he lays there moaning and groaning and whining all night—and then he yells loud for her in the other room to go get him another blanket." She rocked her head from side to side. "It's rare when I can sleep eight hours straight without them waking me up. It drives me nuts!"

"I'm sorry to hear that," I said.

"I'd bet you a cookie he'll be looking *you* up on his computer— and then shouting out to Vicki that he found something about you that doesn't mean anything anyway."

"You'd probably win that cookie," I admitted. "He yells out to Vicki in the next room all night. Don't they sleep in the same room?"

"I'm sure I don't know," she said. "They've never let me in their apartment—not even one toe! But what kind of marriage is that, for heaven's sake? Would *you* share a bedroom with him?"

The visual that flashed through my mind was one I'd have paid a fortune to avoid. But elderly ladies often speak the truth, so I gave her my business card. "If you need me for anything, call me," I said.

She studied my card. "Security. What's that mean?"

"I'm a private investigator. Milan Jacovich." I pronounced my name slowly, just in case she'd ever need it.

"Are you investigating them?"

"No," I said. "Just asking questions on someone else's behalf."

"You should ask *me*. I could give you an earful about them!"

She already had. When I got to the vestibule, I checked the mailboxes once again. Hers was marked "Dorcas Rocker." I'd remember that—but hoped I wouldn't have to.

CHAPTER SIX

K.O.

When K.O. got home, Rodney met him at the door as he always did, meowing happily. K.O. fed him and then cuddled him for a while. Rodney liked this, up to a point, rubbing his whiskers against his owner and purring until he got bored. Once he was installed on the back of the sofa, staring out the window and waiting for outside entertainment—fascinated by watching birds he couldn't get to—K.O. opened his computer and typed out a report on the meeting with Dolores Deluke and what he'd discovered about Loftus and his connection to the county prosecutor, and sent it to Milan Jacovich's computer.

K.O. was better on electronic stuff than Milan, but he didn't know five percent of what his boss knew about local politics and county prosecutors. Milan, in business a long time, knew practically everyone even slightly important in Cleveland. K.O. had spent most of his teens avoiding beatings or rapes in the juvenile detention shower and watching where he stepped in Iraq and Afghanistan. If his Deluke meeting helped Milan on the Loftus case, he hoped to learn how, so he would know what Milan knew.

His e-mail report was detailed—and Milan's e-mail report to him was pretty complete, too, mostly about his visit to Jeff and Vicki Ogrin. He even referred to them as "the Ogres," which made K.O. laugh.

By the time K.O. finished e-mailing and taking notes, Carli was on her way to his apartment. He washed and dried his breakfast dishes, ran a vacuum cleaner over the rug, and dusted the tops of the furniture. Then he jumped in the hot-as-he-could-stand-it shower, shaved, and put on the nicest casual clothes he owned: his only white dress shirt and relatively clean khakis. Then he put away whatever else was in the living room, including the DVD of the film he'd watched last night—an oldie, *The Glass Key* with Veronica Lake and Alan Ladd. K.O. hoped that some day he would be as tough as Alan Ladd was in the movies.

He should have made a reservation at some restaurant, but it was too late now. Besides, he'd never done it before. He had much to learn.

He wanted to provide a snack for his guest—but all he had was half a bag of potato chips, and he didn't even own a decent-looking bowl. He was nervous. Her first time visiting his apartment put a whole new twist on things. He wanted to be classy, fun, and low-key romantic but was worried he'd scare the crap out of her the way he'd done with Dolores Deluke at lunch that afternoon.

Goddamn it! he thought. Why hadn't he grown up normal like everybody else?

Carli rang the doorbell one minute earlier than her announced ETA. Milan and K.O. differed on many things, but they were both annoyed by people who were habitually late.

Further relief came when she kissed him as he opened the door. They'd kissed before, but that one surprised him—almost as much as the shopping bags she brought in with her.

She put her bags on the kitchen counter. "I decided to cook for both of us. Is that okay?"

"You didn't have to do that."

"I don't have to do *anything* except what I want. Do you?"

"Not as much as I'd like."

She reached out and touched his cheek. "Hang in there, Kevin—you'll learn."

She said "Kevin." She touched his cheek. Wow.

She unloaded two steaks, two ears of corn, green leaf lettuce, a cucumber, a package of sliced mushrooms, a bottle of balsamic vinegar salad dressing, and some ice cream—butter pecan. She'd also bought a bottle of Zinfandel. He didn't know what that should taste like but was impressed nonetheless. As soon as she unwrapped the steaks, Rodney jumped down from the back of the sofa, meowing how much he wanted some beef, too, rubbing his whiskers on her leg.

"Well, hi, cutie," she said, reaching down and scratching him behind his ears.

"This is Rodney."

"Well then, hi, *Rodney*."

"I rescued him from a shelter. He's—my best friend."

"That's a good friend to have found."

"So, what can I do to help with dinner?"

"Since you know where everything is, you can set the table."

He looked at his pathetic dining room set. "It's a beat-up table. I wish I'd known we were going to eat in."

"Why?" she said. "So you could buy new furniture? I don't even *have* a dinette; I eat all my meals off the coffee table—on paper plates."

"Then you've come to a pretty fancy place."

It took him two minutes to set the table—the silverware didn't match, and the plates were plastic, not china or stoneware. He didn't have wine glasses and hoped Carli wouldn't mind drinking from dollar-apiece water glasses from Drug Mart. K.O. had tacky salt and pepper shakers and was unsure if he'd filled the one with pepper. He hung around the edge of the kitchen, watching her. She moved like a dancer, and he wondered if some day he'd have to dance with her. He hadn't danced with anyone since junior high school, and he'd sucked at it back then.

She pulled out the broiler drawer and covered the grill with aluminum foil. "Rare, medium, or well done?" she said.

"Surprise me."

"I like surprises."

"Why?"

She washed and tore up several leaves of lettuce and built a salad. "Because when we know each other better, it'll be more interesting."

They ate half the salad before she threw the steaks and corn cobs on the broiler. He wasn't a big salad eater, but the fact that it was her salad and her idea made it taste just fine.

In moments the steaks smelled incredible.

"You'd better open the wine," Carli suggested, "and let it breathe."

"Sure," K.O. said, and then panicked. He didn't have a wine bottle opener. After a moment he remembered his Swiss Army knife and went into the bedroom to dig it out of his top drawer. Thank God it had a corkscrew on it, but his next challenge was *using* it properly.

They clinked glasses—not a melodious clink, but more of a clunk. That's dollar glasses for you. K.O. liked the Zinfandel. He wasn't sure, but it might have been the first sip of wine in his life.

"Mmm," Carli said. "Nice. So tell me, how's the new job?"

"It's okay. I find myself talking to strange people about strange things. I guess I'm comfortable with it—but I need to learn better manners."

"Like saying please and thank you?"

"Like getting answers I want without pissing people off." He told her a bit about his conversation with Dolores Deluke that afternoon—without disclosing why he'd engineered bumping into her in the first place.

She nodded. "That was inventive."

"I thought it up myself—it has a lot to do with local politicians."

"Crooked politicians?" She laughed at herself. "Or is that an oxymoron?" She took another sip, smiling at him over the rim, her brown eyes glowing red from the reflection of the wine. "You're going to be great." Then she frowned, looking concerned. "Nobody's dead this time, are they?"

"No—Milan and I will make sure that doesn't happen."

She reached out again and touched beneath his eye. The bruise from his last fight, when he was working part-time for Milan Securities, was fading to an afterthought purple. Not gone yet, but the touch of her gentle fingers would heal it completely, he knew. No woman had ever touched his face like that before. He held her hand against his face for a few seconds too long.

"Mmm," she said. "So—no more fights, Kevin?"

"I hope not. Hey, nobody calls me Kevin, you know? It's K.O."

"Yes, but the 'K' stands for Kevin, right? Then that's what I'll call you—just because nobody else does."

He ducked his head, not wanting to look too eager. "Call me anything you want."

"Like 'late for breakfast'?"

His cheeks flamed. No wide-eyed innocent, he was twenty-four years old, had spent three teen years in the slammer and much of his young adulthood in the desert, where he desperately yearned for his well-earned two-week leaves so he could repair to somewhere and kick up his heels. But Carli was different—to him, anyway—and her breakfast remark sounded almost risqué.

"I usually don't eat breakfast," he said lamely. "Just coffee."

"Well, finish your whole dinner then," Carli said. "Otherwise you'll be weak from hunger in the morning."

The steaks were perfect, thanks to Carli. He'd never cooked a steak in his life, but he was too on edge to eat much. When they got around to the butter pecan ice cream, he said, "It was nice of you to haul all this food up here and cook it for me."

"I got the idea you weren't the domestic type."

"I wouldn't think the domestic type would interest you."

"Not at the moment. I'm too young for domesticity."

"No boyfriend?"

She shook her head. "Not for awhile."

He thought of all those pictures of her on Facebook—the ones with other men—and wondered which of them was her most recent lover. He wouldn't look through those photos again because he didn't want to know. Instead he concentrated on her being single and drop-dead adorable and having bought him dinner and cooked it in his apartment.

So when she accidentally got a smidgen of butter pecan ice cream on her lower lip, it seemed the most natural thing in the world for him to lean over and kiss it off. It was the best-tasting ice cream of his lifetime.

That was at five minutes to ten. By ten minutes after, they were in the bedroom together. At thirteen minutes after, they were both down to their underwear when the phone rang. The Caller ID said it was Milan Jacovich.

Carli looked at the Caller ID, too. "You'd better answer that," she said, her disappointment almost worse than his. "It might be important."

That's when Milan told K.O. he wanted to meet him in downtown Cleveland, just on the other side of the Detroit–Superior Bridge, right away.

"Don't get dressed up or anything," Milan said. "Just get here."

K.O. didn't say out loud what he was thinking, but he practically snarled. "Right away."

Shit! he thought.

CHAPTER SEVEN

MILAN

A s soon as I got Bert Loftus's hysterical phone call, I called
K.O. and told him to meet me. I didn't know what he was
doing, but he sounded annoyed that I was bothering him. I
threw on a pair of jeans, sneakers with no socks, and a light wind-
breaker over my Cleveland Indians shirt. I didn't imagine I'd run
into anyone who'd care how I was dressed this late in the evening.

Loftus had beckoned me to a small slice of Cleveland a few
yards from the Cuyahoga River that used to be called The Angle.
A century and a half earlier it was a ghetto for newly arrived Irish
immigrants. Things have changed.

When I drove up to the corner of Detroit Avenue and West
25th Street—or as close as I could get, since it was crowded with
cops, reporters, four video units (one for each of the local sta-
tions), and neighborhood hangers-on—it looked like a small-
town carnival preparing to open for business. I counted six patrol
cars with roof lights flashing, turning everyone's faces red, white,
and blue by turns. Bright lights focused on TV reporters—I knew
all their names—making everyone else squint. I ran my fingers
through my thinning hair and hoped like hell no local news re-
porter would point a camera at me. I especially looked for Vivian
Truscott, the Channel 12 anchorperson on the six o'clock news
show, but she was nowhere in sight. News anchors don't person-
ally arrive to do stand-ups on a street corner in the middle of
the night—especially tall, blonde, beautiful, regal-looking news
anchors.

Almost as many people were milling around, mostly for no discernible reason, as had shown up to gawk at the filming of a major superhero movie on the streets of downtown Cleveland.

It didn't take me long to spot my client. On the phone, Bert Loftus's voice was shaky, raspy, and highly emotional, and from the look of him, nothing had changed. He huddled miserably on the steps of the venerable Saint Malachi Church, trying to avoid the TV lights and stand-up reporters who wanted to shove a microphone in his face, shivering despite the warmth of the evening, chain-smoking, and wiping his nose and eyes as if he'd been crying. Cleveland's a tough town, a muscular town, a place where guys don't cry—especially famous, powerful, and unbreakable guys like Bert Loftus, who practically own the city and run it as their own private money machine.

An elderly priest with an impish Irish countenance stood at the top of the church steps with hands clasped behind his back, overseeing the commotion and making sure everyone knew he was only an observer. Saint Malachi is five minutes from the middle of downtown, and everyone has heard of it. I knew about it ever since I was a small kid, even though I grew up on the east side of the city and cut my Catholic teeth at Saint Vitus in the old Slovenian neighborhood. Saint Mal went down in history in 1975 when infamous racketeer and numbers runner Shondor Birns, the head of the Jewish Mafia in Cleveland, was leaving a bar across the street—long gone now—and was blown to bits in his car on Holy Saturday evening. It was one hell of a blast, I recall—people said they heard it from a dozen blocks away—and pieces of him landed right on the church steps where Bert Loftus now sat. It had been an indelible moment for the Catholic parishioners gathering for an eight o'clock evening Mass.

I'm on a first-name basis with some local cops but not the uniformed guys present that particular evening, who didn't want to allow me past the barriers. Some, I was certain—the ones with military haircuts and deadly serious scowls—still only shaved twice a week. I finally caught the eye of Detective Sergeant Matusen of Homicide and waved at him. He approached me with reluctance, probably because he was chatting with a stunning black woman almost as tall as he was. If I'd been talking with her, I'd have been reluctant to leave her, too.

"What brings you here, Milan?" He squished his half-smoked butt to death with his toe; homicide cops never seem able to finish a cigarette. He wore one of his seersucker suits, as he does all summer—and I say "one of them" with hope in my heart, because they all look the same to me. Perhaps he only owns one that he wears every day. It fit him badly; he couldn't decide whether his belly should be covered by his trousers and tightened around his ever-expanding waistline, or slopping over his belt when he buttoned his pants beneath. His standard police weapon made a bump on his hip beneath the jacket.

"A phone call—from Councilman Loftus," I answered.

"He didn't call *me*," Matusen said. "He called the mayor, who got all bent outta shape about it and was on the phone to us to get down here double quick."

"But you're homicide. Did anyone get killed?"

"Not yet. Come on in."

He pulled the barrier aside so I could slip past it and follow him over to where Bert Loftus sat.

"Oh, Milan," Loftus blubbered, "thank God you're here." He stood and wrung my hand in both of his, like trying to squeeze water from a dishrag. The crotch of his gray slacks was wet, the smell of urine hanging around him in the warm air. I was afraid he'd kiss me—or even worse, give me a hug.

I discreetly backed away from him. "Relax and tell me what happened, Bert."

He couldn't find enough breath to get started. Shaking his head as if denying the reality that stared all of us in the face, he wordlessly pointed to his car, parked at the curb a few yards away. Same old Lincoln—except this time there was a bullet hole in the driver's side window and another in the passenger-side window. I strolled over to look, then moved back to Loftus and Matusen. "One shot?"

"Right through, Milan. In one window and out the other," Matusen said, saving Loftus the trouble. "Happened a block from here. The councilman was heading for the Detroit–Superior

Bridge when someone drove up beside him and laid one across his broadside."

"Right beside him?" I looked at Loftus. "Were you and the other car moving, or were you stopped for a red light?"

"Moving," Loftus finally managed to get out. "Going maybe forty."

"In a thirty-five mile zone," Matusen observed.

"Someone was a lousy shot," I said.

Bert's voice, usually modulated and very public, was now almost too high for anyone to hear but dogs. "They tried to kill me, Milan. The bullet went right by my nose—I could damn near smell it—and out the other window." His hand shook as he pointed at his Lincoln.

"Who was 'they'? White guys, black guys, young, old?"

"You think I stopped to see the scenery?" Bert Loftus couldn't decide whether to be outraged or scared half to death. "The minute I heard the shot I ducked down. I didn't look to see who it was."

"Was it the same car as the one driving by the Tiny Bar and shooting at you the other night? Big black sedan?"

"I dunno—too scared to notice." He looked down at his shoes and then at his crotch, covering the wetness behind his hands, as a woman might do if she'd just stepped out of the shower and found a strange man in her bathroom. "Jesus," he moaned, "I pissed myself! How fucking embarrassing is that?"

"It happens to the best of us," Matusen assured him.

I said, "Was anyone sitting in your passenger seat?"

"I was alone. Goddamnit, I'm always alone!"

"What were you doing out tonight—in this neighborhood?"

All at once he didn't know what to do with his hands. "Uh—visiting a friend."

"Which friend is that?"

"You—wouldn't know this person."

"You've paid me money, Bert. Don't fuck with my head."

He lowered his voice to a hiss. "I don't want this getting out."

"I don't care whether you got laid or not. Name, Bert."

Before Loftus could tell me, the black woman who'd been

speaking with Matusen earlier came over to us. Matusen sucked in his gut and tried standing taller. He'd worked under Lieutenant Florence McHargue for a decade and had been her performing puppy, trotting behind her, trying to be unobtrusive. Now he seemed to trail after this one.

She looked at me, trying to figure out who I was and why I was at a crime scene. I didn't recognize her either. The bright TV lights were harsh, but they didn't hurt her looks any. I figured her to be in her late forties, and her eyes were unlike any I'd seen before—a *light* green. I noticed she didn't wear a wedding ring.

Finally Matusen said to Loftus, "Councilman, Detective Sergeant Blaine will take down your statement." Then he looked from the woman to me and back again. "Oh, yeah—introductions. Detective Blaine, this is Milan Jacovich. He used to be one of us, but now he's private."

A perfect eyebrow went up—the left one. "If he were really private," she said to Matusen, "he wouldn't *tell* us his name. Hello, Mr. Jacovich." Sexy voice even when she wasn't trying. Low, competent. She didn't offer a handshake, but cops on attempted murder investigations usually don't.

"Nice to meet you, Detective."

"I imagine it would be. Do you work for Councilman Loftus?"

"I'm self-employed—and my clients are always temporary."

She nodded absently, then took out her notebook and pen and gave all her attention to Loftus.

I stepped away and leaned in to Matusen. "Is she new?"

"She was Cincinnati PD for fourteen years. Before that, she was in Raleigh." Then he added, "North Carolina."

"I know where Raleigh is. When did she start here?"

"Monday morning."

"She'll be busier in Cleveland than in Raleigh. Is she as tough as McHargue?"

"*Nobody* is as tough as McHargue," he said. "But Tobe seems to be a good cop."

"Tobe? That's her first name?"

"You pronounce it like 'Toby,' with a 'Y,' but you spell it T-O-B-E."

"That's a new one on me."

"Me, too. She said it originated in the Yiddish language—kind of like '*mazel tov*'. It means 'luck'."

"Funny," I said, "she doesn't *look* Jewish."

Matusen hitched his shoulders. "Cops don't ask other cops their religion."

Tobe. Nice name, I thought as I pronounced it silently in my head. Different. I watched her discreetly while she interviewed Loftus. Tall, lean, professional—and attractive to boot. I wondered how she'd get along with McHargue. They were close to the same age, both African American, both homicide cops. Would they embrace sisterhood—or gnaw out each other's throats?

I had other thoughts as I looked down the street at K.O. approaching, looking pretty snappy in what were probably his best casual clothes, except it appeared he'd thrown them on in a hurry. He also looked highly annoyed—just the way he sounded when I called him. I hoped he didn't think that the job is only nine to five, because bad people do most of their misdealings in the night.

"What's all this shit about at—" K.O. looked at his wrist, but apparently he hadn't put his watch on. He must have left as quickly as I had.

"It's almost eleven," I said.

"Jesus Christ!" He scuffed his shoe on the sidewalk and shook his head.

"Are you pissed off about something?"

"No."

"Nothing?"

"Nothing *you'd* understand."

I wanted further explanation, but not here. I told him what had transpired. K.O. looked at Loftus, who'd sat back down again and was whimpering. Then he looked at the car.

"He'll probably take it back to Deuce like last time and they'll replace his windows and not charge him anything. Arrogant cheap shit!" he said. Then: "Loftus is on the church steps bawling like a baby who sat in a diaperful of his own shit, and he called you because someone shot at him."

"He called the mayor, actually. But he called me first. The bullet hole in his car window is nothing to ignore."

"He didn't seem upset about the first two attempts. He tried to bargain—to get us to work for nothing—which didn't sound like an attempted murder victim—and he didn't call the police either time, right? But tonight everything's different."

"What's your point?"

"This time the shooting was real, the attempted killing was real, and it scared the piss out of him."

"*Literally*," I said. "Don't let him hug you or you'll be sorry."

"I doubt," K.O. said, "that he'd hug me."

"His car *was* banged up before—you checked the body shop that repaired it. And somebody did shoot a piece out of the brick wall outside the Tiny Bar."

"But he could have lied about the two earlier attempts, or actually staged them himself."

It was a good assumption for a kid who'd only worked full-time as a P.I. for the past three days. "This isn't the time to ask him—not in front of every cop in town."

K.O. glared over at Loftus half pityingly and half something else. "Can we get his ass back in our office?"

I tried not to show how pleased I was. *Our* office. "I'll ask him. You made it here from Mentor pretty fast."

"I drove eighty all the way." He shook his head—still aggravated. "I'd hate to keep *you* waiting."

"I'm sorry—did I interrupt something?"

He shoved his hands into his hip pockets, rolling his eyes skyward like a fifteen-year-old girl as he considered how to answer. "Barely."

Detective Tobe Blaine came back over to us. Her walk, the way she carried herself reminded me of someone else—her squared shoulders, the swagger, the impressive self-confidence. Maybe she'd seen too many Robert Mitchum movies. I introduced K.O. to her as my associate—and again, no handshake, just a curt nod.

"How long have you been on the job, kid?" she asked.

"Too long," K.O. said, "to let anybody call me 'kid.'"

"Whoa, sensitive! Should I refer to you as Mr. O'Bannion?"

"You can call me K.O.—and I'll still call you Detective Blaine, which gives you a leg up on me. Fair?"

Blaine considered it. "Fair enough," she said, a little respect mixed in with the amusement. "So—you both *do* work for Bert Loftus."

"We work for my company—Milan Securities. The councilman approached us to do research for him."

"Research?" She wasn't buying it. "He could hire a college sophomore to do research. What kind of research are you doing?"

"You should probably ask Mr. Loftus," I said.

"Or deal out some Tarot cards. But I'm asking you."

"Loftus is a city councilman."

"And I'm a police officer."

"I don't know what rules you played by in Cincinnati, but here, P.I.'s don't answer questions so easily."

"Cincinnati—how'd you find that out? News travels fast in Cleveland. Well, on only my second day here, I learned all about you, too. You catch killers and bad guys—all the time."

"I only caught five today," I said, "but I slept in this morning."

"Wake up early tomorrow," Tobe Blaine said, "and meet me for breakfast. Nine o'clock sharp at the Big Egg." She pointed vaguely west. "That's right down Detroit a ways."

"I know where the Big Egg is, Detective—I've lived in Cleveland all my life. What will we discuss over breakfast?"

"The philosophy of Keynesian economics—if you know what that is."

"I have a master's degree, Detective Blaine."

"So do I."

"Well then," I said, "I wouldn't miss it for the world."

"If you had the world, your upstairs butler would serve breakfast in bed."

"No way. I hate toast crumbs in bed."

"I hate crumbs in bed, too," she said. "Best you'd remember that." Then she spun on her heel and walked away.

K.O. stood near Loftus but neither spoke much. I whispered to K.O., "I'm supposed to have breakfast with that cop. God knows why."

Loftus had taken off his lightweight sports jacket and was holding it with both hands, covering his pee-stained crotch. I didn't like him, but I feel sorry for anyone who pisses all over himself in public. "Bert," I said gently, "you'll have to come in again tomorrow."

He drew himself up tall. "You'd be better off out on the street trying to find who shot me."

"Nobody shot you," K.O. observed quietly. "You're healthy. Shot *at* you."

"Call it noon, Councilman," I said. "And that means noon. It doesn't mean twelve thirty or two o'clock or *sometime*. It means when the big hand and the little hand both point to twelve. Otherwise, find someone who works cheaper—and on your schedule."

He started to say something else, but I put my hand up, palm nearly in his face. "And I still want the answer to the question I asked a minute ago."

Loftus looked lost at sea. "What question was that again?"

"Who were you seeing this evening?"

Again he lowered his voice. "I don't want my wife finding out—"

"Every reporter in Northeast Ohio knows that somebody shot at you, and everyone else will know what happened by morning, your wife included. I won't mention names—why would I spill the beans to her?—but this is serious. So I want that name."

Bert's eyes were pleading, but the innocent babe look didn't work. Men of wealth and power like Berton K. Loftus think they can do whatever they want without consequences. When they get caught—when their wives find out—they beg for forgiveness. I could forgive Loftus just as long as his retainer lasted.

He began looking around again, terrified that someone would hear him. I handed him my notebook and pen. "Write it down," I said.

Reluctantly he scribbled something down. "This is for your eyes only," he murmured. "If it gets out, I'm fucked!" His handwriting looked like that of someone in their nineties, but when he handed the pad back to me, I was able to read it.

Seena Bergman, he'd written. Below it was her address. I recognized it immediately—an elegant, fairly new building sporting great views of the river, the downtown skyline, and Lake Erie. It was close enough to Saint Mal that I could walk to it. Loftus slouched back toward the steps, trying to keep the TV reporters away by saying, "No comment" over and over again. I took K.O. aside. "You'd better be at the office tomorrow when he shows up."

"Noon? That means he'll waltz in at three o'clock or so."

"Not this time. When you get home, google Seena Bergman, and e-mail me whatever you find. She lives right around the corner, and apparently Loftus was with her until he left and had to duck a bullet."

"He wanted us to think he was shagging Dolores Deluke, too, and it turned out he wasn't. At least, that's what she told me."

"Check Seena anyway. He's anxious his wife not hear about her."

"Lucky him," K.O. scowled. He's always ticked off about something; this evening he was in high gear. "At least *he* didn't get interrupted."

"Did my call interrupt *you*?"

"I wasn't doing anything—*yet*. If you'd called ten minutes later, I wouldn't have answered the phone."

"Sorry. But blame Loftus—or the shooter. Don't blame me."

"Sure, Milan," he said through clenched teeth. "But next time you're getting laid, tell me—so I can call you at the wrong time."

"Why would you assume," I said, sadder than he, "that I'd be getting laid?"

CHAPTER EIGHT

K.O.

Kevin O'Bannion was even more furious driving back to Mentor than he'd been in the first place. What might have been the most romantic and important moment of his life had turned into a forty-mile round trip to hold the hand of a corrupt political whiner who'd pissed his pants. Talk about interruptions!

Carli had left before he got home; he hadn't expected she'd wait. Nonetheless, he was crushed. She'd washed all the dinner dishes and the broiling pan before she left—so thoughtful—and put the remainder of the wine in the refrigerator. K.O. was just angry enough to guzzle the rest of it, right out of the bottle. He knew better than to drink while enraged, but he'd lost the evening he'd planned for and dreamed of—lost it and would never get it back. Getting hammered on wine made a lot of sense.

It wasn't until he went into the bedroom to kick off his clothes that he found Carli's note on the pillow. "Call me." No signature—but below the message was the perfect imprint of her lips in the color of lipstick he'd had to wipe from his mouth as he headed downtown a few hours earlier. His heart turned to butterfly wings.

He studied the note, smiling without knowing it. Was he falling in love with Carli? He wasn't sure what love *was*. He'd never loved anything in his life, except, of course, Rodney. Rodney slept sixteen hours a day, but while K.O. and Carli had had their dinner, he'd prowled beneath the table, hoping one of them might drop something he'd consider good enough to eat. When finally, after the ice cream, they had repaired in some heat to the bedroom, Rodney had been shut out by a closed door.

Now Rodney was asleep on the pillow next to the note. K.O. petted him, scratching gently under his chin, which always made him half open his eyes in ecstasy, but he refused to grant K.O. the privilege of waking up. K.O. carefully folded the little note so the lipstick wouldn't smudge and put it in the bottom of his socks drawer.

Now that he was happy, mellowed out, and no longer furious with Milan, he wished he hadn't finished the wine, as he had work to do. He made instant coffee in the microwave—instant coffee is ghastly, as always, but K.O. didn't own a coffee maker and gulped it down, then made another cup, hoping to clear his head.

The first thing he noticed on his laptop was an e-mail from Carli. He never got personal e-mails from anyone, but she'd sent it as soon as she got home—less than an hour ago. He read it immediately—another extra-short note: "Sleep tight, sweetie. Don't let the bedbugs bite. Me xoxoxoxoxox"

He transferred it to his rarely used "Save" file to look at over and over again. Then he brought up the Google page and typed "Seena Bergman" in the Search box.

There were many sites listed for "Sheena," including a few that mentioned some old TV show, "Sheena, Queen of the Jungle," which K.O. was too young to remember. But it took half an hour before he found Seena Bergman. She wasn't on any interesting sites or in news reports—but she *was* listed in the White Pages, which just gave her address, a building two blocks from where Bert Loftus had been attacked that evening.

Milan was to meet Detective Blaine for breakfast the next morning, so K.O. made his own assignment, setting his alarm for 6:45 a.m. It seemed like the drive to work in the Cleveland Flats got longer every day. He was considering moving closer to town.

That would depend on whether he kept his job with Milan Security.

In the morning he stopped in Panera for coffee and what they call a bear claw, which is bigger than what most people eat for breakfast, before he drove to Cleveland. K.O. couldn't see what Milan disliked about chain restaurants. Panera coffee was better than the instant coffee he made, and he'd refilled his cup there without anyone bothering him. He wondered why anyone would pay for a large coffee when they could buy a small one and keep refilling it.

The other good thing about Panera is that no one leaves a tip.

He crossed the river over the Detroit–Superior Bridge at a few minutes after ten and parked across the street from Saint Mala-chi, where he'd been the night before, although no pee-pants pol-itician quivered on the steps, and there was no watchdog priest in sight. He walked the two blocks to the building in question, went inside, and checked the directory. "Bergman" was listed in apartment 303. He pressed the button and after twenty seconds a tinny female voice answered: "Yes?"

"Ms. Bergman?"

"Who's that?"

"I'm—a friend of Councilman Loftus," he said.

A longish pause, but he could hear her breathing. Then she said, "Stay there for two minutes 'til I buzz you in."

He waited, looking out through the glass door at the sunshine for more like ten minutes than two, until a loud buzz admitted him.

The tiny elevator, which could only carry three people at a time—and only if they happened to be very good friends—rose slowly to the third floor. He got out and looked down the cor-ridor. Seena Bergman had opened her door and stood in front of it, waiting for him.

She looked old enough to be his mother. It was too early for her to be made up and looking presentable enough for visitors, but she had a tan, undoubtedly acquired in a salon and not on the beach, and had quickly slapped on some lipstick and too much mascara, and combed her shoulder-length, badly dyed blonde hair. She wore a relatively short dark blue dress and garish yel-low high heels. Her toenail polish didn't match her fingernails. Around her waist, her pitiless muffin-top was obvious. Her right hand, down at her side, clutched a cigarette. She had the face of a retired stevedore.

She said, "Jesus, you're so young!" Some greeting.

"Can't help it. Maybe I should come back in twenty years."

"Don't be a smart-ass," she said. "Who are you?"

He told her.

"That an Irish name?"

K.O. laughed. "O'Bannion? What was your first clue?"

Her study was so intense, K.O. feared she would check his teeth next. She said at last, "You're friends with Bert Loftus?"

"Uh—more acquaintance than friend."

She puffed, blowing smoke his way. "Okay, then," Seena Bergman said. "Come on in."

Her apartment, though not large, was colorfully busy. Modern furniture, bookcases, and cabinets were alive with roaring hues— bright purple, kelly green, pink. She had lots of plants, too. The broad windows framed downtown, the Cuyahoga River, and a bit of Lake Erie, all summer morning sparkle. The high rent had much to do with the view.

"Sit down. You're pretty young."

He took the purple sofa. "You said that before."

"Surprising, that's all."

"I was supposed to be born at the age of fifty, but my mother screwed up."

Her smile was uncertain, not getting the sarcasm. "I wish you'd called first; I would've fixed myself up. I know what men like. This is pretty early in the morning for me." She crushed her cigarette into a big crystal ashtray. "You want something to drink?"

"No, thanks."

"Coffee? Tea? Orange juice?"

"Not thirsty."

She sat next to him—not close, but near enough that he could reach her if he wanted to. Not that he wanted to.

"So," she said. "How do you know Bert Loftus? Do you work for the city?"

"No, sorry."

She scowled as if K.O. was making her ask too many questions. "What is it, then? Did you do him a favor? Or did he do you one?"

"A favor?"

"There must've been *some* favor involved—or Bert Loftus wouldn't of sent you here for a payoff at ten o'clock in the morning."

"A payoff? Are you supposed to give me money?"

Her lips turned into a humorless straight line. "Is that supposed to be funny? Don't be fucking obtuse. Try not to make this unpleasant for either of us, okay?"

"Try not to make *what* unpleasant?"

She glared at him and immediately lit another cigarette. After her Bette Davis exhale: "If you want me to be crude, fine. Did you come here to get laid, or not?"

Holy crap, he thought. "Hardly."

He didn't mean it *that* way, but she reacted as though he'd smacked her. "Then why *are* you here this early in the morning?"

"I'm working—security, private investigations." He gave her an apologetic look. "I don't have business cards yet."

"You're a private cop?"

"Apprentice private cop. We're doing some work for Councilman Loftus."

Her back stiffened. "Oh, for God's sake. What kind of work?"

"I can't tell you. That's why we call it 'private.'"

Whatever look she'd bestowed on him turned into a sneer. "Don't shovel shit at me, kiddo. Bert Loftus is a crook who's going to prison, and I'll bet he hired you to try and get him out of it."

"That doesn't sound friendly."

"So what? Bert's no friend of mine."

"Have you watched TV this morning or read the paper?"

Haughty. "Do I look like I watch television?"

"Then you don't know somebody tried to kill him last night."

The color fled from her cheeks; now the lipstick looked garishly red on an otherwise white face. "What?"

"About two blocks away. He said he was leaving your place."

Seena looked away.

"Well, *was* he here?"

Her exhale was a long, sad sigh. "Yeah—he was here, all right."

"For . . . ?"

"What the hell do you think for?"

"Sorry to ask you—but are you Bert Loftus's mistress?"

Outraged, she asked. "What kinda nineteenth-century question is that?"

"I can use twenty-first century words, but you won't like them."

She got to her feet and moved to the window, drawing deeply on her cigarette. She blew the smoke toward the glass, but it bounced back at her. "Mistress?" she said. "Grow up, kid. I'm nobody's mistress—I'm a hooker."

"I'm sorry," K.O. said, meaning it. "I didn't know."

She leaned against the window. "I worked for the county for thirteen years—mostly in the assessor's office—and got to meet an awful lot of people. I wanted to be an actress and tried hard until enough people told me I didn't have a prayer of getting an acting career. I was a flirt, I guess—until somebody with money and power made me a proposition. So now I don't put in any more forty-hour work weeks. I live well and smile a lot—not all the time, though."

"It's not a bad life for a hooker, when you get right down to it. I'm specialized. I don't just put out for anybody. I have a select clientele. I get a nice salary, plus tips—and the rent on this joint is paid. So's the lease on my car. I get calls that certain people will be visiting me, and I make sure I'm here and available. And sure, Loftus was here last night—but I don't know anything about what might of happened to him after he left."

"Nobody knows he was here?"

"*I* didn't tell anybody, but God knows who he'd bragged his mouth off to. That's why I was surprised seeing you this morning—without advance notice or anything."

"Well, nobody knew I'd be—visiting."

She almost allowed herself a smile. "My mistake," she said. "When you said you were a friend of Loftus—"

"Does Loftus pay your rent here?"

She laughed out loud, a biting, cutting laugh. "That penny-pinching son of a bitch? He doesn't spend money—he collects it. He comes here every two weeks or so because he has—an arrangement."

"What arrangement?"

"Lots of people in this town have *arrangements*. For some of them I'm part of the deal. How much do I have to explain to you?"

"Who is this arrangement with?"

She shook her head angrily. "I can't tell you that."

"Why not?" K.O. said.

"It's not your fucking business, that's why not. You work for Bert, and you want him to get off easy. Fine—but this has nothing to do with him."

"He's a big deal, right? That means he calls the shots."

"He calls *no* shots in this town, dumb-ass!" Anger teased the corners of her face. "He rides around in somebody's pocket—like everyone else in Cleveland."

"Are we talking about the mayor?"

"Where the hell are you from? Timbuktu? The mayor's got no juice—he won't peek his nose out of his office except to go to church."

"Then who runs things? Come on, help me out."

Seena Bergman crushed out her second cigarette butt. "I'll help you out. I'll help you right out the door," she said, cruising toward it and gesturing to K.O. to do likewise. "My life is none of your concern." She opened the door and stood aside so he could leave. "You're kinda cute for a young kid," she mused. "Sorry we couldn't do business."

"That wasn't why I came here."

"I bet you're not into 'mature' women either, right? You prob'ly have a young, cute girlfriend—young enough to be my daughter. That's okay. Some men have a MILF complex—so it's what I deal with." She looked over her shoulder into the living room. "That's what pays the rent on this joint."

She reached over and pinched his cheek—affectionate, but hard enough to hurt. "So long, newbie. Come back when you grow up and are more interested in women than in girls."

When K.O. got back to his car, he rolled down the windows so he wouldn't roast inside—it was almost noon and the temperature had risen again. He whipped out his notebook and jotted down the high points of his conversation so he could report to Milan all about Seena Bergman later, hoping they'd find out who is powerful enough to pay her rent and so-called salary.

His trip back to the office was a short one, but he chuckled all the way, tickled at the thought of having to explain to Milan what "MILF" stands for.

CHAPTER NINE

MILAN

The Big Egg is a family-style restaurant, but I've never seen a family in there. Maybe it's just the neighborhood. It's on Detroit Avenue on the near west side of Cleveland, moments from downtown. In my youth, it was open 24/7, and if anyone dropped in at, say, three o'clock in the morning, chances were they'd run into someone else they knew. It shut down in the year 2000, was replaced by a Vietnamese restaurant, and then in 2008 was reopened with the old name, new owners, and a new menu. The other big change from the old days is that now it closes at nine o'clock in the evening.

I miss it as an all-night restaurant, but I've aged into being *not* an all-night kind of guy.

Tobe Blaine was already there. Fitted dark slacks, flat black lace-up shoes in which she could run faster than most people and probably kick their teeth down their throat when necessary, and a dark gray blouse over which she wore a bright scarlet Cincinnati Reds jacket. She looked as good in the sunshine streaming through the window as she had the night before on the street in front of Saint Malachi with all the flashing police car lights fighting and winning their battle with the shining moon. When I came in, she barely raised her hand from the table to get my attention. She didn't smile, but didn't seem to be in a lousy mood, either.

I wondered why she wanted to meet for breakfast—maybe an initial sparring between me and a new Cleveland cop in the division where I wasn't much liked by her boss. Maybe she wanted help with the Bert Loftus business. Perhaps she wanted to tell me something—on the order of "Go away and never let me see your face again." I doubted she'd wanted this meeting for the same reason I did—that she was very attractive and I wanted to get to know her better.

"Good morning," I said, sliding into the booth. "Am I on time?"

"I'm not keeping track of the seconds," she said. "Order whatever you want—it's on me."

"Thanks, but I was planning to treat you instead."

She shook her head slightly. "I invited, I pick up the check. Besides, cops don't accept free breakfasts anymore; that myth went out with Princess telephones and eight-tracks."

"I never owned a Princess phone."

"I couldn't imagine someone your size talking on a Princess phone."

"Besides, I just want a cup of tea."

"Order a breakfast, for God's sake. You're a big man—you'll starve to death if you don't eat. There's lots of good things on the menu—and no pictures."

"Pictures?"

"Rule Number One: Never eat in a restaurant where the menu has photographs of the food."

She gave me half a minute to check out the breakfast fare. Then she said, "Come on, I haven't got all day." She waved at the waitress to approach. "We'll have two sausage and cheese omelets—home fries and toast—and one coffee and one tea."

"What kind of cheese and what kind of toast?" the waitress wanted to know.

"Cheddar," Tobe Blaine said, "and rye toast." She finally looked at me. "Is that okay with you?"

"Thanks for asking. I'll have an English muffin instead."

The waitress walked away, scribbling. I said, "Do you always take charge?"

"If you pay for *my* meal, I'll eat whatever you want me to." Popping the knuckles on both hands, she settled against the back of the booth.

"Nice jacket," I said. "Reds fan?"

"I spent many years in Cincinnati. When you're in a particular town, you root for their team. I don't live there anymore, but I like the jacket. Problem?"

"Not with me. You were in Raleigh, too—and no baseball team to cheer for. What did you do then?"

"I followed the Durham Bulls—they're close to Raleigh. I always liked that Kevin Costner movie about them—but I never had one of their jackets. Where did you hear about me?"

"That you're from Raleigh? I have my ways."

"You get around."

"It's my job."

"Well, I have ways, too," she said, "and I heard a hell of a lot more about you than your favorite teams."

"Two guesses where you found out about me, and both of them are Florence McHargue."

"I spent last weekend—off the clock—getting an orientation from her on everything about this town, including you. I doubt she scribbles your name all over her notebook and fantasizes about you when you're not there."

"I try hard to *never* be there."

"But surprise, surprise—I run into you a few days later."

"Do I live up to my hype?"

"The jury's still out—unless you have something to say to me, in which case I'm waiting with bated breath."

"'Bated,' by the way," I said, "has nothing to do with 'bait,' like for a fish. It means 'moderate or restrained.' In case you didn't know."

"Golly gee whiz," she said with a straight face, "thanks so much for letting me in on that juicy subject. I guess the day they taught that in *my* graduate English class, I must've stayed home, sick." She allowed herself a cynical smile. "Jacovich, you are the most pretentious sonofabitch I've ever met."

"I read the dictionary. I'd be wasting that time if I didn't use what I learn."

"Three cheers for you. Did you learn the proper protocol when a cop asks you what you were doing at a crime scene last night?"

"Snap to attention?"

"I'm not joking," she said.

"Okay, I won't either. As I told you, my company is doing some work for Councilman Loftus."

"Loftus," Blaine murmured. "There are three things certain in this life," she said, counting them off on her fingers. "Death, taxes, and Loftus going to jail."

"It has nothing to do with his legal offenses—as far as I know."

"As far as you know, neither does the warfare in Syria—or whatever the hell place they're having a war this morning."

"I try not to read the international news."

"You should, every day. It's better than your detective novels."

"I don't read detective novels; I live them."

The light behind those green eyes danced merrily, reminding me of fireflies. "Nice one, Jacovich," she said. "It's too bad my coffee and your tea aren't here yet, or I'd drink to that."

"It used to be I'd drink to damn near anything."

"Go for it—just so you have a designated driver."

"You're quick."

"Quick? Or fast?"

"I don't know about fast. We hardly know each other."

"So why turn in your badge and gun and stop being a cop? If you hadn't, you'd be retired now with a generous pension."

"Retired to do what? Putter around in my rose garden? I don't have a garden—I live in an apartment."

"Alone," she said. It wasn't a question.

"You found that out, too?"

Blaine shrugged. "It came up in conversation."

"With the lieutenant?"

"No—with Matusen last night."

The waitress arrived with coffee and tea. When she walked away, Blaine waved her hand in front of her face. "Whew! Her perfume could curl your nose hairs. What'd she do, bathe in it?"

"I didn't notice," I said, sniffing discreetly.

"Sorry, I have an acute sense of smell. So—how about this assistant of yours? What's his name—K.O.? He's new."

"New since my last case, which ended a few days ago. He's smart, young, and a hard worker. He wants a P.I. license and works for me so he can get it."

"You hired him to do all the rough stuff for you."

"I avoid rough stuff."

"If I counted the bullet holes and scars all over you, I'd call you a liar."

"Let's make an appointment so you can," I said, and clinked my teacup against her coffee mug. "And I *will* drink to that."

She regarded me through slitted eyes. "Now *you're* the fast one."

"Sorry, didn't mean to be forward."

"Better than being backward. How come you didn't want to be a cop anymore?"

"Why? Are you recruiting?"

"You're too old to recruit."

"Curses! Foiled again."

"Just curious," she said. "I've been at it twenty years, and I don't plan to retire anytime soon—so why'd you quit?"

"I was in Vietnam and lucky enough to come back standing up. Among many things I learned out there was that I hated saluting and shining my shoes. And I looked like a damn fool in a hat. I still do."

"Vanity?"

"No, politics—police politics. I couldn't do that. My best friend did, though, and I had to respect him for that."

"Who's your friend?"

"The late Lieutenant Marko Meglich," I said. "He had the top homicide job before McHargue, and he got it by playing politics. We were best buds since fifth grade."

"I've heard of him. Lost in the line of duty. Sorry."

I didn't explain to her that Marko wasn't exactly on duty when he died, but he was down on the east side of the Flats, putting his ass on the line to back me up. I've never quite gotten over that one. "Yeah," I said.

"He must've been a hell of a cop, and damn good at his job."

"He was. Have you always been a homicide cop?"

"Since my third year in Cincinnati. I'd just made detective, and I asked to be transferred to homicide."

"Why?"

She ran her finger around the edge of her cup. "I was engaged to another police officer. Three months before our wedding, someone shot him. Now I try catching the worst criminals I can."

"Did you catch the man who killed him?"

"My bosses wouldn't let me near that case. They said I was too emotionally involved. Jesus!" She shook her head sadly. "Some other cops nailed the sonofabitch."

"And?"

"And one of the best criminal attorneys in Ohio pulled some strings and fucked around with logic, and the case got thrown out of court." She took a deep breath. "He walked. The motherfucker walked."

"I'm so sorry." I wanted to put my hand on hers but thought better of it.

"He left town a few days later, and if I'd known where he went I would've hunted him down and blown him away myself." She rotated her head around on her neck, and I heard her bones pop quietly. "He joined the army, though, and got himself killed in Iraq."

"There must've been justice in that."

"For him," Detective Blaine said. "Not for me."

The waitress came back with our omelets. When she walked away, Tobe made a gagging face and put her hand up to her nose. "Did you smell it that time?"

"Not really."

"I think it was White Diamonds—a fancy Elizabeth Taylor perfume a few decades ago. Now they sell it in drugstores."

"Are you sure it's White Diamonds?"

She unwrapped silverware from a paper napkin. "My nose never lies."

"Forgive me for asking," I said, salting my home fries, "but just why is it you asked me here for breakfast?"

"Don't use so much salt," she scolded. "Sodium." Then: "Someone tried to assassinate Bert Loftus last night, so I want to know why you work for him."

"I was working for him before last night."

"I figured that, Mr. Jacovich—but my question, in case you've already forgotten, is why?"

"My last name is a mouthful. Why don't you call me Milan?"

"Because I'm a homicide cop right now—and homicide cops don't question people using their first names."

"You're buying me breakfast to question me?"

"Did you think this was a first date?"

"Hope springs eternal," I said.

"Not at nine o'clock in the morning."

"Okay, Loftus approached me and said there had been attempts on his life—twice before."

"Like . . . ?"

"His car got nudged into a ditch a few weeks ago in Lake County. Then someone supposedly took a shot at him outside the Tiny Bar."

She cut into her omelet with the side of her fork. "Why would he hire you? Why not come to the police department? We kind of work for him anyway."

"Because of the trouble he's in with the federal government right now, I don't think he wanted any more publicity."

"You're his bodyguard?"

"No, I don't bodyguard. My job is to find the guy who wishes him harm—and turn it over to the police."

She dug into her omelet, though I just picked at mine. Then she said, "You used the word 'supposedly.' Why?"

"Because it doesn't seem kosher. He might've staged all that shit to make himself look good. He's headed for that country club jail in West Virginia—and even though I hear it's easy time, it's still a jail—so if he can convince a judge someone's stalking him, trying to blow him away, he might get a lighter sentence. He didn't seem that shook up about it until last night."

"What was different?"

"You never met him before?"

She shook her head. "I've been in Cleveland less than two weeks."

"When I showed up at Saint Mal last night, he damn sure wasn't acting. He peed in his pants—from fright."

"Whoever wants him dead knew where he'd be last night. What was he doing before the shot?"

"Getting laid," I said. "He'll admit that to me in my office in about—" I consulted my watch, "two hours."

"He's married," Tobe Blaine said. "Was this a regular girl-friend?"

"Not sure—but I doubt it."

She grew solemn once more. "Don't doubt anything. Loftus is under the FBI microscope every minute. When he blows his nose or scratches his ass, they can tell you the time and place he did it. They must have more pics of him on their office wall than teenyboppers have of Justin Bieber."

"Am I too old to know who Justin Bieber is?"

"Take this seriously, if you know what's good for you."

"I take it very seriously," I said. "When somebody writes me a check to do my job, I take it seriously indeed. As for not knowing what's good for me—I can only dream."

"Well, dream this," she said. "Bert Loftus is up Shit Creek without a paddle because the government is very, *very* angry with him. He's one of the most powerful men in town, which means we cops watch his ass. If we don't, the FBI will be mad at us. If you're trying to get him a light sentence, we'll be angry with *you*—or more to the point, *I'll* be angry with you. You won't like me when I'm angry." She sighed, pointing her fork at my plate. "Finish your breakfast and then go dream someplace else—or else stay here and stare out the window. I happen to have work to do."

We'd left our cars in the rear parking lot, so we said good-bye back there. When I thanked her for breakfast, I put out my hand for a shake, and she regarded it suspiciously, as something not a part of me, or of anyone; again, cops don't shake hands with witnesses. Frustrating—I *wanted* to shake her hand, just to feel her skin. For some reason she finally did take my hand. She said "You're welcome," and gave my hand a little squeeze before letting go and getting into her car.

It was a nice moment for me. Normally I don't have much of an imagination at all.

CHAPTER TEN

K.O.

Milan was already in the office when Kevin O'Bannion arrived after leaving Seena Bergman's apartment. K.O. asked his employer how his breakfast meeting turned out with Detective Blaine, but Milan shrugged it off with a terse "okay," which K.O. translated as being none of his business. If Milan wanted to keep it to himself, that was his ballgame. K.O. was more forthcoming, checking his notebook to make sure he hadn't forgotten anything important, and then told him all about his just-finished interview.

Milan looked annoyed. "What possessed you to go see Seena Bergman on your own?"

"I didn't want to bother you. I *do* come up with ideas all by myself. If my job is only doing what I'm told and then sitting in the corner with my hands folded, waiting for my next order—well, I'm not built that way. Are you mad that I went to see her? Did you want to do it yourself because she's supposed to be Loftus's current squeeze? I doubt that."

"Why?"

"Because Seena's a cheap, nickel-pussy sack of shit."

Milan laughed. "Tell me what you *really* think."

"She's an overpaid, overage, overweight hooker, and Loftus is a regular visitor. Why? Did I spoil something for you?"

"You didn't spoil anything."

"I'm relieved I didn't ask for permission. When I was in

Afghanistan and some towel-head with a rifle took a shot at me, I didn't run to my commanding officer and ask him if I should duck."

"K.O., don't get pissed off."

"Don't piss me off, then."

"And let's find another word besides 'towel-head.' That's right up there with 'nigger' and 'kike.'"

He didn't offer an apology; he was lousy at them. He'd never learned the apology lesson.

He waved his notes at Milan. "You want me to type these up in a report for you? Or should I just eat the pages?"

Milan might have been about to tell him where to shove them, but he gave only a small shake of his head. K.O. guessed that was one more difference between the two of them, and that he could learn self-control just by keeping his eye on Milan.

Milan reminded him: "Bert Loftus is due here at noon."

"I didn't forget."

"Well, don't forget this, either. He's our client; we're on *his* side. And somebody *did* try to kill him last night. I know you're mad at everything and everyone, but you need to mellow."

"Mellow? Great idea—I'll be a fucking pussycat."

"Excellent," Milan said. "You like pussycats, don't you?"

"I like *Rodney*. Everybody else is on probation."

"Does that include Carli, too?"

"If not for you," K.O. said, "she might not be on probation anymore."

"What did I do?"

"You called last night while she was in my apartment."

Milan pulled files from his bottom drawer. "For what it's worth, K.O., I didn't score last night, either."

"You haven't scored," K.O. said, "since Jimmy Carter was president of the United States."

"You weren't even born when Jimmy Carter was president."

"I wasn't born when George Washington was president, either."

Bert Loftus showed up, and this time he was only seven minutes late—and accompanied by another man. It was almost impossible, in a Cleveland summer like this one, to look as wan as Loftus's companion did, as if someone had dug up his grave three weeks ago.

"I'm embarrassed," Loftus said after sitting down, his face flushing. "About last night. I mean, about . . ." He gestured futilely toward his crotch.

"Don't worry, it's forgotten."

Loftus fingered his bow tie. "It's *not* forgotten! There were reporters there. The press is out to get me."

"Journalists have *some* standards," Milan said. He looked at the other man. "Are you going to introduce us?"

"Oh," Bert Loftus said. "This is my—uh, my driver."

The unsmiling driver nodded his head, despite the introduction being almost nonexistent.

"Wait in the car," Loftus said abruptly, and the driver turned on his heel and went back out the door. The noise of him going down the stairs might have been made by one of those zombies in *Night of the Living Dead.*

"What's your driver's name, Councilman?" K.O. said.

Loftus looked amazed. No one ever asked him that before. "Uh—it's Ted."

"Ted what?"

He had to think for a moment. "It's Niculescu."

Romanian, K.O. thought, wondering if Ted Niculescu was just Loftus's driver—or his bodyguard, too?

Loftus shifted uncomfortably in his chair. "You wanted to see me, Milan?"

"For a lot of reasons. That guy—" Milan looked at the door through which Niculescu had gone, "—wasn't driving you last night?"

"He drives me during business hours—or when it's a business event at night. I drive myself to, uh, personal events."

"So you didn't get a look at who shot at you."

"No. I wasn't paying attention to other drivers, or even people walking on the street—not that there were any near the Detroit-Superior Bridge. And after the shot—well, to be honest, I lost control. I was so scared—"

"And when you finally put your head up, the car had driven away?"

"I never even saw what make it was—or what color."

Milan said, "You said your car got wrecked out in Lake County, and someone shot at you coming out of the Tiny Bar. But you weren't very upset about either of those things."

"Why would I hire you if I wasn't terrified?"

"You weren't so terrified that it kept you from bargaining with me for the price," Milan said. "You weren't terrified enough to call the cops the first time—or the second time, either—but last night you called the mayor from your cell phone, and *he* sent the police to take care of you. *Then* you called me."

Loftus looked as if waiting for the cavalry to save his ass. But no one rode over the hill blowing a bugle. "Well—"

"Those weren't murder attempts at all, were they, Bert?"

Someone would have to set Loftus on fire before he'd answer. His wrinkled lips were shut tight and his jaw was aggressively raised and tilted. K.O. said, "Milan, if he tells us, is it like telling an attorney? Client privilege and all that?"

"There's no client privilege—we aren't lawyers. But why would we repeat it?"

K.O. shrugged. "That's true. We're getting paid."

That jolted Loftus out of his sulk with a vengeance. "Goddamn you both!"

Milan said, "I told you to be straight with me. You know what that means—to be straight? It has nothing to do with your sexual preferences; it means telling the truth."

"The whole truth and nothing but the truth," K.O. added.

Loftus arose and paced the room for awhile, like a caged tiger rightly enraged about being *in* that cage.

"You ask a hell of a lot," he finally said through gritted teeth.

"*You* ask a lot. We bust our asses looking for someone trying to kill you—and there's no one to look for because you made it all up."

Loftus was breathing loudly. "Last night was real!"

"We figured that out," K.O. said, "when you pissed yourself."

The councilman glared. Milan had suggested being nice to

him—but to K.O., that was like climbing Pike's Peak on your knees wearing just your underwear. "So what was the purpose? Why hire us to waste our time finding someone who doesn't exist?"

"Jesus," Bert bellowed, "I'm looking at twenty years in prison."

"Maybe more," Milan said.

"I want everyone's sympathy before my sentence! 'Poor guy, sure he took some bribes, but someone tried murdering him— give him a little slack.' After last night I hope to Christ I *do* get some slack."

"All right," Milan said, "let's get to the real business. Who has it in for you? Who might want you to not wake up tomorrow?"

"Everybody."

"Be specific, Bert."

"There are about thirty people who've already been indicted for bribing me to shovel contracts and work their way. But why would they try to kill me now? What for? They're already in trouble."

"What about the ones the FBI doesn't know about? The ones who bribed you?"

"If I told you that I might as well paint a target on my back."

"You already have a target on your back," K.O. said. "Or didn't you notice?"

"K.O.'s right. We can't help you if you don't come clean with us."

"Some of them," Bert mumbled, "are small-time. The federal government wouldn't bother with them."

"We're not federal. We're trying to save your life."

"Let's start small then, Bert," K.O. said. "I dropped into Deuce Auto Repair and talked to Tyler. What's Tyler's last name again?"

"I don't know! We're always on a first-name basis."

"It's Halford," K.O. said. "I looked it up. He fixed your car like he does *all* your repair work—and never charges you for it. That's a bribe, isn't it?"

"It's a favor!"

"Because you're such an important guy?"

"Damn right! You think if the president of the United States drops into T.G.I. Friday's for a cheeseburger, they actually expect him to pay for it? Tyler? Deuce Auto? Small-time shit."

"Slow down," Milan said. "I'm still working on the image of the president at T.G.I. Friday's for cheeseburgers. And it's not small time when you make sure everybody on the city payroll takes their cars to Deuce to be fixed—and Tyler makes more than enough money on them."

"A favor for a favor," he said. His lies were steadfast.

"Who else?"

Loftus held his hands up in front of his face and wiggled his fingers rapidly, as if he were holding two pigeons by the feet who desperately wanted to fly away. "I can't remember names. I'll e-mail you a list if I can put it together." He started to get up.

Milan said, "Don't leave us yet. Talk about Seena Bergman first."

Bert collapsed into his chair. His puppeteer had dropped the strings that kept him upright. "That's personal."

"What were you doing at Seena's apartment last night?"

"What do you *think* he was doing?" K.O. said.

"Is she your steady girlfriend, Bert?"

What began as a chuckle ended up a snort. "Girlfriend? She's about fifty years old. She's nobody's girlfriend."

"What do you call her, then?" K.O. wanted to know.

"Don't get me wrong, I love my wife—been married thirty-one years."

"You love your wife but shag Seena whenever you feel like it."

"It's not like that! She's—well, Seena is special. Kinky." He lowered his head and mumbled the rest. "She does things. Whatever you ask her to do, she does."

"And you love your wife?"

"Of course I do! But do you think my wife'll come downtown after my evening meeting and give me a rim job?"

"Golly," K.O. said, "I never thought of that."

Milan cut in, "Who knew you'd be at Seena's last night?"

"Why?"

"Were they hanging around the Detroit–Superior Bridge, *hoping* you'd just happen to drive by?"

"Nobody knew, dammit!" Loftus fiddled with his tie. "Well, Seena knew—I called and made an appointment."

"No 'Walk-Ins Welcome' sign?"

"K.O.," Milan said softly, but this time he meant it. Then he turned back to Bert. "Mind if I ask how much she charges you?"

"I don't pay her anything," he said. "I usually tip her—fifty bucks or so—but we have an, uh, an arrangement."

"Somebody 'keeps' her, Milan," K.O. said, "and she's available for special people like Bert here."

"Who told you?" Bert snarled.

"A little bird."

Milan sighed, half at K.O. and half at Bert Loftus, who grew more ridiculous by the moment. "Who pays the freight, Bert?"

Bert shook his head.

"Somebody must be pretty powerful to employ a kinky hooker full-time to service people he chooses." Milan hovered his pen above his yellow pad. "Who?"

"No way!" Bert was trying to get himself in hand. "Not important."

"We'll judge whether it's important."

"No!"

"Are you afraid if you blow the whistle on this guy, you won't get to visit Seena anymore?" K.O. suggested.

"Don't be so fucking naïve! He's got my balls in his pocket! If I give him up, he has so much on me that in twenty-four hours, the whole town will know."

"The whole town knows you're going to jail for taking bribes," Milan said. "What's the difference if you're blackmailed for something else?"

"My wife'll find out." He shook his head again. "Everybody will know."

"Know what?"

"Never mind! This can't happen! If you want to walk away, do it—but I won't tell you any more about this. It . . ." He chewed his bottom lip, studying his own lap. "It's a matter of pride!"

"All right," Milan said, and gave K.O. a meaningful look to keep him from saying anything. "We'll drop this for the moment. Tell me about the Ogres."

"Who?"

"Sorry—Mr. and Mrs. Ogrin."

Now Loftus seemed to shrink again—like Alice. "Uh, I don't know them."

"Jeff and Vicki Ogrin?"

"I don't know who you're talking about."

"Everyone in City Hall knows they call your office several times a week. And you've been seen with them, too—at the Tiny Bar."

Looking at Berton K. Loftus, K.O. wondered how he could appear completely innocent of any wrongdoing or lying. He squirmed, wriggled, his hands never still, glancing about for an answer.

"Oh—Jeff and Vicki. Sure." His laugh rang phony. "You throw so much shit at me, I get confused. The Ogrins. What about 'em?"

"They contact you all the time, Bert. Why is that?"

"They—own property in my ward. They like making sure things get done, like filling in potholes and stuff."

K.O. said, "You expect us to swallow that?"

Milan shrugged. "He can be as open as he wants to—or as closed as he needs to. If he won't help himself, it's his choice."

"I don't tell you every time I take a dump!" Loftus growled. "I do what I want, and don't go around blabbing to everybody. I'm in business, for chrissakes."

"You are?" K.O. said. "I thought you were a public servant."

"All right, that's it!" He jumped out of his chair as though it had been plugged in and electrified. "I'm outta here. I have things to do."

"The first thing," Milan said, "is make me a list of names of all your 'business buddies' who haven't been indicted yet. E-mail them to me—and I'll e-mail them to K.O. here."

"K.O.," Loftus said, pointing in his general direction but not even looking at him, "needs to learn manners. I'm a top man in this city, and I expect to be treated with respect."

K.O. braced himself, either to be chewed out right then or the minute Loftus went away. But Milan surprised him.

"You've been stealing for years, Bert—taking care of yourself and letting all the Clevelanders pound sand. There's more than a million bucks that you've acquired illegally, squirreled under your mattress, and when you get out, it'll be all yours, and then you can afford your very own full-time hooker. You don't *deserve* respect."

By the time Milan finished, Councilman Loftus was utterly deflated, a helium balloon two days after the party was over, wrinkled flat and fallen from the sky to hover inches from the floor. Nobody spoke. Milan breathed heavily, Loftus was gasping, and K.O. held his breath so nobody would notice him.

Finally Loftus said softly, "I'll e-mail that list." Then he moved across the room as if fifty-pound weights were tied around each ankle and slunk out the door. K.O. looked at his boss and nodded approval.

"Nice job, Milan. Are we dropping him?"

"We would if not for last night. Now, like him or lump him, we have to make sure he lives long enough to go to court."

"Aren't the police on this?"

"He's not best friends with cops. Never has been."

"Did your breakfast buddy—Detective Blaine—say she'd watch over him?"

"Not exactly. But she told *me* to back off."

"*Me* meaning *us*?"

He studied K.O. for a bit, then nodded.

"Where do I go from here?"

Milan looked at his watch. "To Best Buy—for a laptop to use only for business—and a case to lug it around in."

"What kind?"

"They're pretty much the same. I don't want you playing games on it, or downloading music or movies or porn—it's just for work. Call me when you can, but I won't need you for the rest of the day."

The Best Buy gift cards in K.O.'s wallet were now burning a hole in his pocket. "And what will you do with your afternoon?"

Milan opened up his own laptop. "I'm going to look at your reports from yesterday."

CHAPTER ELEVEN

MILAN

I stayed at my desk for quite a while after K.O. had left the office, thinking about him. He was tough, often rude—and had a perpetual chip on his shoulder. Most of his good teen years—the growing-up years, the exploration years—had been spent behind bars, and his keepers had desperately tried to knock some come-to-Jesus sense into his head, which clashed with his fallen-away Catholic mentality. Now he wanted to be someplace out in the fresh air all the time—without the desert's endless stretches of sand.

I couldn't blame him for being angry.

Or maybe even for using that anger to get in someone's face. Maybe "nice" just isn't in his DNA. And we might have something that could work: good cop/bad cop, with each of us suited to our roles. We'd pummeled Bert Loftus into some sort of submission, and that might be a good thing for all three of us.

I pored through K.O.'s thorough report on his meeting with Dolores Deluke. He's smaller than I am, younger, and not so threatening, but he got more from Dolores Deluke than I would have. I scribbled notes on my own yellow pad, and one name I hadn't thought about jumped out at me. I didn't have to write it down. Like everyone else in Cuyahoga County, I knew this one by heart.

The County Administration Building is on Ontario Street. It's a busy place, but most people in Cuyahoga County aren't really sure where it is. I've been there, naturally—too often. But I'd never knocked on the door of the county prosecutor before.

Jim Hundley's secretary, or assistant, or whatever he calls himself, sat behind a big desk, wearing a blue suit he'd bought off the rack. He did have a plaque trumpeting his name on the desk in front of him: John Michael Belmont III. Yep, that meant he was a *three*. I probably should have known who his father and grandfather were—John Michael Belmont I and II—but didn't really care.

The three guys lounging around in Hundley's office didn't look professional. They didn't seem to be doing much of anything. One cheerfully gnawed on the skin surrounding his thumbnail, one studied the newspaper, mouthing the words as he read them. The third was fascinated with *Hustler*. They all paid attention when I walked into the office and explained to the blue-suited guy at the desk—Mister Three—that I wanted to see Mr. Hundley.

"Did you have an appointment?" His manner was supercilious—he knew I had no appointment, as Hundley's calendar was open in front of him. I offered my business card. He nodded sagely and brutally mispronounced my name. "I've heard of you, Mr. Jacovich."

I doubted that. "Can you tell Mr. Hundley I'd like to talk to him for a few minutes." He didn't move—although the guy chewing on his thumb did, leaning forward on his chair, hands on thighs as if ready to spring at me. The second guy put his newspaper on the floor by his foot; the *Hustler* reader was too involved to bother.

John Michael Belmont III said, "Prosecutor Hundley doesn't see anybody without an appointment."

"Tell him I'm here to see him regarding Councilman Loftus."

"Loftus works for the city, not the county—which we are."

No kidding.

Three Names grew arrogant. "He's too important to drop everything when some perfect stranger walks in and wants an audience with him."

An audience, I thought—like the pope or the queen of England. The county prosecutor was no pope—and if he thought he was, I'd quickly disabuse him of that.

"Then inform Mr. Hundley," I suggested, "that my next visit will be to Ed Stahl of the *Plain Dealer*."

Ed Stahl is a Pulitzer Prize–winning columnist for our local newspaper and one of my closest friends. I tried not to let it bother me that he was one of my *only* friends. But evidently it bothered John Michael Belmont III that I knew him. Ed Stahl has cheerfully crucified almost every politician in Ohio in his five-day-per-week column, and Jim Hundley was no exception.

"I hate to disappoint you," Belmont III said, not disguising his sarcasm, "but Mr. Hundley will be out for the rest of the day."

I didn't believe him. "Where can I find him, then?"

"I don't keep track of his every move. Suffice to say he's not here."

"Suffice," I said. "Oh, well—toodle-oo, then." I'd never said "Toodle-oo" to anyone in my life before, but I enjoyed that moment, and the embarrassed flush on Three's face. I'll store it away in case I need it again.

I headed for the door, passing close to the *Hustler* reader. He was still staring hard at the photograph of the same naked woman and breathing heavily. He looked up at me, obviously irritated.

"Her rack's *too* big," I observed. "But thanks for sharing." I bestowed upon him my most angelic smile and was all the way downstairs and across the street before he figured it out.

I sat in my car making notes that seemed senseless. K.O. must have been doing better than I, because I'd hit one brick wall after another. I drove back to my office in the Flats, navigating a complicated maze of barriers and orange barrels—at least one-third of downtown was under construction.

Bert Loftus wouldn't want to make a list of his cronies and/or acquaintances not yet accused of anything by the feds—despite the fact they were all guilty. But he'd do it, because now, after the attempted shooting near the bridge, he was really scared.

That meant I had to make a certain phone call. I would have rather gone through a root canal without Novocain.

I stood at the window, looking out at the steady flow of the Cuyahoga River as it swirled around the absurd angle of Collision Bend, wishing I could light a cigarette. I'd gone cold turkey on smoking about a year earlier and felt pretty proud of myself—except that I'd not awakened one single morning without desperately wanting a couple of deep puffs.

I went to the phone and punched out the number.

"Special Agent Jeffrey Kitzberger." The voice was tinny over the phone, cutting through static; the local offices of the Federal Bureau of Investigation must have been using a telephone system that went out of date in 1985.

Kitzberger's personality went out of date at about the same time. I'd met him a few weeks earlier while working on my last case, and he presented himself as cold, demanding, and condescending. Movie stars, rock idols, and football players have giant egos, but they can't compare with FBI agents.

For what it's worth, Kitzberger didn't like me any better than I liked him. "This is a revelation—this phone call from you," he said when I'd identified myself. "Are we best friends now? Do we take in a ballgame together—or just hang out in a sports bar and guzzle beer?"

I decided not to let him bait me. "I have a question, Special Agent Kitzberger. Are you in on the Berton K. Loftus deal?"

"Deal?" He was at once on guard.

"His case—his thirty-one indictments. Are you in on that?"

His sigh sounded like a Level 3 tropical storm blowing down a stand of palm trees. I moved the earpiece away from my ear. "My office investigated his situation and bound him over for trial," he said. "Naturally I was privy to all of it. Why do you ask?"

"Loftus is my client."

"Why am I not surprised?"

"Do you have a complete list of those who offered Loftus bribes?"

"What's a bribe?" Kitzberger said, not yet ready to answer. "Being taken to dinner at Lola? Cavs tickets? A weekend at Put-In Bay? Define *bribes.*"

"Don't jerk my chain today, Special Agent—I'm in no mood."

"Neither am I." He was getting comfortable so he could give me more crap. "What's Loftus paying you to do?"

"Keep him alive."

"What do you mean by that?"

"It has nothing to do with the FBI, so I don't think I'll tell you."

"If it has nothing to do with the FBI, to what do I owe the—courtesy—of this phone call?"

I bit the bullet. "Call it a favor."

I had never heard Jeffrey Kitzberger laugh before; I didn't think he was capable of it. This was a great, big, deep-from-the-chest guffaw.

"Thanks," I said. "I live to amuse you."

It took him half a minute to finish laughing. "If you want this favor so badly, you should come here in person so we can talk it over."

I was glad we were on the phone so he couldn't see me wince. "In your office? Another one of your power trips?"

"You won't believe this," Kitzberger said, "but I'm trying to be a nice guy."

"Leo Durocher once said nice guys finish last."

"Who's Leo Durocher?"

"He's in the Baseball Hall of Fame. He managed the Brooklyn Dodgers, the New York Giants, the Chicago Cubs . . ."

"I'm not a baseball fan."

That was one more reason for me to dislike Kitzberger. "For a time he was married to Laraine Day."

"Who's Laraine Day?"

I gave up. "When should I be in your office?"

He didn't waste a second before answering. "Now," he said.

Well, not quite *now*, I thought, dialing another number I knew by heart. I hoped Ed Stahl hadn't left for the day, that he was still hunkered down in a corner of the newsroom at the *Plain Dealer*—the only person in all of Ohio still allowed to smoke his pipe in public because nobody had the guts to remind him it was against the law; otherwise he'd tell the newspaper where they could put his job. Half of all Clevelanders hated his guts and the other half were terrified of him, but he wrote five opinionated columns every week. He was one of the few not afraid to say or write what he really thought—and tucked away in the bottom drawer of his desk was a Pulitzer Prize medal to prove it.

"I was just about to leave, Milan," he said, sounding on edge. It was past five o'clock and he hadn't had the day's first drink yet.

Drinking was bad for his ulcer, or so his doctor told him, but Jim Beam—bourbon on the rocks—was his drink of choice, and he rarely missed his after-hours stopover, either at Nighttown, two blocks from where I lived, or at his latest hangout, the bar at The Mad Greek, which I could see from the bay window in my apartment.

When he drank with me, it was often at the Slovenian-Croatian bar on Saint Clair Avenue, Vuk's, at which I was served my first legal alcoholic drink on my twenty-first birthday. Vuk, the owner-bartender, who's eighty years old and can still twist anyone's head off their neck, doesn't like Ed Stahl much, mainly because Ed dresses like a train wreck—horrible tweed jackets, two supremely ugly ties worn on alternate days, and horn-rimmed glasses that remind most people of Superman's alter ego grown old and tired.

"I'll be at Nighttown," he announced, "if you feel like meeting me."

"Maybe later," I said. "Now I need background."

"When the day comes that you don't need background from me, they'll crown you emperor." I heard him lighting up his pipe and puffing on it. "What do you want to know?"

"Tell me about County Prosecutor Jim Hundley."

Puff, puff. "He's a dick. Next question."

"I tried to see him earlier, but he wasn't in his office."

"He's hardly ever in his office. It feels too much like work."

"Do you have his home address?"

"He won't be there, either. He never is, unless it's to sleep."

"How does his wife feel about that?"

Ed loudly snorted once—his way of laughing. "Ask her."

"So where can I find him?"

"Now?"

"In about an hour," I said, not forgetting Kitzberger was waiting for me. *Another* dick.

"If it were wintertime he'd probably be at Cleveland Chop House or at Johnny's Downtown, depending on whether he wants to hit on some chick at the Chop House bar or hang out with local big shots at Johnny's. But it's summer. He owns a boat he hardly ever takes out, so he's probably at the Sunset Grille—walking distance from where he's berthed."

"Where's that?"

"*Everybody* knows that," Ed said witheringly. "Whiskey Island."

It would be easiest to dismiss FBI special agent Jeffrey Kitzberger as a conceited pain in the ass, but that wouldn't do him justice. He firmly believes everyone else in the world—those who don't carry the same badge and rank as he does, those who clean his floors, serve his food, repair his toilet, and tailor his elegant, expensive suits—is necessary but not important. I'd met him on my most recent case, when he elbowed his way into my office and treated me as if I were an indentured servant.

It was my turn now in *his* office, in a sprawling edifice on Lakeside Avenue overlooking Lake Erie. He was fresh, ironed, coiffed, and shaved, as if his tailor, make-up person, and hair stylist had just rushed in and pressed and fluffed and combed and re-pressed him.

"Do sit down, *Mister* Jacovich," he said. I'd told him at our first meeting that I disliked being referred to only by my last name. "Milan" is fine, or "Mister Jacovich" if one's being formal, but it annoyed Kitzberger when I told him so. Now he puts all his weight on the "mister" like a one-legged pirate leaning on a makeshift crutch.

His office was as I'd imagined it, just like he was—neat, expensive, devoid of personality or the slightest smudge of messiness. "So you're on the Bert Loftus payroll," he said as soon as I sat down.

"He's a client."

"He's a criminal," Kitzberger said, "who accepts bribes and skims taxpayers' money off the top, and who'll sit in jail for every buck he stuffed into his pocket."

"That's what I hear."

"But you take his money anyway."

"By the time it gets to me, it's honest money."

"That's crap."

"From where you sit," I said.

"Well, I'm not involved with him, or any of the other political crooks and bribe-givers. I don't know much about his case—only the reports I've read." With a self-satisfied smirk, he put his hands together like a child saying his goodnight prayers. "Loftus wants you to make things look better for him before he's convicted and sentenced, right?"

"I thought so—but some of what he said was the truth."

"What truth is that, *Mister* Jacovich?"

"That someone's trying to kill him."

That made Kitzberger frown. He leaned back in his throne-like executive chair. "Who is trying to kill him?"

"If I knew, I'd do something about it—and not ask for your help."

"What kind of help?"

"Can you get me a complete list of the other people who are already indicted or convicted in the same case here in town?"

"Why would I do that?"

"To save me the trouble of spending a week looking it up all over the state."

He allowed himself the smallest possible smile. "I don't care how you spend your time."

"Do you care about saving Councilman Loftus's life?"

"Loftus has been indicted for committing a federal crime, stealing taxpayers' money. That is the bureau's only interest in him."

"And you don't give a damn if someone kills him?"

Kitzberger looked to the ceiling—for guidance from up there. "The FBI doesn't deal with murder. According to the laws under which we live, that's the job of local police officers. Not ours."

"Very official," I said.

"Then I'll put it another way before I ask you to leave—and by the way, you'll leave without any information, or any lists you came for. I don't give rat shit what happens to Loftus. If he dies, it'll save the government a lot of money keeping him in prison." He tried and failed to make his face look downright cherubic.

"The bureau will send a wreath to his funeral—to make his wife feel better."

I stared at him for a long moment. That usually makes people uncomfortable, but it hardly ruffled Kitzberger's hair. Finally I said, "You're really something, Special Agent."

"Well," Kitzberger said, "we finally agree on *something*. Don't we, *Mister* Jacovich?"

CHAPTER TWELVE

MILAN

Whiskey Island was only seven minutes from FBI headquarters, and I drove there with my teeth clenched. Hell will freeze over before I ask the FBI, or specifically Special Agent Jeffrey Kitzberger, for *anything* again, I thought. My trip to his office was not only a time-waster; it left me feeling diminished. Kitzberger has that effect on most people. He considers it one of his talents.

At least on Whiskey Island I would be able to breathe in some relatively fresh air. Cleveland sometimes pollutes its atmosphere with steel mills and factories and salt mines—but once on the lake, the usual breeze can clear out your sinuses, at least for a while.

Whiskey Island isn't an island at all; it's a peninsula, bounded on two sides by the Cuyahoga River and Lake Erie and connected to Cleveland at West 54th Street. It was originally home to many families of Irish immigrants and got its name way back in the 1830s when a distillery sprang up there. Sadly, there were no whiskey runners or smugglers at the time, but the romantic name stuck—and so did the booze, because soon there were a dozen saloons servicing stevedores, industrial plant workers, and eventually employees of the railroad.

The Irish moved away to find better work, and during the last century the island was more or less railroad country, home to a salt mine and the legendary Hulett Ore Unloaders—towering, ungainly looking machines. Few people knew what they actually *did*, but many Clevelanders wanted to keep the Hulett Unloaders right there on Whiskey Island for historical reasons, long after they'd outlived their usefulness. Eventually they got moved—during the late 1990s—and Whiskey Island reinvented itself again.

Now there's a sizable marina on the island; the pretty Wendy Park, a lovely picnic spot hosting volleyball and softball leagues; the old and still-deserted Coast Guard station, which would take about a million dollars' worth of repair to turn into a magnificent mansion; a lake beach; low-end rock concerts; all sorts of diverse flora and fauna; and a stunning panorama of downtown. Most of Whiskey Island, as luck has it, is owned by the county.

The Sunset Grille is right on the marina, a stone's throw from the water and overlooking boats and boaters, although landlubbers hang out there, too. The surroundings aren't picturesque, but one visits the Sunset for raucous fun and plenty to drink, whooping it up as if expecting Jimmy Buffet to walk in. The basic foods are ordered from a white board mounted on the wall, after which you stand there with your tray, waiting until it arrives.

It was crowded for a weekday. The sun was on its way down, and boaters, friends, and friend-wannabes had found their way to Whiskey Island from their offices, dressed in what was left of their business suits after they'd peeled off the jackets and pocketed the neckties, or else they were decked out casual-sloppy. In several cases they were paired off with women much younger than themselves. I doubt any of them had brought their wives to the Sunset Grille.

Jim Hundley was luckier than most; he had *two* pretty girls, one on each side of him at the bar, listening to his every word—or pretending to. One of them, the sexy blonde whose white linen shirt was unbuttoned to two inches above her navel, disclosing her forgetfulness to wear a bra, was hanging on his arm. Hundley was louder than anyone else in the bar—and so was his Hawaiian shirt with royal blue palm leaves against a violently red background. Clutched in one hand was a strawberry daiquiri. I don't ever remember seeing a male drinking a strawberry daiquiri in a public bar before, but I guess I hang out in the wrong taverns.

Hovering several feet behind Hundley, sipping from bottled spring water and keeping an eye on everyone, was a thin, wiry character, very pallid with arrow-straight black hair plastered against his head. He wore a short-sleeved white sports shirt and slacks to what must have once been a business suit. His nose, slightly off-center on his face, was like the nasty end of a claw hammer.

I worked my way up to the bar, squeezed myself between Jim Hundley and one of his women friends, introduced myself, and handed him one of my business cards. He frowned before turning on his public-face charm, his welcoming smile as genuine as a four-dollar bill. He pumped my hand and bellowed, "Hi there, Mi-LAHN," mispronouncing the first syllable and incorrectly emphasizing the last one. "Is that what your friends call you?"

"Just the ones who can't pronounce it."

The four-dollar-bill smile diminished to about thirty cents. "My assistant says you were looking for me."

"Your assistant, Whatsisname The Third?"

He didn't like that but only waited a few seconds before chortling at my sarcasm. "That's pretty good. Pretty good, Mi-LAHN. So—how 'bout a drink? It's on me—or on the county, anyway."

"No thanks."

"Aren't you thirsty? Come on, everybody gets thirsty." He waved to the pretty bartender. "Bring this man a Burning River." He informed me with assurance that the beer was from Great Lakes Brewing Company in Cuyahoga County, as if nobody in Northeast Ohio had ever heard of it. The jerk! *Everybody* around here knows Great Lakes Brewing Company. Hundley, though, sounded pleased—the local brewer's taxes paid part of his salary.

He glugged down the rest of his daiquiri. "So—I hear you dropped Ed Stahl's name to try to see me. Well, *I'm* good friends with Ed Stahl. I think you should know that."

Ed Stahl had no use for most politicians, even less for Jim Hundley—so the county prosecutor was already lying to me, hardly stopping for a breath. "You're investigating Bert Loftus?"

"No, he's my client. I'm hoping you can help me."

Hundley shrugged, and the head of the girl who hung on his right arm bobbed as he did so. The other girl didn't bob because Hundley's other arm was now around her, fondling the side of her breast. "Bert and I are friends, naturally. Not good friends, y'know—we don't 'hang out.' We don't play golf together or go out to dinner with our wives—but sure, we're friends. All us politicians know each other in this county." He smiled his faux friendly smile. "I'm not really in politics. I'm in law enforcement—like you *used* to be."

Interesting that he knew all about me. Had he heard of me before? Maybe—but probably when Mister Three told him about me, Hundley had googled me on his iPad.

So he was showing me that he bites. I bit back. "I used to be a soldier, too—but I haven't thrown a hand grenade at anyone since 1973. I still know how, though."

Now even the phony smile was as gone as the final night flight out of Hopkins Airport. "Just what is it you want from me?"

"You're aware of the trouble Bert Loftus is in."

"I read the paper, like everyone else."

"I assumed the county's foremost law officer might know more than I do."

"Bert's a city councilman. That's *city*, not county. I work for the county, remember? Not just Cleveland, but all the rest of Cuyahoga County. So I'm busier than hell doing my job, and I have no idea what Bert Loftus does. That's his business, Mi-LAHN."

It's polite if someone uses your name when they speak to you. When they *overuse* your name—and mispronounce it to boot—it sets your teeth on edge.

"The feds," I said, "indicted him on thirty-one counts—and you don't know anything about it?"

He shook his head. "It's not in my jurisdiction."

"Football isn't in *my* jurisdiction, but I know who's the Browns's quarterback on any given Sunday. The FBI didn't contact you about Loftus?"

"Certainly. I told them what I told you. I have no idea what he might be doing. It's not my area."

"Cleveland *is* your area. It's in your county."

"It is," he said, "but there are other people taking care of Cleveland. The mayor, the city council, the police department . . ."

"Is Seena Bergman in your area?"

His tongue crept out to moisturize his gone-dry lips, then disappeared into his mouth like a scared chipmunk in tall grass. He sucked on the dregs of his daiquiri. "Who?"

"Seena Bergman—a friend of Bert Loftus."

He took both arms from around his female companions and swirled around on his stool to look directly at me, his arrogant smirk gone. "Bert has lots of friends I don't know or haven't met. For instance, I'm a golfer and he's not, so he knows people who don't share my love for the sport, and I know golfers who never met Bert." His head almost quivered as he tried to think up the next thing to say. I didn't want *him* prosecuting anyone I wanted to see go to jail—not in his present nervous condition. "I spend ninety percent of my time working and the rest with my family." How he could say this while half-hammered and draped all over two bar skanks, I had no clue.

"You never heard the name Seena Bergman, then?"

"I might have heard it, but I meet so many people—her name doesn't spring to mind." He looked at his wristwatch—a Patek Phillipe. "I'm sorry, but I can't give you any more of my time today." Then he winked at his companions. "We have things to do, places to go to—and to party on my boat later this evening. Right, girls?"

Two giggles, but no verbal answer. I hadn't expected one.

"But gee," Hundley said—a county prosecutor who actually says *Gee!*—"Thanks for stopping by to say hello, Mi-LAHN."

"Sure, Mister County Prosecutor," I said. "By the way, I don't live in Cleveland—but I do live in your very own county—and I vote. You might want to remember that the next time you mispronounce my name." Then I looked from one young woman to the other. "You can do better, ladies," I said. Then I left Jim Hundley at the bar in his ghastly Hawaiian shirt, stunned, his bodyguard glaring at me, enraged, as if I'd just spread bubonic plague to everyone in the room.

That, I thought, would be a great news photograph for the front page of the *Plain Dealer*.

CHAPTER THIRTEEN

K.O.

Buying a personal computer might have been considered hopelessly old-fashioned by most of Kevin O'Bannion's age bracket, who all now had smartphones—but he needed a computer for work, and choosing a laptop at Best Buy took him less than fifteen minutes. It wasn't the least expensive one—some off-brands looked like they might have been built, he thought, by someone in their mother's basement—but it wasn't top-of-the-line, either. He picked a smaller one, lightweight to lug around.

He wasn't much of a shopper. Men decide what they want ahead of time, walk in, buy it, and take it home—case closed—while women, K.O. figured, took an entire afternoon making the simplest of decisions. Was Carli Wysocki like that? And would he ever find out?

He'd left her in the lurch the night before. (He made a mental note to look up "left in the lurch" on the Internet to find out its origin.) He and Carli had been nine-tenths of the way to consummating their relationship when K.O.'s employer had summoned him because of Bert Loftus's near-fatal experience—and while she'd gamely suggested he answer the phone in the first place, she wouldn't admit she'd been as discombobulated as he. The kind note she'd left on his pillow seemed like a surge of romanticism after a long night alone and a frustrating day.

He stopped at a Subway in Mentor to purchase a foot-long chicken sandwich—specially priced at five bucks—and took it home with him. Of course, Rodney was more interested than usual because he walked in the door with good-smelling food, so K.O. fed him first and held the cat on his lap until Rodney decided there were other things more important, like resuming his window sentry post to tally the number of birds he saw each day.

He opened a bottle of water and unwrapped his sandwich and thought about the lonely evening ahead. He'd blown it with Carli. She had a regular job with regular hours; why would she want a guy called away from advanced *foreplay* to go hold the hand of a crooked politician who'd just been shot at?

He spent five minutes playing with Rodney—a long piece of yarn with a feather on the end was the toy of choice—and then turned on the television. He wasn't a TV fan and had no idea what the reality show he was watching was about. Apparently a group of impossibly pretty young people were sharing a house somewhere and changing sex partners as often as K.O. changed his socks. It took less than two minutes before it bored him, bone-deep.

He sat on one end of the sofa while Rodney fell asleep on the other end—so soundly that he didn't even lift his head when the doorbell rang.

K.O. opened it and took one surprised step backwards.

"Hi, Carli," is all he got out before she threw her arms around him, pulling his head close to hers, and practically putting her tongue down his throat.

As they stumbled together into the bedroom, pulling off each other's clothes and leaving a Hansel-and-Gretel trail from the front door to the bedroom, kissing over and over, K.O. silently thanked the powers that be that he'd ordered neither onions nor garlic dressing on his Subway sandwich.

A cheap bedspread from T.J. Maxx, the blanket, and one pillow were scattered across the floor. K.O.'s head was on his remaining pillow, his arm around Carli, her face planted comfortably in the warm space between his jaw and his shoulder. The sweet scent of her shampoo made him dizzy. His smile was one of contentment.

Carli burrowed deeper, and her voice was almost muffled. "Isn't this where we're supposed to have a cigarette?"

"Huh?"

"In movies—after they have sex, they smoke cigarettes."

"I don't smoke."

"I don't either. I just thought it'd be cool if we smoked."

He wanted to joke that he'd buy a pack of cigarettes for next time, but the fear that there might not be a next time forced him into another silence.

"Are you okay?" she finally said.

"Great. You?"

"Fantastic."

He tried unsuccessfully not to laugh. "I doubt I'm fantastic."

"Don't you know the most important sex organ in the body is the brain?"

"I never heard that."

"Trust me."

"I don't think my brain is all that sexy."

"Not your brain, Kevin—mine." She rolled over and fished the second pillow from where it had been thrown on the floor and tucked it under her head. "It was my brain that brought me over here in the first place tonight."

"You weren't just horny?"

"Of course I was horny, dummy." She poked his chest.

"Well, I'm glad you came over."

She grinned. "You are?"

"Very glad," he said. "Very, *very* glad."

"Just two veries?"

"What?"

"Two. Very *very*."

"There's way more than two—but it's embarrassing to say all of them."

"We don't have to be embarrassed, do we?" She pinched his chin as if she wanted him to smile. "Come on, Kevin, we just made love three times in the last ninety minutes. What's left for us to be embarrassed about?"

"Not embarrassed, exactly."

"What then?"

"Scared, I guess."

"Scared of what?"

"You."

"I don't think I'm scary."

It took him a while to find the words. "I've led a strange life, Carli. Long, boring story. But I never had a real girlfriend before—and I'm scared if I let you get too close, you'll figure what a jerk I am and you'll be gone."

"I'd like to point out that I wasn't invited over here. This wasn't a date. I came because I wanted to."

"You wanted to finish what we started last night."

"No—I wanted to *begin* something tonight." She craned her neck a little and gently licked his earlobe. "We've gone out a few times, Kevin. I wouldn't have seen you that often if I wasn't feeling something for you."

"If you knew about me, you wouldn't be feeling anything. Pity, maybe."

She rested her cheek on her hand. "I don't know *much* about you—but I couldn't ever pity you. You're a strong, tough guy. Not about women, maybe. Not about me. Sure, I'd worry about you. You've been beaten up since I met you—and that wasn't so long ago."

"I wasn't beaten up," K.O. protested. "I won the fight."

"I bet you win most of them."

"Like I said, it's a long story."

"So tell it to me."

"I don't think I could. It's embarrassing."

"Didn't we just say there was no more embarrassment? Come on, I really want to know. I'll get out of bed so I don't distract you. We can go out in the other room and sit on the couch, all right?"

She rolled out of bed and walked naked to where K.O. had tossed his shirt. She started to put it on.

"Wait," K.O. said. "Don't wear that."

"Why?"

"Because," he said, "we came blasting in here so fast, I never got to look at you properly—to look at your body."

She blushed.

"No more embarrassment, right?"

It didn't take Carli long to decide. "You're right," she said. She dropped the shirt on the floor and posed prettily for him, turning around slowly.

"My God, you're beautiful."

"Not beautiful. People say I'm cute, but that's all."

"I think you're drop-dead gorgeous," he said.

"*Too* much," she said. "Can I put your shirt on now?"

"If you have to."

She bent down and scooped it off the floor. When she'd put it on and done up a few buttons, it reached to mid-thigh. "I'm not modest, as you've noticed—but I can't sit and listen to that long story *naked*."

She reached her hand out to him; he took it and got out of bed, embracing her. She put her arms around him, too, her hands gently cupping his buttocks. He kissed her softly, carefully, as if he didn't want her to break, and she kissed him back. There was no daylight between them.

Then they sat on the sofa in the living room, Carli wearing K.O.'s dress shirt with the sleeves rolled up, K.O. in a ratty old bathrobe looking as if he'd stolen it from a homeless Bulgarian beggar, and he told her his life story.

Carli shed a few quiet tears along the way, but they weren't tears of pity and didn't slow K.O. down until he was talked out at almost two in the morning.

"Sorry," he said, leaning forward and putting his hand on her knee. "I lost track of the time. I kept you up way too late."

"I wasn't sleepy," she said.

"Did you notice I didn't mention names of other girls?"

She smiled. "Too many for you to remember?"

"Too many who never even made a ripple in my life. I never figured out how to relate to women."

"You're relating just fine."

He shook his head. "My moods—I'm always mad at something, and you'll worry I'd get mad at you, too. You'll run."

Carli curled up tighter, hugging herself. "You don't know me very well."

"I don't know anyone well. I never learned how to know peo-ple—or how to love them."

"You've got to learn sometime."

"I can't answer that question."

"I didn't ask one."

He pulled the tacky bathrobe's collar up around his neck. "I—don't even know if I love you."

"I don't know if I love you, either."

He looked shocked. "You don't?"

"I'm not sure there's such a thing as real love at first sight," Carli said. "Lust at first sight? Damn right. But love—real love—takes time. So I'd like to take the time, if it's okay with you. I want to know you—and I want you to laugh and be happy."

"But you always smile," K.O. said, "and I never do."

"Wouldn't it be terrible if we were both laughing and smiling all over the place? God, nobody could stand us. And haven't you heard? Opposites attract?"

"I won't be able to smile all the time."

"Well, I won't be able to frown all the time. But if we meet in the middle, maybe things will work out. Whaddya think?"

"I think," K.O. said, "I'm absolutely nuts about you."

She looked at him for a long moment. Then she scooted near to him on the sofa and put her head on his shoulder. "Absolutely nuts about me, huh? Hmm—that works."

K.O. didn't speak, afraid he might squeak like an adolescent whose voice was changing. So he just cuddled her close.

After a while she said, "Let's go back to bed."

"You're staying the night?"

"If that's okay."

"Sure, it's—I mean, don't you have to work tomorrow?"

"It's my day off."

"Oh."

"I know *you* have to work, so we'll get up as early as you want. You have an alarm clock, right? And I hope your shower is big enough for two. I don't suppose you have an extra toothbrush? Don't worry, I won't use yours. We don't know each other *that* well yet. I'll brush my teeth with my finger, okay?"

She stood up, heading for the bedroom, pulling his shirt off over her head and letting it slide off her fingers onto the floor. K.O. couldn't even breathe while he watched the way her ass moved when she walked—but he was actually a face man, and Carli was the prettiest young woman he'd ever seen.

"Coming, Kevin?" she said over her shoulder.

K.O. stood, untied the belt to his robe, and followed her.

CHAPTER FOURTEEN

MILAN

My town is full of nice people. They are open, warm, sometimes funny—huge sports fans, great music lovers of both classical and rock, and dedicated supporters of art, theater, and dance. They're generous; even when times are tough, charities do well here. And Clevelanders love to eat; great new restaurants open here all the time. I wish I could eat out more often, but health issues creep up on people close enough to reach out and touch the age of sixty.

Why was it, then, that ever since Councilman Bert Loftus hired me to protect his ass, I hadn't run into a single person I liked? It worked both ways: None of them seemed to like me, either.

After my run-ins the day before with FBI Special Agent Jeffrey Kitzberger and County Prosecutor Jim Hundley, both of whom I thought of as total shits, I hadn't learned a damn thing. They might even be trying to hinder me. That happens. Nobody wants to help a private investigator investigate.

I came to work first thing in the morning feeling out-of-sorts. In the car I listened to Lanigan and Malone on WMJI 105.7, as I usually do, but I was in no mood even to smile at those funny guys—especially when they're sniping at each other, which is almost an everyday occurrence. On the first step toward a bad day, it threw me off a little when K.O. walked in a few minutes after I did, with a swagger to his step I hadn't seen before. He practically glowed.

"You seem perky," I said. "Sleep well?"

His eyes twinkled when he looked at me. "Not so much."

I saw he carried a new laptop, but I doubted that caused his look of happiness. "Do you have anywhere to go today?"

"Nowhere special. They'll deliver my desk this afternoon."

"Good," I said. "I have a job for you."

"That's why I'm here, boss."

I winced. "'Boss' sounds like I'm either a road gang prison guard or the guy who runs the NCIS team on TV."

"Fine. I'll call you 'Your Majesty.' How's that?"

I ignored the sarcasm. "We're hitting a brick wall on the Loftus case. Get on the Internet and put together a list of everybody who's been indicted and/or convicted that had anything to do with Loftus. Find out who's mad enough to want him dead."

He nodded. "That'll be easy on my new laptop." He tossed the Best Buy gift card onto my desk. "There's a few bucks left on this card. How do you want me to set myself up?"

I considered that. "Use the office address and phone number, and set up an e-mail account."

"Sounds good. So what e-mail address should I use?"

"Make believe I give a damn," I said.

K.O. moved one of my visitor chairs over to the mini-refrigerator that looks like an old-fashioned Wells Fargo safe and set up his laptop so he could work. I was glad he'd be getting his own desk; I've never understood why they call them "laptops" anyway. Who'd want to keep a laptop on their lap for any amount of time? After it's been turned on for a while, the bottom of it grows hot. And if it's indeed resting on the tops of your thighs, there'd be no leg-crossing or stretching. Getting up to walk around or go to the john would constitute a major readjustment.

So K.O. had his job to do, and I had mine: to find and talk to all the other people who, like the Ogres—whoops, did it again, I meant the Ogrins—and Reverend Clarence Whitby, hadn't yet been caught by the feds for doing the same things the already-convicted bribers do.

I was tinkering with my own laptop when Detective Sergeant Tobe Blaine walked in the door—not smiling. She was wearing a summer sports jacket, her badge displayed from the chest pocket. It was too warm to wear a jacket—unless she needed it to cover the Glock carried on her hip.

"You're out and about early this morning, aren't you?"

"No," she said, "I've been in my office since about seven. Watching television." She turned to K.O. at his computer in front of my refrigerator. "I spent most of my time looking at Mr. O'Bannion."

K.O. looked up, startled. Then he rose slowly, closing the lid to his laptop. "I was on television?"

"Closed circuit." She sat in the only remaining visitor chair. "The residential building you visited yesterday has a security system—a vidcam recording who comes and goes—and they have perfect pictures of you going to see Seena Bergman. You rang her bell and waited exactly nine minutes and twenty seconds before she let you in. You were in her apartment for forty-two minutes. Then you left."

Someone else might have looked over at me for assistance, but K.O. kept his eyes on Tobe Blaine, his stubborn streak not far away. "That sounds about right."

She cocked one foot on her other knee. It wasn't how women cross their legs; it was almost macho. "A young guy like you visits a middle-aged hooker at ten o'clock in the morning. Fascinating."

"Sorry I wasn't more entertaining."

I jumped in. "Do you mind my asking why you were watching the videos from Seena Bergman's building?"

"I *do* mind—yes."

"Kevin O'Bannion is my employee. Where he was at ten o'clock in the morning is my affair, not his, because he was on my time. That's why I'm asking."

"I was watching," she said, "because Seena's body was found in the woods last night, near the main entrance to the Metroparks Zoo."

K.O.'s voice almost cracked. "Jesus. What was she doing near the zoo at night?"

"I don't think she was there to see the Elephant Crossing. She'd been beaten up—cigarette burns on her cheek, too. But that's not what killed her. She was strangled." Blaine said, "I'm sure you didn't visit Bergman's apartment yesterday to get laid.

You have a fresh hickey on your neck, Mr. O'Bannion. Hookers don't give hickeys."

"Well," I said, noticing the red bruise on K.O.'s neck for the first time, "*somebody* did."

"I don't care about his sex life," Blaine said. "What was he doing at Seena Bergman's a few hours before she was murdered?"

"Bert Loftus visited Seena just before someone shot at him. That's why K.O. went to talk with her."

Tobe Blaine pondered that. "Interesting."

"Why?"

"Because I saw Bert Loftus on that video from the night before. Okay, what was *he* doing there?"

"Forgive the sarcasm," K.O. said, "but—*duh!*"

"Loftus admitted that to you? Is that why you went to Seena the next morning? Intimate details?"

I nodded at K.O., who pulled his chair over and sat down opposite me, next to Tobe Blaine. She turned her head to him and sniffed—just like a bloodhound.

"Whew!" she said. "What's that aftershave you're wearing?"

K.O. turned crimson. "Uh—I think it's Old Spice."

"You smell like a Mai Tai, and it's giving me a headache. So hurry up and tell me about Loftus."

He looked from one of us to the other. "Do I go first?"

"You know more than I do," I told him, "and Detective Blaine would love to be enlightened."

He cleared his throat. "When the councilman was on the steps of St. Mal freaking out, we asked him where he'd been, and he said he was at Seena's until a few minutes before someone pumped a slug two inches from his ear."

"Did he say why?"

K.O. laughed in her face. She didn't like that much. I jumped in to ease the tension. "Loftus wasn't specific as to why, but he said he didn't want his wife to find out."

"So Mr. O'Bannion dropped by to see her the next morning."

K.O. nodded. "To find out if anybody knew why Loftus would be there that time of night."

"And did you? Find out?"

"Seena Bergman didn't get paid to *talk*."

"This is starting to stink," Tobe Blaine said. "I got dragged kicking and screaming into the attempted murder deal because—well, because I don't usually bother with 'attempted' unless the mayor himself bellows like a gored ox. Now there's a real homicide on my hands, an aging hooker is the victim, and she's been involved with Bert Loftus and Kevin O'Bannion." She pointed a finger at my chest. "And with you, too, Mr. Jacovich."

"Milan," I said, correcting her.

"Mr. Jacovich. When I'm not on duty, I'll call you whatever you want." Her attention returned to K.O. "She didn't mention other names besides Loftus?"

"No. She's pretty discreet for a hooker."

"Most hookers *are* discreet. That's how they stay in business. You say *you* had nothing to do with it?"

"Just what I told you. I'll swear it if you want."

Tobe seemed amused. "On a Bible?"

"I last read a Bible when I was seven," K.O. said, "so I'm screwed."

"Not necessarily. You went because Mr. Jacovich told you to?"

"He doesn't tell me to do anything. I go where I think I have to—and I don't ask for permission."

"Detective," I said, "he went to ask questions. He didn't know Bergman and had no reason to hurt her. So if you arrest him, a lawyer will have him out again before lunch."

"You don't see any handcuffs, do you?"

"Under your jacket," K.O. said, "along with your weapon."

"Smart guy."

"That's why I hired him," I said. "Seena's death is a surprise to us. We're paid to find out who's gunning for Bert Loftus."

"Loftus," she said, "is a crook."

"True. But he still deserves protection."

"Seena Bergman didn't hurt anybody—and she's dead."

"We're not involved with her—just with Loftus. And as of now, there's no law that says we have to stop."

"I *am* the law! So stay out of my way." Blaine rose from her chair and rotated her head until her neck popped. "Don't leave town, Mr. O'Bannion." Then, to me: "Don't *you* leave town, either." She sauntered toward the door.

"Uh—actually I live in Mentor," K.O. said. "And he lives in Cleveland Heights. Does that count as leaving Cleveland proper? Otherwise, neither of us has a place to sleep tonight."

I thought for a moment Blaine was considering blowing us both away for the sport of it. "Don't even think about fucking with my head," she said, and then she was gone.

K.O. said, "Am I in trouble?"

"I don't think so."

"I didn't even know Seena Bergman was a pross. I feel like a dumb schmuck."

"Forget it. She's gone—and nobody else knows."

"*I* know," he said. He pulled his chair back across the room so he was once more using my safe-type refrigerator for his desk.

"Stick around," I told him, "until your furniture comes. I called the phone company. They'll be here this afternoon, too. When you set up your desk in that far corner, you'll need a phone outlet nearby."

"Where are you going, Milan?"

"To chat with my client again," I said. "All about Seena Bergman."

This time, Pam Marek looked surprised when I walked into the anteroom of Councilman Loftus's office at City Hall. "It's early for another beer," she said, rising behind her desk. "Are you just saying hello *again?* Bad timing, Milan. As usual, Bert's about to run off."

"He'd better see me, Pam—before he has to see the police."

"I thought the feds were through with him until the trial."

"This isn't the FBI. It's the Cleveland cops."

That shook her. "Sounds serious."

"You have no idea."

She went into her boss's private office, reemerging thirty seconds later with Loftus behind her, back in his typical outfit—expensive, too-shiny suit and a bow tie.

"What's all this?" he demanded, as if he hadn't hired me to save his life. "What are you doing here?"

"We need to talk," I said.

"I'm busy. I have a meeting—"

"You'd better have a meeting with me—*now.*"

"But," he began, and then stopped. Apparently when I mean business, it intimidates people. He waved a hand at Pam Marek. "Go to lunch, Pam."

"It's early," she said, "and I'm not hungry."

"Then get drunk—or take a walk. It's a nice morning." He motioned me into his inner sanctum.

There were more framed photographs in there, all featuring Bert posing with everyone you've ever heard of in Cleveland. I don't hang pictures of myself all over my office, but then I don't rub shoulders with celebrities. The only movie star I'd ever known personally was dead—killed right here in Cleveland while I was supposed to babysit him—and most top athletes I'd met had either retired or been traded to some other team. As for politicians, well . . .

Loftus didn't sit down. "What's all this about?"

"Nobody contacted you this morning from the police?"

"Why would the police get in touch with me?"

"I guess you haven't heard. Seena Bergman was killed last night."

For a moment he didn't budge—a still subject in a black-and-white photograph, processing reality. Then he staggered back to sit heavily on the edge of his desk.

"They found her body near the zoo."

He put his hand to his forehead to wipe sweat popping out there and on his upper lip—just like Nixon. "Where did you hear about it?"

"It doesn't matter. The cops know you knew her, you were with her the other night before someone tried to kill *you,* and they'll be here any minute. I'm warning you so you'll be ready."

"Ready?" He shook his head. "I don't understand."

"Bert, unless you have an alibi, you're up near the top of their suspect list."

"Suspect? I'm no suspect!" He jumped up to pace the room,

voice rising, arms waving. "I wouldn't kill her. I *couldn't!* What are you, crazy?"

"Relax—don't be flying around the room when the cops arrive."

Moving his shaking hand to his chest, he said, "I'm calm—perfectly calm."

"Where were you last night?"

"Home. I go home every night."

"Some nights later than others. Talk fast, Bert. Seena was a hooker. Did you see her often? Were you a regular customer?"

He squared his shoulders proudly. "Not a customer! I don't pay for sex."

"If you say so."

"Goddamn right I say so!"

"Then what was she? Your mistress? Your girlfriend?"

Shaking his head violently, he said, "She wasn't a girlfriend, exactly. It was different. You don't understand . . ."

"The police won't, either."

He looked heavenward and prayed aloud for Jesus to help him.

"Jesus will wait for you, Bert. Talk to *me* before we have visitors. If you weren't a customer—then what?"

"Somebody—employed her to—entertain certain people."

"Entertain? Did she sing and dance and tell jokes? Bert, with all due respect to the dead, there are hundreds of attractive young prostitutes in town. Why a middle-aged and slightly overweight one? And why you?"

"I—had my reasons," he said.

"So who employed her? Paid for her services?"

He shook his head angrily. "I can't tell you that."

"You'd better tell somebody before they hang you on the wall. The trouble you're in with the feds will fade away by comparison if you're booked for murder."

"I didn't kill her! Milan, you *know* I didn't kill her."

"I hope not, for your sake."

"Then you've got to find the guy who did it!"

"To get you off the hook?"

"For a crime I didn't commit."

"Everyone who's gone to Seena—professionally—will be questioned, too. In about five minutes it's your turn. Why? Why were you one of her frequent visitors?"

"Because she'd do damn near anything kinky!" he almost shouted, and then glanced fearfully at the closed door, hoping nobody else had heard him.

"Kinky? How do you mean?"

"She did whatever you asked her to do—stuff that younger, prettier hookers won't. So—I had reasons."

"Which are . . . ?"

"Gimme a break, Milan. I won't discuss my sex life with you!"

The door opened, right on cue, and Detective Sergeants Tobe Blaine and Bob Matusen walked in, unannounced. Blaine said, "Guys talking dirty this early in the morning? Hello again, Mr. Jacovich," she said. "You move fast."

I nodded. "Moving targets are harder to hit."

"Councilman Loftus," she said, "I'm Detective Sergeant Blaine. We met the other night. And you know Detective Sergeant Matusen."

Loftus hadn't gotten himself under control yet. "Milan told me about Seena Bergman. I have no idea what—uh—I'm as much in the dark as you are."

"We're not in the dark. We'd like you to accompany us to police HQ so we can talk to you privately."

"Oh. Well, I have a meeting."

"The meeting with us is more important."

His eyes pleaded with me to save him, but there wasn't a damn thing I could do. He said to Blaine, "Am I being arrested?"

"It's not an arrest. It's a request. You'll be back in two hours."

"Unless you confess," Bob Matusen added. It was the first time since I'd known him that he tried to make a joke. This was a bad one. It got no laughs.

"You won't handcuff me, will you?"

"That won't be necessary. Detective Matusen will drive you and bring you back," Blaine said. "I'd like to speak to Mr. Jacovich now, though."

Bert Loftus followed Matusen out the door with his head down, shoulders slumping. It was his idea of a perp walk, but there were no cameras, no crowds, and no one called him a murderer.

Tobe waited until she heard them leave the front office. Then she said, "Nice job—running over here to warn him I'd be coming."

"That's why I get paid."

"I think you scared the crap out of him. He smelled of fear."

"Your sense of smell is very dramatic."

"Sometimes it's a curse."

"Tell me, then—what aftershave lotion did I put on this morning?"

"Oh, goody," she said, "a pop quiz. Well, I don't think you're wearing aftershave. But you shampooed your hair before you left the house, right?"

"Very good. What kind of shampoo?"

"This isn't a game show."

"If you say so. Do you have more questions for me, Detective?"

"Not really. I just want to have a discussion."

"Here in City Hall?"

"Why not? Do I have to buy you breakfast again?"

"It's closer to lunchtime. Want to grab a bite? On me, this time?"

"Yesterday was a get-acquainted meal; today it's a homicide. After Bergman's body was discovered, the night-shift cops saw O'Bannion on the building's security tapes. They also explored Seena's very interesting closet."

"Her closet?"

"Not the one where she keeps her clothes. A special closet—with whips, paddles, handcuffs . . ."

"A dominatrix?"

"Yes and no," Tobe Blaine said. "There are packages of adult-sized diapers stacked neatly in one corner. We also found some child outfits. Little print dresses, long white socks, little white panties. She was submissive when she was paid to be."

I shook my head. "That doesn't fit in with the whips and cuffs."

"Apparently Seena went both ways—or God knows how many other ways."

"That's how some people make a living."

"There was other stuff, too, like tiny vidcams artfully hidden in her living room and bedroom, and more than a hundred tapes, labeled with dates and initials. She must have set up the cameras herself."

"Tapes of what?"

"You can imagine. It'll take our guys days to get through them all. Interested in seeing some?"

"Not in the slightest. Why would she make tapes of her clients?"

She folded her arms across her chest. "Take your time—figure it out."

"Blackmail?"

"Bingo!"

"Who was she blackmailing?"

"I won't know until we've seen the tapes." She nodded at the chair behind Loftus's desk. "Some of them are of him."

"Is that why you took him downtown for questioning?"

"I took him because he'd been to Seena Bergman's apartment just moments before somebody shot at him. True?"

"True."

"Or maybe those tapes marked B.L. aren't of him."

"They might be Burt Lancaster's, then. Except he's dead."

Tobe's eyes sparkled. "Anything's possible. Maybe this year the Browns will win the Super Bowl, too."

"Never say maybe," I said.

CHAPTER FIFTEEN

K.O.

K.O. had moved from working atop the mini-refrigerator to his own part of the room with his laptop and his recently acquired gleaming ivory telephone atop his new desk. He'd jotted on his legal pad several names: people who had either been accused, indicted, or convicted of bribing, cajoling, or somehow making Cleveland councilman Berton K. Loftus do favors for them.

It was a lengthy list:

Bridget Carfield—former deputy city administrator who got her job by bribing Loftus with $15,000, paid to him over eighteen months. She'd been convicted and sentenced to nearly five years, her prison stay to begin in November.

Donald Kaltenborn—real estate developer who made millions constructing low-cost housing on Cleveland's east side. His bribes to Loftus totaled $94,000 over five years. His trial was set for late September.

Bruno "Buster" Santagata—construction contractor. He made $170,000 worth of repairs and additions to Loftus's house and charged him $800—hoping to land a job with the city, probably as director of the Housing Authority. He didn't get the job but was repaid when Loftus sent some major city construction contracts his way. Convicted, awaiting sentence.

Glenna Pollard—Common Pleas Court judge, convicted of paying Loftus more than $22,000 to appoint her brother-in-law and two of her best friends to high-level city jobs. Her brother-in-law has also been indicted.

Sergei Chemerkin—arrested and charged with racketeering in cahoots with Bert Loftus, including buying stolen jewelry and other valuables in Connecticut and Massachusetts and shipping them to Cleveland for resale. He was out on $100,000 bail, awaiting trial.

William Gorney—He flew Bert Loftus to Miami and Las Vegas to eat, cavort, and patronize some glamorous and expensive prostitutes. Eventually he took Loftus to New Orleans to party, ending with 30-yard-line seats for the Super Bowl, in return for which he was able to supply Cleveland with almost all its cement, gravel, and blacktop to repair streets and roads. His trial was scheduled for just after the first of the year.

There were twenty-three more names, and K.O. copied them dutifully, hoping this case would be over before he had to plow his way through all of them. He'd never heard any of them before, but now he made a mental note to subscribe to the *Plain Dealer*.

His laptop was now set up with his new account name, NEOHIOTIGER. He put the laptop into sleep mode, made sure the phone was set on voice mail, then locked up the office and went downstairs to his car.

He hoped he wasn't going to cause any trouble—or *get* into trouble—for what he was about to do.

Bert Loftus lived in a mini-mansion sprawled over three acres and as close to Lake Erie as one could go without getting wet. The various levels of the house itself were hard to count from the outside—either three or four stories. K.O. saw modifications and additions had been made, and the rolling lawn that swooped down to the street might have been mowed and weeded to perfection five minutes earlier.

The doorbell played the familiar Big Ben chime. The door was opened by an attractive woman of about fifty, wearing gray slacks and a lighter-gray blouse, her short, dark blonde hair casually styled, her lipstick and makeup low-key.

"Hi. Are you Mrs. Loftus?"

Her nod was tentative. "Who are you?"

He introduced himself, telling her that Milan Security was laboring on behalf of her husband.

"The councilman isn't here during the day," she said, and then mumbled softly, "He's hardly here at all."

"Actually, ma'am, I wanted to talk to you."

"If you call me 'ma'am' again, I'll have to kill you. I'm not your mother, your teacher, or the queen of England, either."

She led him to an easy chair in the living room facing wide glass doors that opened out onto the lake. The manicured backyard plantings and flowers were summer lush, and the cool air blew pleasantly through the room.

"Nice breeze," K.O. said.

"You didn't come here for the breeze." She plopped down onto her gray-green sofa. "Can we get on with this?" Jana Loftus's tone and manner were brusque as she toyed with her single-strand pearl necklace. "What can I do for you?" She seemed on edge, and very down—probably because Bert was heading for a federal prison for bribe-takers and other abusers of power. And when the Cleveland cops finished with him, another cell might be waiting, this time in a state prison where they keep murderers.

"We're trying to determine," K.O. explained, "who might be so angry at your husband that they attempted physical violence."

"Many people are furious with him. He's screwed practically everyone in the county—and beyond. And I use the word 'screw' advisedly. You'd have to ask *them* if they're into violence." She glanced out at the lake. "I'm not violent, either—but if I were, I might want to try killing him, too."

"Do you mind me asking why?"

Her laugh was forced, phony—she sounded like an audience member at a TV show taping being cued to laugh by an overhead "Laughter" sign. She found nothing about this amusing. "He's a cheat. A cheating politician, a cheating elected official, a cheating husband—and a lying son of a bitch. Surprised? Don't be—unless you don't know any politicians personally."

"Not many."

"Assholes, every one of them—hypocrites who lie and steal, and pocket money that isn't theirs, hand over fist," Jana Loftus said.

"Some get away with it. Others—stupid bastards—get caught."
She sighed. "Bert's one of the stupid bastards."

"You're aware of his car accident a few weeks back."

"Of course. It's the family car—*our* car, not the one he tootles
around in that's owned by the city. Council members use city cars
during the day, or in the evening when they have some politi-
cal whoop-de-do to attend—or they have drivers. Do your home-
work."

K.O. quietly wondered whether the president of the United
States even remembered how to drive. "I'm doing homework
right now. What did Bert tell you about the accident?"

"He said someone rammed his car and pushed him into a
ditch." Her hands flapped around looking for a cigarette before
she remembered she'd quit smoking. "He dined with somebody
connected to somebody else important, but he wasn't specific—
and I didn't ask. I never ask. Stupid me." She looked away. "I
wouldn't be surprised if some irate husband tried to kill him. He's
such a slut!"

"Why do you stay, then?"

"What?"

"I don't mean to get personal."

"That's what you're doing," she accused. "You're getting per-
sonal."

"When I need to. You don't have to answer that question."

"I don't have to answer *any* question. You're not a cop."

"Private investigator," K.O. said, "hired to keep your husband
from getting killed."

She took a moment to decide. Then: "Fair enough. Okay, I stay
because of the money. Without him I couldn't buy a sausage Mc-
Muffin. Oh, he has nothing big in the bank; the FBI crawled all
over us after he was convicted."

"Where does he keep it, then?" K.O. asked.

"I don't have the foggiest idea. By law, half of whatever is his
belongs to me, but he never tells me how much he has. He didn't
sew it into the mattress, that's for sure. I sleep on it and I'd feel
the bump—like the Princess and the Pea."

"Safe deposit box somewhere?"

Jana shook her head. "The feds could find that in a second."

"Maybe you should go through his papers. He has an office or a study here in the house, doesn't he?"

"I couldn't even begin to look—I wouldn't know where or what to look for. Besides, they searched this house like a murder suspect's place. Everything went on the floor in piles. Whatever interested them got taken away, and it took me three days to put all that shit back where it belonged."

K.O. didn't tell Jana her husband was, at the moment, atop the suspect list for the death of Seena Bergman, and that the local police would tear the house apart again, looking for anything the FBI hadn't already found. "Does he have an outside business? Some holding company where he might deposit his cash and no one would know?"

Jana shrugged. "If no one knows, then I wouldn't know either, would I? Look, if Bert doesn't pay back all his bribes to the government, they'll strip him of everything, so he won't come out of prison in a few years and start living high on the hog again. They'll take the car, the paintings off the wall, his stocks and bonds. They'd take this house, too, if they could, but it's in my mother-in-law's name—Bert set it up that way years ago in case he got caught—so I guess I can keep it. If they take the furniture, though, I'll sit on apple crates and sleep in a sleeping bag for the rest of my life."

"There must be people who've bribed him who haven't been indicted yet."

"He doesn't share information with me." She stared at the wall. "He doesn't share much of anything!"

"Do you know the guy at Deuce Auto Body Shop?"

She shook her head. "Bert always takes care of the car."

"How about Reverend Clarence Whitby?"

"We don't go to church. I've heard of him—but never met him"

"How about Jeff and Vicki Ogrin?"

"Nope, sorry."

"Everyone calls them the Ogres. Your husband knows them."

"My husband knows *everybody*—bartenders, businessmen, city hall workers, bookies, and hookers. He gets around a lot. I can't remember the last time he was home for dinner."

Jana stood quickly and strode over to one of the open windows, leaning against the jamb and staring out. She took deep, almost desperate breaths, enjoying one of the few times Lake Erie was calm and blue and placid. "I wonder sometimes if Bert remembers *my* name."

Bruno Santagata, called "Buster" by those who knew him, lived in Bedford Heights, southeast of Cleveland, although his construction office was right in the middle of Bert Loftus's ward. His home wasn't elegant but a nice-looking piece of property; were it on the market, its asking price would be three hundred thou or more.

When K.O. pressed the bell, Buster Santagata answered the door himself, decked out in baggy blue trousers, flip-flops, and a short-sleeved white rayon sports shirt that might have been bought at Kmart. K.O. placed him in his mid-fifties, short and thick without being fat. His wavy once-black hair was sprinkled with gray. "Buster" is a name, like "Biff" or "Butch," that smacks of aggressiveness, and Buster's looks and attitude fit his name.

Once more, K.O. went through his introduction, telling Santagata he was working for Bert Loftus, which would be somewhat awkward until he got his business cards. He wasn't invited into the house. Instead they stood in the atrium, with only a screen door to keep out the summertime insects.

"I called your office," K.O. told him, "but they said you were home."

"Where the fuck did you think I'd be?" Santagata growled, extending his left leg to show K.O. the ankle bracelet he wore. "I'm under house arrest—a goddamn prisoner in my own home. If I even walk to the curb for the morning newspaper, the feds'll be all over me like a cheap suit."

"That's tough."

"Tell me about it."

"Maybe you should tell me."

"I'm not gonna tell you the time of day. I'm in enough trouble already."

"Are you angry, Mr. Santagata?"

"If you were headed to jail, wouldn't you be?"

"Are you mad at federal prosecutors?"

"Among others."

"Anybody else?"

Santagata squinted at him through one eye. "You work for Loftus, right?"

"I work for Milan Security. Loftus is one of our clients."

"Well, your 'client' is a prick."

"Why? He sent some big projects your way."

"So? I did a shitload of work on his house and charged him practically nothing, 'cuz I wanted a job with the city—but he wouldn't give it to me."

"That job—housing director—would've paid how much? Around $125K a year? Those construction jobs made you more money than that."

Before Santagata answered him, a young man of about seventeen came clattering down the stairs; his Rock and Roll Hall of Fame T-shirt hung over his jeans. He stopped when he saw K.O.

"Where you going, Steven?" his father demanded.

The kid shrugged. "Ashley's house."

"For dinner?"

An affirmative nod, not accompanied by eye contact; the kid's mouth was a thin slash across his face. He appeared quietly furious.

Santagata said wistfully, "Who's gonna eat dinner with me, then?"

"Who gives a shit, Dad?" Steven brushed past, jostling his father. A spring at the top of the screen door kept him from slamming it loud and hard.

"Damn kids," Santagata mumbled. "You raise them and they turn on you. Nobody gives a damn about me—but I counted on him." He leaned against the wall next to the doorway. "You're almost as young as him—my son. You spend a lot of time with your old man?"

"No."

"Don't you get along with him?"

"We're in separate universes," K.O. said. "But *my f*ather didn't steal anything."

Santagata crossed his arms defensively. "So how come *you* get a private eye job like this? You're messin' with important men in this town—like me. Powerful men—and you're so damn young!"

"When I killed people in Afghanistan, I was even younger."

The color fled from Santagata's cheeks. "Are you here to hurt me?"

"I'd rather not." K.O. squared around to look directly at Buster Santagata. "If you got that job from Loftus, you could skim a hell of a lot more money and put it in your pocket, right?"

The old man looked away. "Comes with the territory—or it's s'posed to."

"That's why you're pissed off at Loftus."

"It's his fault my kid talks to me like I'm shit. He knows he'll have to go live with his mother in Toledo when I'm a jailbird."

"Are you mad enough at Loftus to kill him?"

That shocked Santagata. "Kill him? Are you nuts? I don't like him—I wouldn't piss on him if he was on fire, *that's* how much I don't like him. But *kill* him? I'm a crook, but I'm no murderer."

K.O. took a step closer, hoping he wouldn't make the other man even more nervous by standing too near him, but he wanted to get a closer look when he asked him: "Do you know Seena Bergman?"

"Seena? I never met anybody in my life named Seena." Santagata showed no emotion whatsoever. Either he was the best actor in the world, or he was telling the truth. "Who is she?"

"Just a woman I know."

Santagata nodded. "So why did you ask?"

"Just—wondering," K.O. said.

When K.O. got back to the office, Milan hadn't returned. He sank into his new chair, realizing he'd been standing a lot that day and his feet hurt. He'd learned a great deal and wanted to bang out a report for Milan to read at his leisure.

But always in the back of his head—whether he was looking up names, or getting an earful from Jana Loftus, or even standing uncomfortably in the entryway of Bruno "Buster" Santagata's home—was Carli.

K.O. was not inexperienced at sex. When he got sent away, he'd only been fifteen and hadn't had time or opportunity to find out much about it. In juvie, he learned how to protect himself from a fellow inmate—answering threatened rape with merciless violence. But when he was freed, he caught on quickly. He even endured a ghastly night of "speed dating," spending less than eight minutes talking with each woman, exchanging information and rating in his head whether or not she stimulated his imagination or his gonads, to decide which one he might see again or which one he might take to bed that evening.

Involvement with local women in Iraq and Afghanistan was out of the question; they both would have been killed, perhaps even for speaking to each other. The military was different; there were plenty of female soldiers among whom he circulated. One in particular had interested him in a surface way; she was a Specialist 4th Class and very married to another soldier, a master sergeant, deployed somewhere in Europe. She and K.O. drifted into a nonemotional affair, bedding together a few times each week until she flew to Germany, where her husband had been transferred. So that relationship had ended, and during his leave time K.O. found his way to Istanbul or New Delhi, where it was easy to meet women who were close to his own age, somewhat attractive, and available.

As a civilian back in Northeast Ohio, he kept to himself and kept his emotions tamped down and cold like a burnt-out campfire site in the middle of a dry forest.

Until Carli.

Everything changed then, culminating last night in what K.O. believed was the most amazing sex he'd ever had. It was different, important in a way no other entanglement had been important.

He got a cold pop from the office refrigerator and began typing up his report, rendering his meetings with Jana Loftus and Buster Santagata, adding his own observations.

"There's no question," he wrote, "that Loftus has everybody hot under the collar. But he never did anything to make someone want him dead. He took bribes, put the money where the feds can't get to—and cheated on his wife. (BTW, neither Santagata or Mrs. Loftus have ever heard of Seena Bergman.)"

He looked at his wristwatch.

"It's almost 7 o'clock," he typed. "I'm going home. CU in the AM."

Driving north on the I-90 freeway, he thought about his recent accomplishments. He'd made a friend of Suzanne Davis, and she'd introduced him to Milan Jacovich, who'd hired him until he could apply for his own license as a private investigator—the first time he'd actually had a job when not wearing a military uniform. He'd found himself in three work-related fights in the past few weeks, met some fascinating people on both sides of the law—and then Carli, who taught him the difference between fucking and making love.

Not bad, K.O. thought, his car edging a few miles over the speed limit. Not bad at all.

CHAPTER SIXTEEN

MILAN

The Third Precinct Police Department on Payne Avenue gets older, seedier, and more tired-looking each time I visit—but I'm older and seedier, too. After Vietnam, the Roaring Third was my home-away-from-home when I was a badge-carrying cop, along with my best friend Marko Meglich. We'd had a fist-fight in the school playground when we were ten and became fast friends after that. But I hated the bureaucracy and handed in my badge to become a private investigator, while Marko reveled in the police department's byzantine bureau politics and eventually became head of homicide.

Now that job is held by Lieutenant Florence McHargue. She doesn't dislike me nearly as much as she had for the past ten years. I'd finally taken her to lunch and we ironed out *some* of our differences—but we aren't best friends forever, either. So I was less than comfortable when I ran into McHargue in the hallway. She blocked my way, fists on hips.

"So," she said, "you're working for crooked politicians."

"Bert Loftus is my client, but I have nothing to do with his legal troubles."

"Is that what they are? Legal troubles? They'll lock him up and throw away the key. Now *that's* legal troubles."

"You're lucky. The feds took care of it so you won't have to."

"I have my own troubles. Like the aging hooker who got killed—what's her name? Sienna?"

"Seena," I corrected her. "It saves you a syllable."

Tobe Blaine came out of her office and slowed down when she saw McHargue and me together in the hallway.

"I figured you'd be over here today," she said.

"I should have called first."

Tobe nodded. "You should have."

"Don't waste my detective's time," McHargue said to me.

"Yes, ma'am." I looked at McHargue and Blaine, side by side. An interesting duo, I thought: McHargue a few years older with more gray hair; Blaine a few pounds thinner and a few inches taller. They were both stunning-looking women, although Blaine was more sexy—and both were hardnosed cops, rigid, demanding, and authoritative.

McHargue took no nonsense from anyone. She gave terse orders and expected them to be carried out. She was efficient, successful, eschewed departmental politics (as far as I knew), and struck awe into fellow police officers and lawbreakers alike.

Tobe Blaine looked as if she could punch the crap out of you.

McHargue caught me comparing, but for some reason didn't hit the ceiling as she usually did; instead she shrugged. "Stay on top of this Sienna thing, Blaine," she ordered, and marched off down the hallway. People also walking in that hallway, including beefy cops twice her size, moved discreetly out of her way.

Tobe Blaine leaned against the wall. "Are you here this morning to announce who you think killed Seena? You're not supposed to," she said, "nor are you to stick your nose into a capital crime. So if you're here to tell me what you shouldn't know in the first place, I'll be very cheesed off at you."

"I'm hoping you can tell *me* something. It's probably your coffee break time; come on, I'll buy you a donut."

She drew herself up to her full height of five foot ten or so. "Do I look to you like I eat donuts?"

She'd probably never touched donuts in her life; she had the body of an athlete at least twenty years younger. "Then," I said, "may I buy you some broccoli?"

We got into my car and headed for the Superior Deli on Superior Avenue. After we'd driven a few blocks she leaned toward me, sniffed, and said, "Still not wearing men's cologne—but your shaving cream smells like peaches."

"If you walked on four legs they'd have you at the airport sniffing out drugs in suitcases. What's the deal with your nose?"

She moved away from me, looking out the side window. "It's hyperosmia."

"That sounds like a 1950s horror movie."

"I figured you'd never heard of it. Hyperosmia is an increased ability to smell things most people can't smell—some of which are annoying. It comes with cluster headaches and migraines—often with Addison's disease, like JFK had. Part of the adrenal gland doesn't function properly. But I missed out on Addison's. My—*smellability* comes naturally."

"Sorry about the shaving cream, then."

"I use stuff—shampoos, lotions, hair spray—that is either unscented or doesn't give me headaches. Like lavender."

"I don't own anything lavender."

"It's not a male-type smell—and you're a male-type guy."

I tried not to laugh. "I love being a male *type*."

She chuckled. "In my job, sometimes my super-sensitive nose comes in handy."

"When you discover the murder victim several days later?"

"Yuck! But yes."

When we walked into the Superior, I said, "What does your nose tell you about this place?"

She inhaled, then lifted one eyebrow. "The coffee's too strong, the bacon's crisp—and they use too much grease to fry their eggs."

We sat at a booth. Tobe just wanted coffee—not broccoli. I had tea and an English muffin. I'm a sucker for English muffins.

"Are you a tea addict?" she said.

"I prefer coffee, but it's not good for me anymore."

"Aging, huh?"

"Gracefully. Have you watched all Seena's videotapes?"

"I didn't see many of them; I made other cops watch them. The first dirty movie ranges from amusing to exciting to silly. By the twentieth dirty movie you think seriously of becoming a nun."

"Don't nuns watch dirty movies?"

"The next time you see a nun," Tobe said, "ask her."

"If the nun had seen Seena's tapes, what would she say?"

The waitress returned with our order. Tobe waited until she was out of earshot, then said, "Sister Whatserface would piously tell you a lot of important men in Greater Cleveland have kinky sex preferences."

"Was Seena the producer, director, and star of all of them?"

"Yeah—I wish I could complain to her. There was a vidcam in the heating duct near the ceiling in her bedroom and a remote control taped underneath her night table. Amateur stuff."

"I wonder if Seena blackmailed these guys."

Tobe shook her head. "I don't think so. Not yet."

"What was she waiting for?"

"Something big—and that'd make one of her clients desperate. A big score, a big moment. It's one thing to squeeze some politician, but when he announces he's running for electable office or is ready to close a huge deal, that's something else again."

"But they don't pay their way with her—not directly," I said. "Someone set her up—apartment, car, money, et cetera."

"And who was that?"

"Loftus wouldn't say."

She nodded. "Maybe *I* should ask him."

"Is he a suspect?"

"He doesn't *seem* guilty, but I've been wrong before."

"About what?"

"About becoming a cop," she said, dust-dry with a sarcastic slant. "I always wanted to be an alligator wrestler."

"Okay, don't tell me. I'll find out someday."

"You will, huh? You have a pretty high opinion of yourself."

"Sure—I'm a private eye. So Loftus is on tape. Who else?"

That raised her eyebrows. "You expect me to tell you? Are you joking? You work for Loftus, so I'm talking to you—but you're *not* on my homicide team, so I'll thank you to mind your business."

"Oh. You're welcome."

"For what?"

"You thanked me to mind my business," I said. "When someone thanks you, you're supposed to say you're welcome."

She shook her head in exasperation. "You're a funny bastard."

"Glad I made you laugh."

"I didn't laugh."

"I saw the laugh behind your eyes. Okay, then—can you tell me what's on the Bert Loftus tapes?"

"Loftus likes being handcuffed and dominated. You remember the scene in *Pulp Fiction* where the slave comes out of the basement wearing that mask covering his whole face? Well, that's the kind of mask Seena Bergman put on Loftus."

"Whips, too?"

"No. Whips leave marks. She used a paddle on his ass, though—scolding him for being a naughty boy. She wound up fucking him, too—while calling him nasty, humiliating names."

"Who else is on those tapes?"

"You don't really think I'll tell you."

"Why not?"

"Because you don't carry a badge. What I'm saying to you is friend to friend."

"I like being your friend."

"Goody." She gulped down most of her coffee and looked around, gesturing to the waitress for a refill. "I know Mark Meglich was a legend on the force—and that you were close. I know sometimes he helped with your cases."

"When I asked him to."

"Well, I'll help you whenever I can," she said.

Now I was surprised. "That's really nice of you."

"As long as you don't interfere with police business."

"Are you my friend, Tobe?"

"Tobe, is it? Are we on a first name basis now?"

"If we're really friends, we use first names."

"The jury's still out on that—and for God's sake don't tell Mc-Hargue we're friends, either."

"Everybody is scared of McHargue."

"I'm not scared of her; I respect the crap out of her. We're alike—both black women, and both tougher than a ten-minute egg. She's not exactly the president of your fan club, but she's my superior, and that's how it'll stay."

"I hope you and I will stay friends as well." I touched her hand lightly with my own, then quickly removed it.

She looked at me closely, for much too long a time. Then: "Are you hitting on me?"

I finished my tea. "The jury's out on that, too," I said.

"You're not paying me," I said to Councilman Bert Loftus, "to get you out of a murder rap."

Loftus wasn't wearing his suit jacket, even though his office air conditioner was set cold enough to hang meat. His bow tie was bright red with white polka dots, making him look like a circus clown. He looked nervously at the closed door. "Shh, do you want the whole world to hear you?"

"Just pray the police won't get mad enough at you to publicize what you've been doing with Seena Bergman."

Bert's fingers fluttered to his face. "Don't—*joke* about it."

"From what I hear, it was no joke."

He sank into one of his own visitor chairs and reached out shakily to grasp the edge of the desk. "It's nobody's business."

"You're a public figure! *And* political. It's everyone's business if you so much as scratch your ass. You should've known better. How long were you at police headquarters yesterday?"

"Five hours, maybe more. They put me in a room all by myself for a long time before they even came in asking questions."

"Who was there?"

"Matusen and the nigger girl."

Something behind my eyes took a twist to the left. I stepped forward until I towered over him in the chair. "If you ever use the 'N' word in front of me again, I'll personally—*personally*—make sure that all Seena's sex tapes starring you with your pants down goes viral."

His next sound was between a sob and a whimper. "Don't frighten me."

"You *better* be scared of racism. Do I make myself clear?"

He shuddered, nodded.

I backed off a few steps. "Now—you're what they call a sexual submissive, is that right?"

"No!" He swallowed. "No, not all the time. It was something—

different once in a while." I waited. "Listen, she entertains—ah, shit, I mean *entertained*—a lot of people."

"Kinks," I said. "Fetishes."

He closed his eyes for more than two seconds, then opened them again. "That's her thing," he said. "Fetishes. Listen, she was fifty years old! I could get all the *young* pussy I wanted. I'm a big man in this town."

"You'll be a big man in federal lock-up, too," I said. "You'll look snappy wearing that bow tie with those orange jumpsuits."

His eyes flashed anger. "Now you're being cruel."

"Yeah, but I'm still steamed about your racist slur. So she was a specialized hooker—but you never had to pay for it."

"No."

"And she wasn't your full-time mistress?"

He shook his head.

"Then *someone* was paying her."

"The way I understood it," Loftus said quietly, "she was like an employee of a holding company. I don't even know what a holding company is!"

And we elected him to take care of our city!

"Are you living in a Bolivian tin mine? Who said you could do whatever weird thing you wanted with Seena and not pay for it? A holding company? That's a firm that produces nothing. It just owns stock of other companies. Holding companies don't own stock in prostitutes."

This time the pause was at least fifteen seconds long. "I don't—remember."

"You actually told the police you don't remember?"

Now he looked stubborn. "That's right."

"Your lousy memory will put you in jail, Bert."

"I'm going to jail anyway."

"For a few years in a fed lock-up country club for guys like you. But murder puts you in hard-core prison—maybe for life."

His eyes filled with about-to-be-shed tears. "I don't want to die in prison."

"Then who introduced you to Seena Bergman?"

His whole body quivered. "I—can't tell you that, Milan."

"Can't? Or won't?"

"I'd be too afraid."

"More afraid to tell than to die in prison?"

"Don't push me on this! It's off-limits, okay?"

"Fine—but I'll find out anyway."

In his outer office as I was leaving, Pam Marek called to me from her desk: "Hey, I'm free for a beer after work today."

"Rain check," I said.

She'd told me again she wasn't looking for a relationship, but I began not believing her. I wasn't looking for a relationship, either.

At least, not with *her*.

CHAPTER SEVENTEEN

K.O.

K.O. was up early, with a long list of things to do for Milan. After his shower, he chugged down two cans of energy drink so he could run around for most of the day. He played catch-the-string with Rodney until the cat decided it was time for his morning nap and curled up on a blanket in the corner. Then K.O. tucked his new laptop under his arm and headed toward Cleveland. Thirty minutes later he was on Shaker Boulevard, just east of Shaker Square.

Bridget Carfield's apartment was in a high-rise, only about a thousand feet west of the Cleveland city limits. Living beyond that line would have cost her job as deputy city administrator. K.O. had been admitted graciously, and now, looking out her window wondering why anyone pays a healthy rent for living next to the RTA tracks on Shaker Boulevard, K.O. observed her to be African American, short and square, with swept-back gray hair and red-rimmed glasses. She was a chain-smoker; half-filled ashtrays were all over her living room, and smoke hung in the air like an early-morning fog.

A stack of folded cardboard moving cartons indicated Bridget Carfield was packing to leave. K.O. had never considered what prison might be like for a woman, and he felt sorry for her as she ushered him into the living room surrounded with belongings she might never see again.

She seemed resigned enough to her immediate future, though. "I did my job," she said. "Nobody gets rich on a city salary, so I maybe cut some corners, busted my butt for a little extra money so I can live well after I retire. Everybody does it, and some get caught. That's what happened to me." She sucked the smoke from what was left in her cigarette, blew it out noisily, and stubbed the butt into the nearest ashtray. "Well, if you see anything here you might want—paintings, picture frames, anything like—I'll sell it to you, cheap." Her sigh was sad and audible. "I can't take it where I'm going."

"I hope I'm not bothering you, Ms. Carfield."

She snickered. "You're not. Most friends have forgotten my phone number anyway, so I don't see many people anymore. Want a pop or a beer?"

"No, thanks. I just have a few questions."

"Take your time, Mr.—sorry, what was your name again?"

"Kevin O'Bannion, but people call me K.O. I work for Milan Security."

"Milan Jacovich? I know who he is. I've met him. Are you a private investigator, too?"

He nodded. "In training."

"I'm already convicted, so there's not much I can tell you."

"I want to ask about Councilman Loftus."

She looked to the sky. "Oh, please! The government investigated him up the ass—and when they found I'd slipped him a chunk of money to get my job, they nailed me, too." She shook her head slowly. "Stupid."

"How long did you have that job?"

"Two and a half years," she said, "and I'm sentenced to twice that long in prison. It doesn't seem fair."

"Are you angry with Bert Loftus?"

"No. Why? He delivered what I bribed him for."

"He'll go to trial because of that."

"That," Carfield said, "and a lot of other things. It doesn't look good. Bert makes the right sort of noises, but he has no use for black people—which isn't different from lots of others." She smiled gently. "Maybe you, too."

"When I was fighting in Iraq and Afghanistan," K.O. said, "I didn't notice what color the guy fighting next to me was."

"Bert sure noticed the color of my money—green."

Her husband chose that moment to enter the room. He was skinny with a subtle paunch, close to sixty, and was losing his hair. He'd apparently lost his manners decades earlier.

"What are you talking with this kid for?" he railed, yelling at her but glowering at K.O. "He doesn't mean crap to anyone, and you'll just get yourself in more trouble."

Bridget sighed. "Mr. O'Bannion, this is my husband, Jack Carfield."

K.O. extended his hand but Jack Carfield ignored it. "Send him away, Bridget. He's not on your side!"

The woman took his elbow and gently led him toward the door he'd just entered. "Nobody's on my side, Jack," she soothed. "Just you. You're the only one on my side."

The older man seemed to pout. "I'm always on your side, Bridget."

"I know, baby. Now run along—Mr. O'Bannion and I are doing just fine."

Jack Carfield looked as if he'd cry. Then he squared his shoulders and, with one last look at K.O., left the way he'd come. Mrs. Carfield ran a hand through her hair.

"Sorry," she said. "Mr. Carfield is in the beginning stage of Alzheimer's, and sometimes he can't quite get it together. I swear to God, I don't know what'll happen to him after I go to jail. Our daughter will probably look after him—but she's married with three kids of her own, and she doesn't have a lot of patience."

"I'm really sorry," K.O. said.

"Forget it. It's not your problem." She opened a silver box on the coffee table and took out another cigarette. "You want to buy this cigarette box, cheap?"

"I don't smoke."

Bridget Carfield flicked her lighter and puffed. "I should quit. Maybe I will. I won't be able to afford cigarettes anyway."

"Ms. Carfield, have you ever met a woman named Seena Bergman?"

"I don't think so. I wouldn't forget a name like Seena; it's unusual."

"Never heard of her before?"

"No—and she probably never heard of me, either. Why?"

K.O. thought for a moment whether he should tell her Seena was dead or if he should lie. He decided on the latter.

"She used to work for the city."

"I don't know everyone in Cleveland—or half the people heading for jail, especially city workers. Even a former mayor."

"I don't think I was in town for that," K.O. said.

"Oh, the mayor was dirty. But the feds graciously allowed him to escape doing the FBI walk—"

"What's an FBI walk?"

A corner of Carfield's mouth lifted in amusement. "The Walk of Shame—a special name when the feds are involved."

"Do you have plans for yourself—down the line?"

"You mean when I get sprung?" She giggled, amused by her own slang. "Nope, no plans. I put money into savings and stocks. I didn't steal anything, except maybe the job, so they won't empty out my bank account. And I'll put my stocks into a protective trust until I'm active again. I don't have to be tough," she said. "Federal women's prison isn't full of murderers and crazies."

"You have to be tough no matter what prison you're in."

"How would you know that?"

He considered, then told her. "Three years in juvie."

"Wow."

"No murderers, but I had to take care of myself. Behind bars— behind *any* bars—you either get tough or you get broken."

Sergei Chemerkin lived on the other side of Cleveland, in Middleburg Heights, just off Turney Road. Everyone knows about Cleveland's ethnic neighborhoods—Italian, Irish, Slovenian, Hungarian, and the like—but few locals realize that the Turney Avenue area is very heavily populated by Russians. Like many Eastern European immigrants, Russians had settled in Greater Cleveland in the early twentieth century, most to work for the railroads.

Chemerkin had been arrested and charged with racketeering in cahoots with Bert Loftus. He had deep criminal contacts on the east coast, and had made a fortune buying stolen jewelry and other valuables in Connecticut and Massachusetts and shipping them to Cleveland for resale. Loftus had quietly collaborated with him—after all, stealing expensive jewelry and things wasn't actually *hurting* anyone except insurance companies—and pocketed his 15 percent fee for Chemerkin's profits. The Russian was free now on $150,000 bail; he'd paid the 10 percent in cash, which he'd had right there in his pocket as he stood in court during his arraignment.

When K.O. arrived at his home, a very large dog was barking in the backyard. Sergei Chemerkin opened the door, wearing a collarless shirt, peasant-style, and a pair of bright red parachute pants. His feet were barely encased in leather open-toed sandals, and he was at least three inches taller than K.O. He held a glass of tea. He didn't seem welcoming to visitors and was put out when K.O. identified himself. He didn't step aside, but blocked the doorway, wanting to know why K.O. had "invaded" his home.

"Why I should tell you nothing?" Chemerkin demanded. He still had remnants of his Russian accent, though he'd lived in Ohio for twenty years or so. "Nobody put me on trial yet. If I tell you secrets that are none of your goddamn business, you gonna rat on me. *Then* where I gonna be?"

"I don't work for the government, sir. I work for Mr. Loftus. I'm trying to find out who is angry with him and who isn't."

"Everybody mad at Loftus—one way or the other."

"Why?"

"'Cause he's dumb. He thinks he does what he wants and nobody gonna say shit to him. Maybe that works for him here—but not where I come from. That's why we all going to jail."

"You might be deported."

"Hey! I'm American citizen. I vote, pay taxes. I ain't even gone back to Russia for eleven years. I go to church—Saint Sergius Russian Orthodox. I even go to the monastery out by Hiram—by the college—where the monks live."

That impressed K.O. "I didn't know there was a Russian monastery at Hiram College."

"You don't know lotsa things. I even hang out the flag on the Fourth of July."

"I salute your flag, Mr. Chemerkin—but you steal, too."

"Who cares? Everybody in America steals, right? If you in the church, you steal—that's why churches are so rich. If you in the business, you steal by fucking the other guy. If you in the Congress, you steal worse'n anybody else. Jesus, ain't nobody here that don't steal. So what's the big deal? Me, too—I steal, but I got caught." He took another sip from his sweating glass of tea, wrapped with two paper napkins.

"That's why you're going to jail."

"Maybe," Chemerkin rumbled. "We'll see."

"Really? You have important connections?"

"Nobody here can fuck with FBI. I got friends other places."

"Where?"

"None a your business."

"Am I supposed to guess?"

"Ever been to Brooklyn, boy? Brighton Beach?" Chemerkin's smile was nasty, full of contempt. "They chew a guy like you up and spit you out in the street like bubblegum."

"Never had the pleasure."

Chemerkin laughed. "Pleasure? You stick your nose where it don't belong in Brighton Beach, you find out what pleasure is. But you go there to eat in a Russian restaurant, now *that* is real pleasure. In Cleveland?" He rocked his free hand back and forth. "Not so much."

"So your fences are in Brooklyn?"

"Fences?" The Russian frowned as if he'd never heard the slang expression before, although K.O. was certain he knew exactly what the word meant.

"You don't actually do the theft, do you, Mr. Chemerkin? Except two or three times removed."

"You ask too many questions. I don't like that. You got a lousy attitude." He put a fist on his hip. "You think you're tough?"

"I *know* I'm tough. You want references? But I didn't come here to fight with you."

"Damn good thing. I fight dirty."

"I don't think you do—because if you really fought dirty, you wouldn't be telling people about it. You'd just do it."

Sergei Chemerkin just stared at K.O. for a long moment. Then he threw his head back, roaring a hearty laugh. "Son of a bitch— you're *right!*" He stepped aside and motioned K.O. to enter. "Come. Have a glass of tea, maybe shot of vodka—the good kind, not the crap they sell here—and we talk." He cocked his head and bestowed upon K.O. a wink. "I tell you all you wanna know about Berton K. Loftus."

Judge Glenna Pollard's home was right in the middle of Bert Loftus's bailiwick, not too far from the lake. She was in her late forties, and when K.O. arrived to speak with her, she was wearing designer jeans and a man's white dress shirt with the sleeves rolled up. She didn't much look like a judge, but then K.O. had never seen a judge not wearing black robes. He wondered idly whether Glenna Pollard dressed that way under her austere robes, then dismissed the thought.

Her husband, Lionel Pollard, was there, too, also dressed informally. He wasn't glad to see K.O. He'd opened the door, and when K.O. introduced himself, the husband just bellowed his wife's name and then walked away, leaving K.O. standing on the doorstep.

Glenna Pollard was agreeable enough once K.O. was seated in her living room and didn't seem too bent out of shape about her upcoming prison sentence. "There's not a damn thing I can do about it now," she told him, sipping on a water glass full of vodka, "so I'm trying to make the best of it. And it's a federal prison, so I probably won't have to live every day with murderers or prostitutes or major drug dealers. Maybe they'll give me a job inside that I'll like—maybe feeding the ducks and geese, or working in the library."

"You seem to be taking it very well, Judge Pollard."

"What's my other choice? Get hysterical and cry all day for the next three years? Listen, you get caught making a mistake—well, let's be honest, doing something wrong—and you have to pay the price." Her mouth became a wry grin. "I paid a big price to begin with—about twenty-two thou to Bert Loftus. If I had one wish, I'd love for that never to have happened."

"Was Loftus the one who squealed on you?"

"Oh, no—why would he do anything like that? Actually the government found out about me first—my giving money to him in exchange for favors. That's how he wound up in shit."

"And your brother-in-law?"

"Leonard?" She stopped for a deep breath. "He had an executive job with an electrical firm out in Bainbridge—until they downsized him. He kicked around looking for work for about a year until I found him a job with the city housing authority—worth about a $110K a year."

"And Loftus offered him that job?"

"Sure—after I paid him for it."

"Ouch," K.O. said.

"It was supposed to be an investment for me. Leonard was to pay me back once he started that job. But he never gave me one red cent." She rolled her eyes. "He's such a fuckwad—and now he's on his way to prison, too."

"Is that why your husband seems angry? Because his brother's been convicted?"

"No, because *I've* been convicted. He's pissed off, resentful, and he's so sullen that he can't smile anymore, can't even meet someone's eyes with his own." She rubbed her forehead as if suffering from a headache. "He'll spend the next three years rattling around in this house, living on less than half the money he's used to. Naturally I won't collect any salary while I'm in a cell, and when I get out I won't be judging—or lawyering, or anything else—with my conviction hanging around my neck. So my guess is that Lionel will divorce me while I'm inside." She shrugged sadly. "He hasn't said so, but I know him pretty well, so it won't be that big a shock. Or else he'll find himself a girlfriend and not tell me about it until I walk back in the door."

"Sorry," K.O. said. "So—are you mad at Loftus because of all this?"

"Hell no. He did me some favors, and I'm grateful to him."

"So grateful that you bribed him?"

"Young man," Glenna Pollard said—and now her attitude was that of a judge and not of a convicted felon, "call it whatever you want, but that's how politics operates. That's how the city operates. I was a well-paid attorney for eighteen years, but I wanted to be a judge so I could use some power, make things happen."

"For yourself?"

"Of *course* for myself! For me, my friends, relatives. If you don't look out for yourself and those around you, you're nothing but a goddamn fool."

K.O. got to the office after four o'clock. The two shots of genuine Russian vodka he'd drunk in Chemerkin's house had mellowed him, and the three or four Russian *prianik*—a fattening pastry covered with white frosting—made him forget about having lunch. So did Judge Pollard's attitude. Somewhere she'd learned to accept the bad with the good.

Three boxes on his desk contained the brand-new business cards Milan Jacovich had ordered for him. They looked just like Milan's—blue printing on a white card, with a handprint in the center, like forensic examiners might find when they were lifting fingerprints from a crime scene. In one corner was printed "Kevin O'Bannion," and in slightly smaller letters beneath, "Associate."

K.O. inserted some cards in his wallet to be passed out when needed. He'd never owned a business card in his life, nor had he needed one. Now he was official—a Somebody. He no longer had to run around in 120-degree desert heat with a load of equipment on his back, carrying a death-dealing rifle. Now he was a professional.

He was inordinately pleased with the idea of whipping out one of his cards and presenting it, with flair, to Carli Wysocki, in the hope that she'd put it in one corner of her mirror at home so she'd see it and think of him every time she washed her face, combed her hair, or put on make-up. For the moment, though, he needed to write a memo to Milan, telling him all Chemerkin and Pollard had shared with him.

Chemerkin and Loftus had worked together, stolen together, profited from the illegal activity, and both had been caught with their hands in the cookie jar. He'd even gone into lengthy explanations of what had been stolen in Boston and in several upscale communities in Connecticut, like New Canaan and Hartford: diamond bracelets and necklaces and earrings, high-end wristwatches like Rolex and Patek Phillipe, computers and iPads and big flat-screen TVs. Chemerkin had purchased them directly from the thieves for twenty cents on the dollar, brought them back home to Cleveland, and resold them for nearly three times as much, thanks to the quiet assistance of Councilman Loftus, who knew exactly where the booty could be peddled and was rewarded with "things of value," both for engaging in racketeering with Chemerkin and for making "favorable personnel decisions" about city jobs for friends and associates.

K.O. also wrote a shorter report on Bridget Carfield. Her criminality, he noted, was more passive than active, but she'd go to jail anyway.

Checking his own e-mail, he read Milan's notes to him regarding his latest face-to-face with Loftus, mentioning that Seena Bergman was employed by a nameless holding company. Possibly that holding company would have something to do with the attempts being made on Bert Loftus's life.

K.O. didn't expect any more office visitors that afternoon, so he reexamined his list. Still twenty-five names to go. The next in line to be interviewed had an office on the east side, which would mean when he was done, K.O. would be that much closer to his own home.

He hoped he'd get there before Rodney got too hungry and set out to destroy something out of revenge.

CHAPTER EIGHTEEN

MILAN

I pored over K.O.'s list of the indicted and convicted politicians and bribe-givers in Cleveland. I'd heard of some of them, naturally; if they were important enough, they were paraded for all to see on the evening TV newscasts. Others were brand new to me, names in jobs that were obscure.

It's not that different in any big city—the corruptibility of power and privilege is contagious. The Clevelanders who'll go to jail didn't start out being evil or rapacious, but when they grew powerful, they deluded themselves into taking whatever they wanted, as much as they wanted, when they wanted it.

It was their due.

That's why 99 percent of people in the world are mad as hell at the other one percent.

Flirting on the edge of illegality happens to everyone—some police officers, too. I thought about Marko Meglich. When he was head of homicide on the Cleveland P.D., he was incorruptible. His closure rate on capital crimes arrests was somewhere around 90 percent. He was damn good at what he did.

Yet, when he was walking the beat, and later, when he moved up, I wondered whether Marko ever looked the other way from things that were illegal but nonvicious. He was a canny political being, at least within the department, and I'd bet the farm that he'd "fix" the traffic ticket of a buddy without batting an eye, or help out an important guy who might in the future return the favor in a different way—Marko's way. One doesn't earn a gold lieutenant's badge without political skill and savvy.

I hoped my doubts were fruitless. Since childhood I'd had no better friend in the world than Marko, and I prefer to recall him as a completely honest guy—and a good cop. Maybe the word "completely" didn't belong there, and that bothered me.

That led me to consider Lieutenant Florence McHargue, but only for a moment. She's so honest, I feel the urge to rise and sing "The Star-Spangled Banner" when she walks into the room. She got *her* gold star by being twice as tough as anyone else. Did she have friends? If anyone in the department knew, they weren't telling. She was married, though I didn't know who her husband was nor what he did. I doubted he was a cop, at least not a local one, but I couldn't imagine McHargue hooked up with anyone who wasn't a straight arrow and as serious about the law as she is.

Which nudged me into possible scenarios with Detective Sergeant Tobe Blaine. She was damn attractive, blindingly fast on returning powerful verbal serves, and almost as tough as her direct superior. She was a native Ohioan, but the differences between her hometown bailiwick, Cincinnati, and my native Cleveland are as vast as those between Omaha, Nebraska, and Timbuktu. Except for her hyperosmia—her uncanny sense of smell and her reaction to scents and odors near her—I didn't know much else about her.

My opinion, based on nothing but my instinct, was that she was as honest as the day is long. So I wanted to get to know her better, to spend time with her when she wasn't firing questions at me about Bert Loftus's sins and peccadilloes, time where we could relax and talk and not have to answer our cell phones and then run off to right someone else's wrongs. Time to find out about each other.

I wanted very much to kiss her.

Many female cops date and wind up marrying other cops; a common understanding of the job and its dangers makes those relationships work. I wasn't a police officer, not anymore. I wondered if Tobe Blaine would even go out with me if my job and hers might get in one another's way.

Besides, she might not have considered kissing me.

I'm lousy at dating and generally unsuccessful with women. My marriage was stolen out from under my nose, and my subsequent romances hadn't lasted much longer than a baseball game going into extra innings. I hadn't dated for more than a year when I recently became enchanted by a very pretty schoolteacher. The feeling seemed to be mutual until she couldn't accept my dangerous profession, and the almost-romance withered and quietly passed away.

Now, Tobe Blaine appeared at the edges of my life. *Detective Sergeant* Tobe Blaine—too damn many syllables to say before I even got to the name itself.

I put her out of my mind; there was work to do. I wondered what K.O. was up to at the moment, but he often "does his own thing" before I know about it, and it invariably works out. Instead, I continued studying the long list of those Clevelanders we hadn't interviewed yet who'd illegally or unethically done business with Loftus, wondering which would be angry enough about going over the side with him that they might want to eliminate him permanently.

I was interrupted. I'm often distracted by office drop-ins, and while it grates on my back teeth, it's part of the job. This time, though, it was a part of the job I was reading about at that very moment.

Being a Slovenian growing up in the Slovenian-Croatian neighborhood of Cleveland, I can easily spot an Eastern European face. This one was connected to a man whose sports jacket and slacks were expensive but off the rack, as they didn't quite fit the rest of him—especially the bulge under his left armpit. His eyes were as blue and cold as the Arctic Ocean.

"You are Milan Jacovich." Not a question. He poked himself in the chest with his thumb. "Sergei Chemerkin." He spoke with a discernible accent—probably a Muscovite, a Moscow native.

"What can I do for you, Mr. Chemerkin?"

He pointed at one of my chairs. "I sit down?"

I waved him off his feet, and he spilled slowly into the chair, folding his hands over his stomach, a pose most often associated with much heavier men. "You work for Bert Loftus, yes?"

"Yes, I do."

"Why?"

"Why do I work for Bert Loftus? That's private business."

"Bullshit."

I wonder why so many people use that same expression. Why *bull* shit? Is it any different than that of other animals? Not lion shit, not elephant shit, not antelope shit, not snake shit, not even the female version, *cow* shit. Why do bulls impact so strongly on our casual conversation? Maybe because it sounds better in Spanish: *Caca de toro.* "A young kid from your—" He waved his hand vaguely around my office, not sure what he should call my operation. "He come around my house and talked to me today."

"Would that be Mr. O'Bannion?"

"How do I know his name? A stranger. He told me he work for you—and he asked me lotsa questions about Loftus."

"It has nothing to do with you, Mr. Chemerkin," I said.

"It got all to do with me—and Loftus. I'm going to fuckin' *jail*!"

"You're going to jail because of yourself, not him."

"That's what *you* say." Chemerkin sighed. "So, what you do for him? Get him a haircut, make him throw away his fucking bow ties, make him look good before they lock up his ass forever?" He shook his head sadly. "And he pays you for this."

That made me smile, but only a little. "I get paid for what I do."

"How much?"

"What?"

"How much Loftus pays you?"

"Are you my accountant?"

He laughed aloud, but his eyes weren't smiling. "Fine. I pay you double."

"Double?"

"Twice as much as what Loftus pays you."

"And what do I have to do for that?"

"That's the good part," Chemerkin said. "Nothing. You do nothing. You do nothing for Loftus no more. I write you a check, double, for that." He pulled a checkbook from his inside jacket pocket. "I write it right now, yes?"

"You write it right now—no!"

He scowled. "I'm gonna have trouble with you? But I pay you double! You and the young guy, too."

"Not double, not triple, not anything. There won't be trouble, because I'm not doing business with you."

Chemerkin stood up and leaned over the desk to shout right in my face. I don't know what he had for lunch, but his breath was most unpleasant. "You don't know what trouble *is!* You gonna be goddamn sorry not playing ball with me."

"Russians know about baseball? Good—here's another baseball expression for you. You're out—caught stealing!" I jerked my thumb over my shoulder like an umpire. Then I gently pushed him away. "Now back off."

He looked as if he wanted to reach for the handgun I knew he was carrying—but he thought it over and changed his mind. "If I get extra jail time for what Loftus say about me—I come looking for *you.*"

"You found me this time," I said cheerfully. "You'll find me again. Oh, by the way—I need to ask *you* a question."

He didn't answer me; he just growled.

"Do you know someone named Seena Bergman?"

"Is that Russian name?"

"I don't think so."

"Then how I should know this person? Who is it, anyway?"

I shrugged. "She died. I thought maybe you might know her."

"I know her because she died? Fuck you, man! Don't ask me no more questions!" He started for the door, then spun around and pointed a finger at me. "An' tell that O-something kid—I gave him *vodka*, and some pastries, too—if he knock on my door again, I shoot him in the balls."

His exit actually amused me; guys like Chemerkin don't leave in a huff. He might have been with the Russian mafia, or wanted me to think so. There is one in Cleveland, although small and generally ignored by the authorities. Russian mob guys always play tough; they just don't talk about it.

I listened as he stomped down the stairs and started thinking about K.O. He was bone-deep hard and as good a fighter as anyone I know, but he was unable to pack a firearm, even for protection. That might get him hurt, or even killed. Would his juvenile-offender record keep him from getting a carry-concealed license? I'd have to ask someone about that.

What, then, *was* Chemerkin's problem? What did my case have to do with him? Unless he was behind the attempted assassination the other night, or knew something about Seena Bergman's death.

I dialed a number most familiar to me but was surprised at who answered.

"Homicide Division, Detective Sergeant Matusen."

"Milan Jacovich."

"Milan? Are you calling to help us? Or you want us to help *you*?"

"Sort of," I said. "I'm calling to speak with Detective Blaine."

Matusen took too many seconds before he answered. "She's not in the building right now. Anything I can help you with?"

"I want to run a name by you. Sergei Chemerkin. You know the story on him?"

"I know stories about everybody in this city, and as far as I can tell, he hasn't killed anybody. But I don't know much besides what I hear around this place."

"And what do you hear?"

"Chemerkin's a thief, busted by the FBI—but everyone knows that. It's been in the paper and on the news."

"He's mad at Bert Loftus."

"Mad at Loftus? Take a number."

"Is he Russian mafia?"

"He's Russian and he's rich—but I don't think he's mafia, not where you could see it. Hey, this ain't Brooklyn—it's Cleveland."

"Thank you for telling me this is Cleveland. So Chemerkin's no physical threat, then?"

"Everybody's a physical threat if you push them the wrong way."

"He carries."

"What?"

"A firearm," I said.

"How do you know that?"

"He just walked out of my office, angry as hell—and I saw the bulge under his jacket. Besides, who wears jackets in this heat unless they're hiding something—a beer belly, or a gun?"

"I could check if he's got a license to carry, but I don't think he's dangerous. He's a crook, but I doubt he's a killer."

"If he decides somebody needs shooting, that won't matter—but look it up for me. As a favor."

"A favor for you?"

"I thought we were friends."

"We are friends—sort of."

"Then can you sort of find out if he has a license to carry?"

Another pause. "Okay."

"And my new assistant, Kevin O'Bannion. I'd like to get him a license to carry, too."

"For what?"

"For protection, in case things get bad."

"So—do it."

"Yeah, but he's got a juvie record. Assault and battery in Lake County, when he was fifteen. And he used his fists—no gun."

"I dunno about that. I dunno what goes on in Lake County."

"The U.S. Army gave K.O. a gun," I said, "when he was in Iraq."

"Well," Matusen said. "I'll ask about a license, if it'll help."

"I'd appreciate that."

He took a brief time-out again. "So, should I tell Blaine to call you when she comes in?"

"That's okay," I said too quickly. "Don't bother."

"No bother. You want to ask *her* about this Chemerkin guy?"

"Uh—yeah, that's why I called."

He snickered—an unpleasant sound under the best of circumstances; hearing a snicker on the phone is especially vexatious. "How come it is," he said, "that you didn't ask *me* on the phone, then? It sounds like you wanted to talk to her—*specifically*. Did you?"

I quit blushing when I was about forty—it's more often a younger person's problem—but now my cheeks flamed red. I'm very private, so it aggravates me when somebody like Matusen makes personal comments. "I—wanted to ask her about Chemerkin."

I could hear amusement in his voice; I'd never known him to laugh at anything, or even seen him smile. "Blaine's been in town less than two weeks. How would *she* know about some local putz when I lived here my whole life? Know what *I* think, Milan? I think you got a thing for her. Am I right or wrong?"

"None of your business." I took a breath to even myself out.

"Course not," Bob said, dripping cheerfulness. "So, when she comes back, should I tell her you called her?"

"That's not necessary."

"Well—screw it, I'm tellin' her, anyway."

I made a special effort being gentle when I clicked the phone off. Damn Bob Matusen anyway! Not only would he tell Tobe Blaine I'd called her, but he'll undoubtedly squeal to Lieutenant McHargue, too. And the last thing in the world I'd choose to discuss with Florence McHargue was my attraction for Tobe Blaine.

I had more pressing things to mull over. Matusen didn't think Sergei Chemerkin was a threat. Now, I'm no genius—but if a guy walks around with a firearm holstered under his armpit, he's damn well dangerous!

Which possibly meant that he's the alleged perp who'd been after Berton K. Loftus, who took a shot at him near the Detroit–Superior Bridge. And if that's true, Loftus *needed* to hire a bodyguard who'll go with him anywhere—a bodyguard who packs a bigger and more dangerous gun than Chemerkin.

CHAPTER NINETEEN

K.O.

Donald Kaltenborn's office was past University Circle, where much of Cleveland's artistic heart is located, including the Cleveland Museum of Art, the Cleveland Institute of Music, and the elegantly beautiful Severance Hall, where the Cleveland Orchestra makes its home, as well as Case Western Reserve University, University Hospitals, and its sister, Rainbow Babies and Children's Hospital. Kaltenborn was further east on Euclid Avenue, where the buildings very quickly turned older, more tired, and kind of tacky—at least on the outside. On the inside, Kaltenborn Realtors was elegant. It's almost as if Donald Kaltenborn had too much money to spend decorating and furnishing his office space, and had done so without much taste.

He himself occupied what felt to K.O. like a throne room. His desk was big enough to land a fighter plane on, and both desk and chair were installed on a carpeted three-inch riser, making Kaltenborn seem taller and, by design, more important than anyone else. That's probably why he didn't stand up from his huge high-backed executive's chair to shake Kevin O'Bannion's hand.

He studied K.O.'s business card and then looked up. His hair was dirty-blondish, made darker by all the goop he'd put on it each morning to make it lie down, giving him the Gordon Gekko look. His blue eyes were small and cold, and his wan complexion testified to his aversion to the sun.

"Milan Security," he said. "Is that that private detective fellow? Milan Voinovich?"

"Jacovich," K.O. corrected him. "Voinovich was our governor—before he became our U.S. senator."

"Yess," Kaltenborn almost hissed. "So are he and Voinovich related?"

"Jacovich and Voinovich?" K.O. suppressed a laugh. "I don't think so."

"Hmph! So—what do you want with me?"

K.O. asked Kaltenborn the usual questions, probing at his feelings toward Berton K. Loftus. He got the impression Kaltenborn didn't care one way or the other.

"Sure, I know him," Kaltenborn admitted. "He threw a lot of business my way over the last few years. No crime, right?"

"That's not what the FBI says."

"Screw the FBI. People do favors for friends all the time—and friends do favors for them. That's how the world works. Suppose there's this chick, see? And she needs somebody to paint her apartment, wash her car, maybe drive her to the airport so she don't have to take a cab. So you do it for her—as a favor, right? Makes sense to anybody, doing favors. She wants to show her appreciation, she wants to do you a favor back? So she gives you head. She got something she wanted, you got something you wanted. No harm, no foul, right? That's favors."

K.O. knew his job was to be polite, just like Milan—but sometimes he couldn't help himself. This was one of those times. "Are you saying, Mr. Kaltenborn, that Councilman Loftus funneled lots of high-paying business to your realty company as a favor, and you gave him a blow job?"

Kaltenborn puckered up his mouth, but his glare didn't indicate he was ready for a kiss. "Smart-ass punk," he said, oozing contempt. "Watch your fucking mouth, sonny-boy, or a guy ten times as big and tough and important as you are can *make* you watch it."

"And what big, tough, important guy is that, sir?"

"The same important guy who's gonna make sure when I go to trial in the fall I'm gonna get off without even a wrist slap, that's who." Kaltenborn sat back in his chair with a satisfied smile that didn't change anything about his eyes. "You're way in over your head, kid. You and your boss, Voinovich—he's over his head, too."

"Jacovich—Milan Jacovich."

"Who? Who is he again?"

"You know," K.O. sighed, preparing to leave. "Senator Voino-vich's cousin."

K.O.'s verbal joust with Donald Kaltenborn had put an idea in his head, one that wouldn't go away. He had to chase it down, and it was early enough for him to explore it.

Lexia Wilhelm wasn't a name with which Kevin O'Bannion was familiar. "Lexia," he thought, was probably a shortened version of Alexandria—like "Alex" or "Sandy." He had known a "Zan" in junior high school, another Alexandria shortcut. The surname "Wilhelm" sounded German.

He'd floundered around on the Internet for almost two hours earlier that day, trying to discover who owned the apartment building he'd so recently visited—the one in which Seena Bergman had lived. Eventually he'd found a company named Pequod Managers listed as owner of the piece of upscale real estate on the west bank of the river, and only after he'd searched further did he ascertain that Pequod Managers was a holding company based in Cleveland, and its CEO was Lexia Wilhelm.

He found no one by that name on the online White Pages. There were lots of Wilhelms, but no Lexias.

Then he googled her. There was no Lexia Wilhelm anywhere, and when he tried Alexandria Wilhelm, he saw within two seconds that there were more than 29 million links for him to plow through.

Twenty-nine *million*. He thought, there must be a better way.

He might call the cops for the information, but although he'd enjoyed only brief meetings with Lieutenant McHargue and Detectives Bob Matusen and Tobe Blaine, he was fairly certain no one knew or trusted him on the Cleveland P.D. And why would they? He didn't even live in Cleveland.

However, there was a policeman he *could* call. He looked up the number in his pocket notebook, then called the Mentor Police Department in Lake County and asked to speak with his own arresting officer, his champion and his sometime guide.

"Sergeant Jake Foote."

"Sarge, it's K.O."

"Hey, kiddo, what's happenin'?" That clear-your-throat kind of voice was familiar to K.O. He spent a few minutes talking with Foote, telling him about his new full-time job with Milan Jacovich, and spoke a bit about Carli without getting all mushy and stupid about it.

Then he said he wanted a favor.

"Need a few bucks?" Foote asked.

"Thanks, but I'm okay. I need to find out something about somebody, and I don't have the computer programs you do."

"Is this a Cleveland person?"

"I'm not sure. It's the CEO of a holding company called Pequod Managers. I never heard of them, either."

"Let me give it a try, then," Foote said. "What's his name?"

"It's a her—or I think it is. Lexia Wilhelm."

"Spell it."

K.O. did.

"And she's the CEO of this Pequod Company?"

"According to the Internet. But there's no record of an office location for Pequod—just a P.O. box."

"Doesn't sound kosher to me. I can't pry that information out of a post office without an official warrant signed by a federal judge."

Foote's computer keys clicked as he hummed a nonmelodic song under his breath. After a few moments he said, "This is no piece of cake for a Lake County police officer, K.O. I don't have the same downloaded programs Cleveland cops do. Give me half an hour; when I find anything, I'll call you back. *If* I find anything. Where are you?"

K.O. gave him his cell phone number. "If you find out who she is, can you get an address for me, too?"

Foote hummed some more. "This isn't just some chick you have the letch for, is it?"

"Like I told you, I've already got a girlfriend. This is—well, I'm investigating. It's my job."

"Gotcha," Foote said. "I'll be back to you."

After the call, K.O. checked his wristwatch. He couldn't think of anything more to do until he heard back from Jake Foote. He wanted to call Carli, naturally; he *always* wanted to call Carli. But it was still too early; she'd probably just gotten off work, and if she were already home she'd be changing her clothes, reading her mail, checking her e-mail and her Facebook. Besides, he feared his caring for her might smother her if he wasn't careful. He didn't want to be in her face every minute of the day. Be cool, he thought.

Now that K.O. was a private investigator—or on his way to becoming one—he wished he could be cool. Even Milan was *sort* of cool—some of the time. He could be a pain in the ass, and he probably believed everything he ever read in his life, including the so-called healthy ingredients printed on prepared food that was mostly all crap. But Milan allowed him to follow his own hunches.

If K.O. badly screwed up on this case, he'd be summarily canned, which would mean he wouldn't be able to find another P.I. apprenticeship, at least not in Northeast Ohio, and that would end his career plans. He had no back-up work idea because the only thing he'd ever done well in his entire life was to kill people in the desert. He'd been efficient at that, but it wouldn't look good on his résumé.

He wanted this job—badly. He'd been an actual employee for only a few days, but God help him, he loved being an apprentice private eye. And now that he had his own desk and phone . . .

He took a few minutes to enjoy himself, the new high-backed executive chair, the way he'd positioned the desk in the office so he could look out the window at the river and its fairly active boat traffic, and across the water to the downtown towers and to Progressive Field where the Indians played baseball.

He opened up all the desk drawers, thinking what he could put in each of them. The bottom right-hand drawer would be perfect for a Sam Spade bottle of booze and two glasses. That's what all black-and-white movie private shamuses had going for them, liquor in the desk drawer—but he wasn't much of a drinker, and he didn't suppose Milan would approve of it in the office.

K.O. sighed. Life was like that; nobody's dreams come true as perfectly as they'd wish.

So he filled up his waiting time playing solitaire on his lap-
top—frustrating because he hardly ever won a game. He'd play
solitaire with a real deck of cards at home, and frequently cheat—
but there was no cheating on a computer! Foiled again.

Forty-seven minutes later, his phone rang. Jake Foote on the
line.

"I found out who Lexia Wilhelm is," Jake said. "So sit down,
kiddo—because this is gonna knock your socks off."

The house was in Bay Village, overlooking Lake Erie just sixty
feet north of its back door. A large swimming pool was at the
rear of the house, just in case nobody really gave a damn about
the lake. When K.O. made his way up the long sidewalk, he could
hear loud music playing, not inside but from around the back. He
rang the doorbell and waited.

After a minute, he rang it again.

Jake Foote had said the house was listed as belonging to Lexia
Wilhelm, but the ownership might be constructed that way to
avoid taxes—or for other reasons. That led K.O. to make his trip
out to Bay Village, at the far western end of Cuyahoga County. He
couldn't remember ever having been in that suburb before, but
from the look of the beautiful sprawling homes on the beach, he
understood why. The residents of Bay Village, in the part of it that
kissed the water, were economically comfortable. K.O. had never
been economically comfortable in his life.

His wait felt endless, and he considered leaving—but he still
heard the music playing. He rang the bell once more, leaning on
it hard for fifteen seconds.

A woman came around the side of the house. Her ankle-length
cover-up didn't cover much of anything, as it was practically
transparent, showing a black bikini matching her black head-
band. Her handsome face was long, Modiglianilike, and looked
sorrowful beneath her tan. Her sunglasses had light blue lenses
that didn't obscure the dark brown of her eyes. In one hand was
a half-full highball glass.

"I hope you're not selling anything," she said, "because I'm not
buying." Not cold, but not very warm, either. "You ring that door-

bell like it's your religion." She sipped her drink. "What can I do for you?"

"Mrs. Hundley?"

She frowned. "Where did you get this address?"

"My name is Kevin O'Bannion. I'm with a security company— Milan Security."

"We already have a security system, Kevin O'Bannion. It works just fine, thanks. Now, if there's nothing else . . ."

"Most people call me K.O."

"In five seconds I won't be calling you anything. I'm busy."

"Was your maiden name Lexia Wilhelm?"

She took off her sunglasses so she could see K.O. better. "You've done some homework."

K.O. shrugged.

"Look, I'm not going to stand out front here in my bikini for everyone driving by to look at. I'm assuming you won't go away anytime soon."

"I'll only keep you a few minutes."

She considered it, then nodded. "Come on." She turned and went back around the side of the house. Her legs were long and so were her strides, and K.O. tried keeping up with her without running.

She went through a wrought-iron gate to the swimming pool. K.O. followed, noticing one poolside chaise longue stretched out nearly flat and covered with two colorful beach towels. On a table next to it was an ice bucket, four Cokes in the white cans the company hoped would fool people into thinking they were caring for endangered polar bears, and a bottle of rum, although there wasn't much of it left. Lexia Hundley dropped her wraparound, made one slow turn so K.O. could get a good look at her bikini-clad tan, and then melted slowly onto her accustomed spot. She wasn't being seductive, but her body was willowy for a woman almost fifty, and she probably liked showing off.

Beside her on the deck was a boombox. K.O. didn't recognize the music—Johnny Hartman singing along with John Coltrane's tenor sax—but he caught on that it was mellow and slightly sad. Lexia lowered the volume a tick, then jerked her thumb over her shoulder. "Grab a chair from over there if you're staying for a while. Want a drink? All I have is rum. Or Coke. Or rum and Coke." She almost giggled. "Quite a choice, huh?"

"Thanks, but I don't drink rum."

"I started doing rum when I was sixteen."

"Rum and Coke is a kid's drink?"

"It is," Lexia said. "I just never got out of the habit. Cheers." She finished her drink in two gulps. "So—you got our address, which isn't listed anywhere—and arrive at five in the afternoon. Are you here to shoot my husband?"

"The county prosecutor?"

"Everyone he ever put behind bars has a hard-on for him. That's why our address is secret."

"Well, I'm afraid I didn't bring my gun."

"Shit," she said, mildly remorseful.

"I came to see you," K.O. said.

She put her sunglasses on again. "I hope you enjoyed the view, then, because that's all you'll get."

"*Is* your maiden name Lexia Wilhelm?"

She nodded languidly. "You probably know everything else about me, too—my favorite color, favorite movie, shoe size and bra size. You don't want a drink, you won't get laid, and you're not anxious to leave—so what are you doing here?"

"Just asking questions. Are you CEO of a company called Pequod Managers?"

She cocked her head to one side as if taken by surprise, then sat up and poured herself another drink. "Pequod—that sounds familiar."

"You're the chief executive officer and you *think* it sounds familiar?"

"I own things I don't even know about—businesses, companies, tax shelters. I even own this house—although I personally never paid a nickel for it. Every so often my husband sticks some papers under my nose and I sign them. That's business, and I don't really 'get' business, so I don't pay any attention. So I *might* be—what is it again? The Pequod? I might be the CEO of a holding company called the Pequod."

"Do you know where it's located?"

"I haven't the foggiest idea. Middleburg Heights?"

"Not even close," K.O. said. "Try the Cayman Islands."

"I don't know where the Cayman Islands *are*," Lexia said.

"You should know—because your so-called holding company is sitting on over $4 million in a Cayman bank."

She turned a few shades paler beneath her tan. "Four mill?"

K.O. nodded. "That's a round figure."

She fell back on her lounge chair, flipping her glasses up on her forehead. "I had no idea . . . I know some of that stuff I own is so *he* won't have to answer for it—probably real estate and things—but four million bucks!"

K.O. sat quietly, watching Lexia Wilhelm Hundley absorb the information. Finally he said, "Another question, if you don't mind."

"If I do mind, will you not ask it?"

"Is Seena Bergman a name you might know?"

It was subtle, but K.O. watched the muscles harden in her face. "No. Who's she? One of Jim's bimbos?"

"I don't know."

She leaned on one elbow, holding her drink in her other hand. "Jim's a slut. Mister Big-Shot-dot-the-I county prosecutor. I know about it—always have. I show up at his political whoop-de-dos, and stand by his side and smile like an idiot during elections. Otherwise, we live separate lives. Half the time he doesn't come home at all—which is okay because half the time I don't come home, either." She leveled a red-tipped finger at K.O. "Is that what all these questions are for? You trying to find out about my sex life?"

K.O. said, "Nothing personal, but I don't give a damn about your sex life. I just wondered if you know who Seena Bergman was."

"Was? What do you mean, 'was'?"

"Nothing. Sorry, I was just curious."

"Did anything happen to this Seena Whatever-her-name-is?"

Now K.O. was flustered. "It's got nothing to do with you, Ms. Hundley. Forget it, okay?"

Lexia Hundley arose, reaching for her cover-up. "I won't forget it! And if I find out who this woman is and if she has any connection to my husband, I'm going to have *your* ass for breakfast!"

She shrugged the garment on and hugged it to herself, ignoring that it was see-through. "I don't really know who you are, buddy, nor do I care, but you're starting to be a major-league pain in the ass. I'm sure you know the way out." She pointed toward the gate. "And stay out."

When K.O. got to his car, he drove it west for a few more blocks, turned down a side street, and parked for a few minutes while he jotted down everything he'd found out that afternoon.

Pequod Managers somehow belongs to the county prosecutor, Jim Hundley, K.O. thought—in his wife's name. She says she knows nothing about anything she signs. He'd been around long enough to read reactions and body language, and he believed Lexia Wilhelm Hundley didn't know who Seena Bergman was, nor anything about her—but she'd come to terms with her husband's promiscuous ways.

Apparently she had a few of those, too.

K.O. didn't worry about himself in that department. Unlike many guys his age, who would screw anything that moved, he felt in his heart that when sex is right, it's *right*. And Carli Wysocki was right for him.

Would it last? No one knew the duration of real love, certainly not K.O. And he thought of his boss, who had been attracted to a woman who decided their relationship should end before it got started, uncomfortable about a romance with someone who's frequently in danger of getting killed.

K.O. hadn't come close to death when he was on the edges of the last Milan Security case—he'd been in two fistfights, winning both of them. But he wanted to call Carli anyway and assure her he wasn't in danger.

He drove back to the office and parked his car where he usually did. As he headed for the iron gate across the front door, a man approached him on foot. K.O. was a quick study when it came to strangers, and he noted the man was slim—skinny, if the truth be known—with jet-black hair combed straight back, and a hawklike off-center nose like an axe.

"Excuse me, sir," the man said. "We're looking for the guys who run the iron shop there on the first floor, but apparently nobody's there. Do they go home that early?"

K.O. couldn't remember any occasion in his life when he'd been referred to as "sir" before. Now he found it pleasing, even respectful. Maybe he was growing up after all. He relaxed. "They go home when they've finished working," he said. "But I work upstairs, and they hardly ever tell us when they're leaving—"

And then something was clamped over his nose and mouth from behind—a cloth or a handkerchief, wet and very sweet-smelling. His automatic response was to claw at it with both hands, but it took less than five seconds before he lost consciousness and drifted down into a fog-colored darkness in which the ambient sounds—the traffic, the river, even the breathing of the man who'd asked him that question—seem to have been coming from far away, perhaps in another dimension. There was no way he could know what would happen next—and he found himself not caring one way or the other.

CHAPTER TWENTY

MILAN

When I drove into my lot and saw K.O.'s car where it usually was, I didn't think anything of it. We didn't really have assigned parking places, but I always parked in the same space, right next to the main door. Most of the guys who worked at the iron gate shop left their cars around to one side of the building, and K.O. had taken to parking out in the middle of the lot, about twenty feet away. It really didn't matter. The parking area could have held a hell of a lot more cars than had ever been there at one time.

What surprised me, though, was that the front door and the iron gate across it were locked, which they never were when K.O. and I were inside. Why discourage drop-ins who hopefully came here to spend their money?

If K.O. wasn't in the office, where had he gone to, and why had he left his car behind?

Upstairs, I dialed his cell phone number, but the call went directly to voice mail. Kevin O'Bannion's generation connects entirely by cell phone. Although I don't believe he has that many friends, I'd never known him to shut his cell phone off or, even worse, *lose* it.

What the hell, I thought, maybe he'd forgotten to charge the battery.

I booted up my computer to see whether he'd e-mailed me a report on his day's activities; that had somehow become what we each did at the end of the work day.

Nothing.

Maybe he was off somewhere researching or interviewing—
but I didn't think so. It was past six; talking to anyone involved
with Bert Loftus was usually a daytime job.

Had Carli gotten in touch with K.O. today? Had she driven
downtown from where she worked, in Beachwood, and picked
him up so they could go out to dinner together, and that's why his
car was still in the lot? If so, he would have e-mailed me—even
told me what restaurant they'd visit, or at least scrawled a note
for me to find on my desk.

I was working at not worrying about him when the phone
rang. Late for a client to call, I thought, then snatched it up hop-
ing to hear K.O.'s voice.

Instead it was the not-so-dulcet tones of Special Agent Jeffrey
Kitzberger.

What a surprise.

"Hmm," he said. That was his greeting. No "Hello," no "This is
the FBI," not "Hey There, this is Jeff calling." Just "Hmm." Then
he added, "You work long hours. I figured you'd be home by now."

"Then why'd you call?"

"Curious. How's the Loftus case coming along?"

"Fine," I said.

He waited for further explanation, but I was damned if I'd give
it to him.

"Fine? Just 'fine'? Fine doesn't give me much to go on."

"I'm supposed to give *you* something to go on? I remind you
that this case was none of your business—and further, when I
asked *you* for assistance, you sent me packing."

"I don't get paid to help you solve your piddly-ass cases."

"And I don't get paid to help you solve yours."

"Yes," Kitzberger said, "but I'm the *government*."

"Woo-hoo!" I said. "If you're the government—you person-
ally—how about giving out more jobs to Americans who had
theirs pulled out from under them?"

His pause was only milliseconds long, but I caught it. "That's
not my job."

"*I'm* not your job, either. You're looking for something about
Bert Loftus and hoping I'll give it to you. So what do you want—
and why do you want it?"

I heard steady, rhythmic breathing through the phone as he considered his next move. "This is FBI business, y'know. Classified."

"Then what I know is classified, too—which means I'll give you the time of day and nothing else."

"Look," he said. I think he started beginning sentences with that word when President Obama made it popular. "Look, Bert Loftus is trying like hell to get out of going to jail."

"Wouldn't anyone?"

"Yeah, but—" he said, and then stopped.

I waited.

"Are you aware he's spilling his guts to the bureau, to the federal prosecutors, to anyone who'll listen—fingering people who haven't been indicted yet in the hopes of getting his own sentence down to a minimum—or thrown out altogether?" His laugh was totally mirthless. "He spent most of today talking about Reverend Clarence Whitby." Then he lowered his voice as if he didn't want anyone to overhear. I wondered why; he *was* in his own office. "Twenty percent of what Whitby collects in the offering plate on Sundays finds its way into the Loftus pocket, or to other people's businesses that Loftus diddles with—in exchange for Loftus breaking his butt to give Whitby every business break, inside stock trading information, and bargain real estate deals about foreclosed houses. And," he added, "real estate variances, whenever possible."

"I spoke with Whitby a few days ago," I said. "He didn't give me squat."

"Just imagine, then, what he's going to talk about to *us*."

"And you want me to tell you what he told me. Is that it?"

Kitzberger sounded relieved. "I'm glad you understand, Mr. Jacovich."

"What I understand, Special Agent, is that you desperately want to shut up *my client* when he's trying to save himself from going to prison for the rest of his life. Am I close?"

Kitzberger said, "I wouldn't call it *desperate*."

"Call it whatever you want—I'm through talking to you."

"You might get a subpoena."

"For what? Running my business honestly? How about if I just

sit on my hands and wait for the process server to walk in here
and hand me one."

"It might happen," he warned.

"Have you always been a bully? Or just since you joined the
bureau and read all about the life and times of J. Edgar Hoover?
Have a terrific evening."

And I clicked the OFF button on my phone, smiling. He'd
babble to his shrink tomorrow that someone hung up on the FBI.

It was indeed time to go home. I switched off my own com-
puter, dusted the top of my desk and that of K.O., closed the win-
dows, and was about to walk out the door when somebody else
walked in.

"I wondered if you'd still be here," Tobe Blaine said. She took
off her sunglasses and put them in her over-the-shoulder purse.

"I was just leaving."

"Bob Matusen said you called me this afternoon."

Mental note: Kill Matusen. "Yes, to ask about Sergei Chemer-
kin."

"How would I know anything about Sergei Chemerkin?"

I shrugged.

"So you asked Bob instead?"

I nodded.

"Liar liar, pants on fire," she said. Then she laughed. "Bob says
you have a thing for me."

"I don't even know what a 'thing' is."

"What are you, seven years old? I'll put it so you can under-
stand. You've got the hots." I looked stunned; she pressed on.
"Horny. Dirty mind. Sex-starved. Get my drift?"

I was unbearably uncomfortable, not knowing whether to sit
or stand—and had no idea what to do with my hands. "That's
crude."

"Sex is crude—if you do it right."

"It's not about sex," I said. "I want to know you better." And
how lame was *that?*

"Like you want to get to know some second-string linebacker
for the Browns?" She walked over to me. "Would a linebacker do
this?" And she put both hands on the back of my head and pulled
me close to her for an amazing kiss.

When I finally got my breath back, my arms were still wrapped around her. "A linebacker, huh?"

"I actually kissed a linebacker once. You do it better." She smiled. She'd not smiled openly at me before. "I hope I didn't cross any boundaries. Are you bothered by the interracial thing?"

"Not at all. I hope you aren't, either."

She shook her head. "I was engaged to a white guy, once—three quarters white, anyway."

"I'm—sorry what happened to him."

"Me, too. But you move on, whoever you are."

"You're moving on to me?"

"Let's say I'm open to new ideas," she grinned. "And you kiss pretty good, so . . ."

"I had help."

"I do my best," Tobe said. "I know you've been divorced for-ever—and from what I hear, there's nobody special in your life right now."

"And where do you hear that?"

"I'm a cop—I hear everything." She poked me gently in the chest. "You know about that; you used to be a cop yourself."

"Many moons ago."

"It's like riding a bike. You never forget."

I laughed and finally moved away from her. "I can't remember how to ride a bike."

"Well, you remember how to kiss."

"My last kiss was decades more recent than riding a bike."

"It'll come back to you," she said. "Just—climb on."

We had dinner at La Strada on East 4th, a street a few blocks from the Indians' ballpark. Ten years ago, that street was nothing special: wig shops, pawn joints, and ghostly empty stores. Now it's a lively block in the heart of downtown, lined with top-notch restaurants. La Strada was named for an Italian movie, thanks to owner-chef Terry Tarantino, who also owns La Dolce Vita in Little Italy. The menu was eclectic Mediterranean, with Italian, Greek, and Moroccan dishes making it unique. Tobe was new in town, and this was her first trip to East 4th.

"Fancy restaurant," she said.

"Not fancy; you can tell that from the prices. It's just good."

She studied the menu. "Hmm. No hummingbird thighs on toast points. Too bad."

"No bumblebee flank filets, either. Sorry."

She was teasing, and I teased right back—but I could see she was impressed. I was hoping she'd like my city.

She finally chose the lamb shank—for her, lamb was an adventure—and I ordered the Fettuccine Fellini.

"You know all the good places to eat," she said, sipping Grey Goose vodka.

"There's little of Cleveland I don't know about. And if I don't, my pal Ed Stahl does; he writes a column for the *Plain Dealer*."

"So you two are your own personal police force."

"Not exactly. He helps me with—background."

"I wish I had a newspaper buddy who knew everything. So what's his background on Seena Bergman?"

I lifted my shoulders and then let them drop. "I haven't asked him about Seena. That's your case, not mine."

"Do you think your case and my case and maybe a couple of other cases are all somehow tied together?"

"Probably," I said, "but I'm bending over backwards not to get in the PD's way—per your instructions, remember?"

She grimaced. "That's the trouble. Putting Bert Loftus in jail is the FBI's problem. Keeping him safe is yours, and Seena Bergman's murder is mine. And Loftus was a customer of Bergman."

"Not a customer. Someone else paid for her services."

"Who?"

"If I knew, I'd tell you."

"Somebody's damn well going to tell me. Why was Bergman dumped out by the zoo?"

"It's lonely there. People work the graveyard shift, but they wouldn't be outside the zoo, so they wouldn't see or hear anything. Another reason: It's far enough away from where Seena Bergman lived so the killer wouldn't be noticed by a neighbor."

"Killer," Tobe said, "or killers."

"You think there was more than one?"

"I'll know more when I get the autopsy results, but she wasn't shot, beaten to death, or raped. She was strangled. I'd love to know if she tried to defend herself, as she probably would have against a single attacker."

"Good thought," I said. "You must be a smart cop."

"Too smart for my own good. I shouldn't think about murder now. This is supposed to be a romantic dinner, right?"

"I'm trying my best."

She winked at me. "You're doing fine."

I looked at my watch—8:45. She said, "Do you have a late date with somebody else?"

"No, but I'm concerned I haven't heard from Kevin O'Bannion at all today. That's not like him."

"Maybe *he's* having a romantic dinner."

"He's newly in love, or lust, or whatever you call it—with a very pretty girl, too. But I keep getting his voice mail. He always answers his phone because he's anxious to hang on to this job." I took a sip of Greek beer; it wasn't Stroh's, because few good restaurants serve it. "He eventually wants his own license—to open his own company."

"Do you think he wants to take over yours?"

"Let him dream on," I said.

"Try calling him again."

"I don't want to be rude when I'm sitting here with you."

"Rude is okay." She cocked one eyebrow. "*This* time."

I dug my cell phone out. K.O. didn't answer. Frowning, I said, "I guess he'll explain it tomorrow."

"Maybe you should look for him. He's probably okay, but you *are* in a dangerous business, and you're dealing with Bert Loftus. Someone tried to kill *him*, so . . ."

"I don't want to leave you sitting here, Tobe."

"If you thought we were going to tear each other's clothes off before we get in the door—well, this *is* a first date, Milan, not the start of a honeymoon."

I laughed in spite of my embarrassment. I wasn't expecting the tearing off of clothes that evening—but it *had* occurred to me.

"Tell you what," Tobe said. "Let's look for K.O. together."

"Terrific idea. But there's no big rush—his battery may have died. We should finish dinner first."

She nodded, taking another bite. "Good. No way I'm walking away from this lamb shank."

Half an hour later we drove back to my office in her car, mine having been left there before dinner. K.O.'s car was right where he'd parked it. Next to it, looking as if it had been stomped on, was what was left of his cell phone. I hadn't noticed that earlier.

"I don't like the look of that," Tobe said. She reached into her pocket, extracted a rubber glove and a plastic food bag, and daintily picked up the cell phone. "I don't suppose he's with this new girlfriend, or maybe with someone else?"

"I doubt it. But why the smashed phone?"

"Can you call his girlfriend and ask her?"

"Carli Wysocki—her number's written down somewhere in the office."

"Good," Tobe said. "It's too early for me to put out a BOLO, but I'll ask the guys at Third to be looking for him." And she took out her own cell phone.

The iron works on the first floor had their own entrance around the corner, but when I bought the building and informed them I wouldn't be raising their rent any time soon, they reciprocated by building and installing an iron gate across the front door for an extra dollop of security. I fumbled with my keys to open it.

"The last time I saw an iron gate like this was at a federal prison," Tobe said.

"With these nice little iron leaves on it?"

Her eyebrows raised a little. "Let's just say that tonight I'm in a noticing mood."

I unlocked the gate and the main door, and Tobe and I went upstairs. When she stepped inside my office, she whispered, "Wow!"

"Wow? You've been here before. Why the 'Wow'?"

"Offices look different at night," she said softly. "Lonesome. And the rhythm inside your head is different, too—more quiet. No sunshine coming through the windows, no bustle." She almost blushed then. "No kissing."

"Homicide cops spend half their time in their offices at night—with other people around."

"You're right. Still—it just feels—alone in here."

"Until I hired K.O. a few weeks ago, I worked by myself. It was always lonesome."

She paused, then straightened her back—ramrod-straight, like a U.S. Marine. "We're here now, so it's not so lonesome."

I took two steps in her direction, but she held up her hand. "Call K.O.'s girlfriend first. Then we'll see what direction this evening's going to take."

"Make yourself comfortable," I grumbled, and went to K.O.'s desk. She wandered over to the window and smiled; downtown Cleveland always looked its most beautiful at night when all the lights were on. She opened my little refrigerator that looked like a safe but didn't see anything to drink in there that suited her.

I rummaged around in K.O.'s drawers until I found a pocket-sized address book. Despite the difference in our ages and experience, K.O. was old-fashioned, just like me, actually writing things down instead of listing everything he cared about on his cell phone.

Carli Wysocki had two numbers after her name, both with a 216 area code. One K.O. had labeled "C" for cell phone and the other "W" for work. I dialed her cell number on my own phone.

"Carli? It's Milan Jacovich. K.O.'s boss."

She sounded startled. "Oh. Well, hi there."

It was almost ten o'clock; I understood her surprise. "I'm sorry to bother you this late," I said. "Is K.O. with you?"

"He sure isn't. He hasn't called me, either. I called him several times but kept getting kicked over to his voice mail."

"So you don't know where he might be?"

"No," she said, "and he usually calls me every evening." Wistfully: "I hope he hasn't dumped me."

I grinned, looking over at Tobe. "Carli, the sun might rise in the west tomorrow—and it might snow up a blizzard, even in August. But I guarantee you haven't been dumped."

Carli's laugh was like the gentle tinkling of a tiny wind chime. "Kevin says you're always right. I hope you are this time."

Kevin. Not K.O., *Kevin*. Apparently his real name was only for his lady love's use. For the rest of us, K.O. would have to suffice.

"Carli, if he calls—and he will—have him call me. Okay?"

"If he doesn't call you," she said, "I will." I believed her.

I clicked off and shrugged at Tobe. "No dice."

"Call his other friends, then. Somebody *somewhere* knows where he is."

I nodded. I called Suzanne Davis's voice mail. Then I looked up Jake Foote in K.O.'s tattered little book. Again, two numbers, marked "H" and "O." It was late, so I dialed him at home.

Jake Foote's rough voice must have been used hard all his life. I introduced myself, and he thanked me for hiring K.O. when he needed it most. The polite chit-chat lasted for about forty-five seconds. Then I asked if he'd heard from K.O.

"Today," he said, "asking me to look someone up for him."

"To look someone up?"

"It sounded strictly business. I looked up a Lexia Wilhelm. Apparently she's the CEO of some company. Pequod."

"Pequod? Like in *Moby-Dick*?"

"Yeah, Pequod Management. Nope, my bad—it's Pequod Manag-*ers*. Considering whales and whale ships, it must be something pretty big, but I couldn't find out what. Wilhelm was Lexia's maiden name; now she's married to your own county prosecutor."

"Jim Hundley?"

"That's the man," Foote said. "Why don't you ask K.O.?"

"I can't find him. I thought you'd know where he was."

"'Fraid not. I'm home with my wife." A quiet little cough didn't help his voice any. "Is Hundley in trouble?"

"He's an asshole, but I can't come up with anything solid."

"Hundley being an asshole is no news flash," Jake Foote said. "Even the prosecutors in Lake County are better than him."

"That makes your job easier."

"Yeah, by one percent or so. Hey, you and I oughta meet— maybe a lunch somewhere, or just a drink or two."

"That sounds good, Jake—but right now I'm more concerned with K.O."

"Gotcha," Foote said. "He'll be all right. He's spent his whole life learning to take care of himself."

I thanked him, hung up, and told Tobe about Lexia Wilhelm Hundley. She listened quietly, her fingers drumming the arm of her chair. She'd have made notes if this were a police matter.

"Have you met Hundley?"

"No," she said, "but it's just a matter of time. We should talk to him—now."

"It's late."

She tossed her head. "Police detectives don't have time frames."

"He's probably not home."

"That's even better—talking to his wife is more important. If she's asleep, we'll wake her."

"That might piss her off."

"If it does," Tobe said, "she can call a cop."

Lights were on downstairs when we drove up to the Hundley home in Bay Village. Either Lexia was still awake or she'd gone to bed leaving every lamp burning. When we got to the front door and I pushed the button, we could hear jazz playing inside.

"Maybe her old man's home," Tobe said.

"Doubtful."

Movement was going on inside, possibly someone bumping into things. I rang again, and finally the door opened.

Neither of us had met Lexia Hundley before, so we were un-prepared for a middle-aged woman wearing a transparent cover-all over a bikini at nearly eleven o'clock at night, weaving danger-ously and waving a smudged highball glass containing the dregs of a drink. It took her a while to focus on us, and when she did, she became angry—or as angry as one could get while drunk on their ass.

"What the fuck is *your* problem?" she snarled.

Tobe Blaine flashed her badge. "Good evening, Ms. Hundley. Detective Sergeant Tobe Blaine, Cleveland Police Department."

"Who?" she demanded. Tobe repeated her name and stuck her badge under Lexia Hundley's nose.

"You're Cleveland P.D.," Lexia observed. "This isn't Cleveland. It's Bay Village. You got no jurisdiction here."

"I'm not arresting anyone. Is your husband here?"

"Not home. Sumbitch is *never* home, damn his eyes. Come back tomorrow."

"Actually we were looking for you," Tobe said.

"Why? What'd he do *now?* Somebody finally shoot him?"

"Nobody shot him," I said.

Lexia shook her head. "Shit! I wish I'd shot him myself when I had the chance." She zoned in on Tobe. "I coulda, y'know. I got a gun—upstairs someplace. I coulda shot him while he was sleepin' off a drunk." Her statement made her laugh. "That's what I oughta do—sleep off a drunk." She went nose-to-nose with Tobe. "You think I'm drunk? You're so goddamn smart; you think I'm drunk?"

"I think you'd better call me tomorrow," Tobe said, and dropped one of her business cards into Lexia Hundley's highball glass. "As soon as you wake up and start feeling better."

The county prosecutor's wife stared at the card in her glass without touching it. Then she said, "I won't feel any better sober than I am drunk—so what's the difference?" She shifted her gaze toward me. "Come on in an' drink with me."

"Not tonight," Tobe said.

Lexia reared back. "Not talkin' to *you*, bitch. Talkin' to him. He's hot."

"Sorry," I said, "but I'm with her."

Her shoulders slumped, and she held on to the door jamb to keep from falling on her face. "Tha's my trouble. Everybody's with *somebody!*"

She struggled with her balance, then turned around and swayed back inside, not bothering to close the door. If we were robbers, she'd have awakened the next morning to find herself badly hungover in a completely empty house.

We stood on the doorstep for a while, until Tobe pulled the front door shut. "Not talking to you, bitch," she said, chuckling quietly.

"This might shock you," I said, "but police officers are often spoken to like that in Cleveland."

"'Bitch' wasn't the word bad guys in Cincinnati used when they talked to me. So, do we look for the county prosecutor tonight?"

"I have no idea where he is. I know where he drinks, but he usually has company every night."

"Female feminine lady company?"

"Sometimes more than one. But he doesn't stay in the bar with them this late."

"His object is to take them elsewhere and do dirty things? I'd hate to walk in and interrupt him. I can watch porn any old time. You can track him down tomorrow."

"Come with me while I look for him?"

"May I remind you," she said as we walked back toward the car, "that this is *your* case, all about *your* protégé. It's not mine. I want that woman's killer. Now if *Hundley* got murdered, I'd know which suspect to gouge first."

I opened the car door and got in. When I was a kid, I was taught it was polite to open a car door for a woman. But she was doing the driving, not me—and besides, there was no point being chivalrous to a high-ranking female cop who could have busted my nose with one punch.

She slid beneath the steering wheel and the car rumbled to life, making a U-turn on Lake Road and heading back downtown. She didn't look over at me but smiled when she said, "Hot, huh?"

"*I* didn't say that. So—are we going back to the office?"

"That's where your car is."

"Oh." I waited a minute. "Where do you live, anyway?"

She didn't take her eyes from the road, but her brows were raised, and she lifted one corner of her mouth in a smile. "Why? Do you want me on your Christmas card list?"

"Naturally."

"Then ask me again around the first of December. In the meantime, let me know tomorrow what's up with K.O. I hardly know him, but he's a kid and I worry about him."

"I will. I wish neither of us had been worried about him tonight."

"Why?"

I shrugged. "Things might have gone differently for us."

"Pretty sure of yourself, aren't you?"

"No," I said. "Just—fantasizing."

"Hoping."

"Not really."

"That's good," she said. "This *is* a first date."

I nodded. "But you were the one who kissed me."

"That doesn't mean we go pick out matching wedding rings. A kiss is just a kiss."

There's only one response I know of: "A sigh is just a sigh."

With her right hand she brushed her hair away from her face, still quoting *Casablanca*. "Milan," she sighed, "this could be the beginning of a beautiful friendship."

CHAPTER TWENTY-ONE

K.O.

It was dark, or at least it seemed so because K.O.'s eyes were closed. His other senses were creeping back to him bit by bit, although he wasn't sure if he'd been unconscious for a few minutes or for several days. The first thing that returned to him was his sense of smell—stale, damp warehouse smells, cigarette smoke, body stink that wasn't his own. His lips and nose were sore and irritated, but he didn't know why, and the inside of his mouth was parched and dry.

Chloroform. He'd never smelled chloroform before, but he recognized the symptoms. He'd read about chloroform in an army combat manual, or perhaps a paperback mystery novel. It was part of a Freon refrigerant. He never overthought his own health—he kept himself in good physical shape and rarely got so much as a cold or a headache—but he recalled that chloroform could cause liver damage.

He tried breathing deeply but wasn't sure where his liver *was*, so he couldn't discern whether it was injured. He could feel, even on such a warm August night, the coldness of the hard floor—cement, probably—on which he'd been stretched out.

Feeling his own fear.

He heard sounds like playing cards being snapped, and muddled male voices, too, although K.O. couldn't understand the words—not yet. He decided to keep his eyes shut until he scoped out his situation.

This was a strange moment. He'd been in dozens of fights in

his short lifetime. He'd been punched, kicked, and choked, and had learned how to be tough and how to survive. In all that time, in all those battles, he'd never lost consciousness. Now someone had knocked him out with a chloroform rag that anesthetized him within seconds.

It took him another minute or so to realize he was lying on his right side, his hands tied together behind his back. He didn't know if he was being watched, so trying to ascertain how tightly he was bound didn't seem a good plan. Besides, if they tied him up, they probably did a good job of it, whoever they were.

He thought over the last few days, running through his activities in his mind. What had he done to make someone angry with him? To whom had he spoken? The guy from the auto body shop? The Russian nutso? The middle-aged hooker who'd come on to him? Dolores Deluke, the one he'd taken to lunch who worked for the county prosecutor's lawyer? Or maybe, he thought, Bert Loftus himself, who openly disliked him. The city councilman had secrets, as any politician does. Had K.O. uncovered a few of them without even realizing it?

The reminiscence didn't help much, so he forced himself to wake up more, careful not to move as he listened to the sounds.

Snap! Snap! went the cards. Then:

"Calling on two."

"Shit."

Pause.

"Twenty-six. Dammit, I was one jack away from gin."

Another pause, pencil scratching.

"You owe me sixteen bucks and change."

"Another game. Double or nothing."

"Nah. Sick of playing gin rummy anyway. What time is it?"

"Almost nine."

"It's nearly dark out. Can't we get going?"

"Don't be a schmuck. There are plenty of boats still out on the lake—and people hanging around the harbor. Want them to see us?"

"Guess not."

"I don't wanna go to prison for murder."

"Who the fuck does?"

The sound of a chair scraping. Footsteps on the hard floor, coming closer. Breathing beside and above him. K.O. opened his eyes to slits, hoping no one would notice. Brown shoes badly in need of a shine, inches from his face.

"What if he never wakes up?"

"Tough shit. If he dies now it'll save us the trouble."

A sniffle. Footsteps moving away. "I'm not crazy about the idea."

"You weren't crazy about icing the whore the other night, either. You do your job—or else quit and get a real gig mopping floors at Burger King."

"I hurt people before in my life. But I never—ah, screw it."

Another chair being pushed back. Another set of footsteps. A match being lit, a deep inhale, a loud exhale. "Don't think too much. It's like taking out the trash. You just do it. Right?"

"Yeah. I guess."

"Well, don't guess. And stop analyzing it—we got another couple hours at least."

"So—what if he wakes up?"

Long pause. Then: "Jesus, I never thought about it. I dunno. Talk to him, I s'pose. Or don't. Whatever you feel like."

Mirthless laugh. "What if he don't talk nothin' but Arab?"

"He's no fuckin' Arab. I think he's Irish or something."

"I don't care if he's North Korean! Don't make this personal!"

"If I don't, nothing'll get done!"

Chairs scraping again—the sound of shuffled playing cards.

K.O. opened his eyes a little more. Two men sat opposite each other at a card table. One, big and rather stupid-looking, was shuffling the cards, the skin around his fingernails reddened where he'd gnawed them. The other was very thin, sallow as a teen vampire in a "Twilight" movie, with an off-center hatchet nose that didn't match the rest of his face. Both smoking cigarettes.

It was now time, K.O. thought, to get active. He rolled around and groaned so they could hear him.

They looked over. Big Dumb Guy said, "Look who's awake."

Hatchet-nose grunted, stood, and strolled over to K.O., looking down at him the way one might look at road kill while out on a stroll. "Don't give us no trouble, or you'll be sorry you did," he threatened. "Just lay there and shut up."

K.O. tried to make his voice soft, weak, frightened. "Water," he gasped, realizing he meant it. He licked his lips. "Water."

"Where you think you are? A restaurant?" Hatchet-nose growled, then turned and went back to the table, giving K.O. a chance to look around a large open room that might have once been a small industrial shop, not used for manufacturing in decades.

"Lemme give him some water," Big Dumb Guy whined. He got up, took a water bottle from the table-top, and walked it over to where K.O. was lying.

"I can't exactly drink it by myself," K.O. said.

"I look like a waiter to you?"

"Give me a break, huh?" K.O. said. Big Dumb Guy shook his head in disgust, kneeling down on the floor next to K.O., tipping the half-full water bottle to his lips. Good Samaritan.

The chloroform had made K.O. thirsty. He gulped down almost all the rest of the water and tried not to think about the fact that he was drinking out of the same bottle as this stupid-looking thug.

It was the other one, Hatchet-nose, who interested him most. He was the one who'd approached him in the parking lot, which meant he was the smart one, the one who does the talking. K.O. waited until both men were sitting at their card table again before beginning a conversation.

"Will you tell me why I'm here and why my hands are tied?"

"No," Hatchet-nose said.

"I didn't do anything to you. If I did, you gotta tell me."

"Shut your face."

"It's not fair!"

"Fair?" Hatchet-nose was on his feet again, almost charging across the room to where K.O. was stretched out. "This is no grade school softball game! *Fair?* Jesus!"

K.O. thought Hatchet-nose might kick him in the face or the ribs, and he braced himself for it. It never came.

"You stick your nose where it ain't none of your business, an' fuck up people who're worth more'n fifty of you!" Hatchet-nose went on. "So that's why you're here, asshole."

K.O. processed that. He *had* been sticking his nose into things, asking questions, and making reluctant witnesses uncomfortable But that *was* his business—the job description of a private investigator. Asking questions that can be rude, drawing answers from recalcitrant observers, and putting the many pieces together in hopes of forming a complete picture.

Nearly everyone he'd spoken to in the last few days was irritated with him—but K.O. couldn't imagine them ordering him chloroformed and kidnapped. Bert Loftus wouldn't dare. Lexia Hundley didn't have any reason to do so. The guy from the auto shop—K.O. couldn't even recall his name—probably forgot about him ten seconds after he left the office. Seena Bergman wouldn't have revealed her discussion with a stranger like K.O., even though she hadn't given him the information he sought.

So why was he here?

And more important: What was going to happen next?

K.O. swallowed again, thankful for the water. "Where do we go from here, guys?"

"Shut your mouth or I'll shut it for you," Hatchet-nose growled.

"Hey, easy," Big Dumb Guy told his partner. Then he looked down at K.O. "You relax, too."

"How can I relax when I'm lying on my hands?"

Big Dumb Guy looked confused. Then: "Figure it out." He tossed the empty water bottle off to one side with some other junk over against the wall—beer cans, more empty bottles, wadded-up paper, a few ancient pizza boxes. This place wasn't used anymore; if it were, *somebody* would clean it up once in a while, sweep the floor on which he now lay, or at least take out the trash.

Big Dumb Guy lumbered back to sit down opposite Hatchet-nose and stared at the walls, the ceiling, his shoes, or at just about anything else except their bound captive. Hatchet-nose dealt out solitaire; K.O. looked at them both.

The warm evening temperature was up into the healthy seventies. Neither of K.O.'s guards wore jackets; Big Dumb Guy had on a polo shirt with blue and red stripes, making him look like a six-year-old on his first day back at school. Hatchet-nose wore a creamy-white short-sleeved dress shirt, over khakis. Not tucked in.

All right, K.O. thought—unless one or both of them strapped handguns to their ankles, at least Big Dumb Guy wasn't armed. Hatchet-nose might have heat hidden under his untucked shirt, but would he use it?

K.O. didn't know if this vacant building was close to other, occupied buildings, or on a busy street with foot traffic. No—unless fans were walking to or from a major sports event, there isn't much foot traffic *in* Cleveland. And he couldn't see his wristwatch, so he had no idea what time it was.

He weighed his options and took a risk. "What will you do with me? Shoot me?"

Hatchet-nose's glare gave K.O. an inadvertent chill that made the hair stand up on his arms and neck. "No, but I could kick your fuckin' head in till your brains spatter all over the place. So shut up, goddammit!"

Big Dumb Guy looked almost sorrowful. "Hey—that's not necessary."

Hatchet-nose snorted, angrily slapping down his cards. K.O. raised his voice so both men could hear him. "Whatever's going down here, I got the right to know."

"Uh—we're gonna go somewhere. Later."

"Where?"

Hatchet-nose threw his cards down. "On a little boat trip. You'll make a hell of a sailor."

Big Dumb Guy seemed embarrassed. K.O. gulped some stale air and let it out slowly as the realization hit him hard, forcing his stomach up, pressing against his lungs, making it difficult for him to breathe or swallow.

They planned on taking him out on the lake to drown him.

He wasn't frightened. His combat tours where the chance of tripping a hidden bomb and being blown to pieces was part of life had taught him fear was a waste of time. But he didn't like the idea of drowning in Lake Erie, so he quieted down for about fifteen minutes while he decided what to do.

Big Dumb Guy was humming softly, a tune no one could recognize. Hatchet-nose glared at him for a while, then snapped, "You wanna turn off the radio?"

"Huh? What radio?"

"Knock off the goddamn singing, *that's* what radio!" He shook his head in exasperation.

"Oh. Sorry, I didn't mean to."

"Listen to yourself and you'll stop!" Hatchet-nose ran a hand through slicked-down hair. "You sound like somebody choked a squirrel!"

"I *said* sorry!"

Hatchet-nose made a sound through his teeth like someone extinguishing a cigarette in a cup of cold coffee.

K.O. remained silent for about five minutes longer, then cleared his throat again. "Hey—I gotta go to the bathroom."

"Who cares?"

"Come on, man!" K.O. whined.

"So piss in your pants," Hatchet-nose snarled.

"Hey." Big Dumb Guy. "We're gonna have to stay here till late—like midnight. In this heat, if he pees himself, he'll be stinking by then. Come on, think about it, man."

"Aw, shit!" Hatchet-nose mumbled. "Well, I'm not gonna hold his dick for him. Whattya think, I'm some sorta homo?"

And in that moment, K.O. knew he was going to win.

Big Dumb Guy hauled himself up from the table and lifted K.O. to his feet. "Over there," he said, giving K.O. a little push.

They walked across the large room to a door in one corner. Big Dumb Guy opened it and ushered K.O. inside. There was a single filthy toilet; probably no one had used the building or its facilities in decades. Despite running water, there was also a grossly dirty sink. No towels.

"Unzip me," K.O. said.

Big Dumb Guy's eyes opened wide. "Hey, man, I'm no queer!"

"Then untie my hands. Don't look scared. What do you think I'm gonna do? Punch you out? My hands'll be busy."

Big Dumb Guy pondered this problem until finally K.O. said, "Hurry up, man; I can't wait much longer."

A major sigh. Then: "Don't try nothin' funny." Big Dumb Guy fumbled around and untied the hands; K.O. rubbed his chafed wrists. His toilet monitor placed one large hand at the back of his neck and squeezed hard. "You try anything smart, I'll rip your head off."

"Just want to take a leak," K.O. said. Shaking his hands to get the circulation going in them, he turned, unzipped his pants, and began relieving himself.

The hand on the back of his neck got tighter, and he glanced over his shoulder to see that Big Dumb Guy—being a men's-room gentleman as most adult males are, no matter what their station in life—had turned his head discreetly away.

K.O. turned slightly and urinated all over Big Dumb Guy's leg.

For a moment the recipient didn't move, shocked statue-still. Then, horrified, he stopped squeezing K.O.'s neck and backed away.

That's when K.O. punched him under the chin, directly on his Adam's apple. Big Dumb Guy staggered back against the wall, making a horrible noise as he tried to breathe, clutching his throat. K.O. stepped forward and drove his fist wrist-deep into his stomach. Big Dumb Guy sank to his knees, his face almost purple, and then K.O. clubbed him just behind the ear with the hard, rigid edge of his hand. That left him the only person in the tiny bathroom still conscious.

He rubbed his wrists some more to improve circulation, zipped up his fly, and stepped out into the big room again. Hatchet-nose, hearing the commotion, was rushing toward the bathroom, spewing enraged obscenities as he came. As soon as K.O. stepped out of the bathroom, he was hit by what could best be described as a flying tackle.

Hatchet-nose was smaller than K.O., so the collision didn't wind up in tangled limbs on the floor, but it did knock K.O. to one side, and when he struggled to get his feet solidly beneath him, Hatchet-nose swung a roundhouse right toward his head. He only managed to partly avoid the blow, which landed near his ear. He shook his head to rid himself of sudden ringing in his brain.

The wild swing had taken Hatchet-nose off balance, too, and before he could straighten up, knuckles smashed into his mouth, knocking out one of his front teeth and loosening two more.

Blood ran down his chin as he reached into his pocket and produced a switchblade knife. The sound it made when he clicked it open sounded to K.O. like cymbals crashing.

It's going to be *that* way, K.O. thought as he set himself. His memory kicked in, unbidden, to a time when he was only fifteen years old, and another juvie prisoner, older and bigger and meaner, had challenged him in the same way. The knife, naturally, was not a switchblade but a spoon pilfered from the dining hall and scraped against concrete for months until it became a deadly weapon. K.O. had never dealt with a knife-attacker before, but he'd been in enough fistfights to have learned how to handle himself like a matador, moving within a hair's breadth of out-of-reach. In that fight, he'd only been cut on the forearm; no blade had ever touched him since.

He didn't look forward to dealing with another sharp blade— but he was glad he'd guessed correctly about Hatchet-nose not having a gun tucked into his pants.

The first swish of the knife toward K.O. didn't cut him, but it caught the loose front of his shirt and sliced it open. Hatchet-nose's first thrust missed by less than an inch, but the momentum spun him left, giving K.O. a straight shot at his ribs with a deadly left-hand blow traveling less than a foot, shattering the bones with an audible crunch.

Something else K.O. learned in jail, and later in combat: When throwing a punch, don't ever believe you're in some sort of drunken dust-up in a saloon's parking lot because you looked the wrong way at somebody's girlfriend. The object of the fight, always, is to do the worst possible damage to your opponent. The broken ribs made Hatchet-nose grunt and stagger away, gasping for breath. Then K.O.'s kick to his knee put him on the ground and drove his kneecap around to one side of his leg, turning his grunt to a scream. A second kick to his wrist broke it cleanly and sent his knife sailing across the room.

He looked up, shocked and almost pleading—but K.O. had to make sure the battle was over. His next blow smashed into Hatchet-nose's jawbone, just below his right ear, making his eyes bulge and then close as another tooth flew from his mouth. He sprawled onto the floor—out of fight, and out of his senses.

K.O. folded the switchblade closed and shoved it into his pocket. Rubbing his sore knuckles, he stepped over Hatchet-nose, looking around for an exit. A steel door led out of the room, and when he pushed it open he found himself on the second floor of some building or other. He had no memory of being brought in here. He ran down a long flight of uncarpeted stairs to what he figured was the street door, but that was locked, too, from the outside. He had no way of getting out.

Trapped.

Eventually the two men upstairs would awaken, and though they didn't have guns and were too badly damaged to do K.O. much harm, he might have to render them unconscious again.

He worried he might kill them.

He'd killed before.

So he wanted to escape more than ever—but the steel door to the street was impenetrable.

He looked back up the stairs, remembering that on the landing halfway between the first and second floors was an opaque window.

K.O. loped up there within seconds and tried wrenching up the window, but it hadn't been put there to be opened—just to make the front of the building look somewhat more attractive, although buildings like that were never meant to look beautiful in the first place. He felt the glass with his fingertips. Then he went all the way back upstairs and into the room where he'd been imprisoned.

Big Dumb Guy and Hatchet-nose were still out cold. K.O. scanned the room for something hard to pick up. He had no idea what this room used to be, nor the building; he explored without knowing what he looked for.

Empty pizza boxes. A plastic fork from some fast-food joint. The empty plastic bottle of water that Big Dumb Guy had given him. None of them good for much of anything.

And then, on the floor beneath a table once used for manufacturing something, K.O. found a dust broom—wide brush mounted on a long wooden handle. He picked it up, hefted it, and, concluding it was better than nothing, took it back to the landing.

He made five attempts, dashing at the window with the broom in his hands like the lance of a jousting medieval knight, before it cracked the opaque glass. It took him a few more mighty runs to break out the glass completely; then, with the handle, he knocked out all the sharp shards that could severely injure him.

The street was dark, although he couldn't tell what time it was; they had taken his wallet, his cell phone, and his watch after he'd been overwhelmed by the chloroform. He didn't really know Cleveland that well, but he thought he might be somewhere in the East 30s, north of Euclid Avenue. No traffic. No pedestrians. Quiet as a tomb.

Sticking his head out the window, he saw he was about fifteen feet above the street—a long drop. He shivered.

What if he broke his leg? What if he fell wrong and broke something else, his hip or his shoulder? He'd have to lie there for a long time, possibly until morning when local workers in adjacent buildings began arriving for their early shift. A broken leg and shoulder would entail a painful wait—but if he hurt himself some other way and he was bleeding, that *could* be fatal.

He hoped a car might drive by. But what if the car was somehow connected with the two men he'd left snoozing upstairs—and what if, unlike those guys, the driver had a gun?

Oh, what the hell, K.O. thought. He grabbed the sill, pushed his body up, and swung his legs out the window.

CHAPTER TWENTY-TWO

MILAN

I was asleep, dreaming nice dreams, when I was awakened by the ringing of my doorbell as if someone's life depended on it. Fortunately I can wake up quickly and be ready for anything. I glanced at the clock on the dresser, cursed aloud at the lateness of the hour, and rolled out of bed, draped my bathrobe over my otherwise nude body, and padded into the living room to find out who it was.

"It's K.O.," came the voice over the two-way speaker. "Ring me in, okay?"

I pushed the button to let him in downstairs, then re-tied the bathrobe belt, turned on some lights in the living room, and opened the apartment door when I heard him out in the hall.

He looked like hell. His shirt was torn in the front, his clothes were a mass of wrinkles, and dirt was smudged on his face, hands, and pants. One side of his face, in the general vicinity of his ear, was bright red. The areas around his lips and nose were reddish, too—not chapped, exactly, but more as if he'd put something irritating on his face. It had grown cooler outside, but he looked as if he'd been sweating.

"My God," I said, "you look awful. Want a drink of water?"

K.O. almost croaked a yes. I got a bottle of Deer Park from the kitchen, and he drank it down like he'd been lost in the desert for a month.

"Better?" I took back the empty bottle. "So it's the middle of the night. Is this a social call?"

He was out of breath. "I have to sit down a minute."

"Be my guest. Want me to whip you up a late supper?"

"Fuck you," K.O. said without rancor. He limped across the living room, favoring one ankle, and sank into my sofa.

I sat down. "What's going on, K.O.?"

"It's been a long evening."

He took half a minute to pull himself together, then sucked most of the air out of the room with a prodigious inhale. "Well—to start with, I was kidnapped."

He started to tell me more, and then stopped, struck silent with his mouth foolishly open, as Tobe Blaine came out of the bedroom wearing one of my long-tailed dress shirts commandeered from my closet, and not much else. She hadn't bothered combing her hair, either.

"Good evening, Mr. O'Bannion," she said, as cool as if she'd been fully dressed and wearing her weapon and a badge.

K.O. apparently couldn't think of a damn thing to say. Finally: "Well, I'll be a son of a bitch!"

Tobe took it well and laughed. "You were kidnapped?" She sat on the other end of the sofa. "I want to hear about that."

"I was chloroformed this afternoon," he continued with a shaky voice. "I woke tied up on a cold floor in some empty firetrap. I was threatened with drowning and finally attacked with a switchblade knife, and I had to beat the shit out of two guys. But now—well, now I'm really, *really* surprised."

"I was a little surprised myself," I said.

Tobe's manner changed; now she was the lead detective on an attempted homicide gig, even though she was nearly naked under that shirt. "How many people? Just the two men?"

K.O. nodded.

"Where did this happen? The chloroform part."

"Downstairs in the parking lot at Collision Bend. One guy came up and asked me a question about the ironworks and another one snuck up behind me and clapped something stinky over my face. The next thing I knew, I was an inmate—all over again." He hugged himself without realizing it. "I hate that shit."

Tobe turned to me. "Pen and paper." It wasn't a request. At

least she hadn't given orders in the bedroom. I fetched a yellow legal pad and a ballpoint pen. "Okay," she said. "Start at the beginning, Kevin."

"K.O. That's how I like to be called—K.O."

"I'll call you whatever you want after I hear what you've got to say."

He slumped back on the sofa, gaining confidence as he spun out his recent history. I noted the swelling at the side of his face and the red marks around his wrists, so I knew he wasn't creating this story out of whole cloth. Obviously he hadn't tied himself up, either.

He started from the time he woke up, as Tobe scratched feverishly on the pad.

"The window was about fifteen feet off the ground," K.O. finished, "so I sprained my ankle a little bit." He shrugged. "Adding it all up, I've been hurt more than this in a fistfight in jail."

"We're not done," Tobe said. "So you jumped out the window. How did you get from the east side of Cleveland to up here in Cleveland Heights?"

"I couldn't call anyone—and I had thirty-nine cents in my pocket, so I couldn't get a cab. Anyway, no cabs cruise that neighborhood in the middle of the night. So I trudged up to Chester Avenue and stood on a corner with my thumb out, hoping someone'd take pity on me."

"Did they?"

"The first guy who picked me up must've thought I was a male hooker, because he offered me thirty bucks to let him blow me."

"That would've got you a cab," I said.

"So I got out fast at around East 105th Street. After half an hour I finally thumbed another ride who drove me here."

"Another gay guy?"

K.O. laughed. "Three black girls who live in the Heights and go to school at John Carroll."

"Did they want your body, too?"

"Don't think so. They felt sorry for me—I was limping, and my shirt was all torn."

"You beat the crap out of both kidnappers?"

K.O. shrugged painfully. "I fight dirty."

Tobe said, "Let's go back to the warehouse, or wherever you were. Did you get the address?"

"I didn't stop to write it down. I just got the hell out of there, fast."

"You don't know what street you were on?"

"Again, I didn't look. In the east thirties, north of Payne Avenue."

"You didn't get the kidnappers' names? Even a first name?"

He shook his head. "No one introduced us."

"How 'bout a description?"

"One was big and dumb. The other guy was short, skinny, and mean. He was the one who had the knife." He winced. "Oh, yeah, I forgot. Here." He pulled the switchblade out of his pocket and tossed it to Tobe.

"They could have bought these at one of a million stores," Tobe said, examining it. "Pawn shop. Army-navy surplus. Sporting goods. I don't suppose you picked it up with rubber gloves or a handkerchief so we could get his prints?"

"Not hardly. But I didn't wipe it off, either—so you'll find my fingerprints on there with his."

"Or a hundred other people as well—including mine. You shouldn't have tossed it to me. That's evidence—that you fucked up."

K.O. looked crestfallen. "Sorry."

"Let's move on," Tobe said. "Attempted murder? How do you know the kidnappers were going to drown you?"

"They said so."

"They told you so?"

"In so many words."

"So they're dumb shits. That's a good start. Come down to headquarters tomorrow."

"I think that's today," K.O. said.

"I didn't ask you what time it is!" Tobe snapped, annoyed. Then, more softly, "Come at eleven o'clock. I'll put you together with an artist—so we can identify these bastards."

K.O. nodded.

I said, "Do you want me to drive you home, K.O.?"

He looked from me to Tobe and back again. "That's okay—I can see you're busy."

"Are you all right to go get your car and then drive home?"

He grinned—the biggest actual grin I've ever seen on K.O. "I think I'd better."

"Why?"

"Because tonight," he said, "I'm sure as hell not going to sleep *here*."

I'd summoned a taxi. While K.O. waited for its arrival, he called Carli, at my suggestion. "Don't be specific," I warned him. "Just tell her you ran into some trouble and couldn't call her, but that you're okay now."

"I figured that out," he muttered. "I'm not five, y'know."

"We know," Tobe said, more amused by the situation than I.

He wanted to call Carli from the other room, since everyone could hear what he might say on both the living room and kitchen phones, but I insisted he not make his call from the bedroom. My clothes and Tobe's were scattered all over the floor in there, and I doubt he'd want to sit in the midst of all that on the edge of a very unmade bed and chat with his girlfriend. Things were embarrassing enough as it was.

When the taxi driver laid on his horn downstairs, I took down my personal handgun, a Glock 9mm, from the top shelf of the closet. "You know how to use this?"

"Gee, no—the army taught us that when we were attacked, we should speak very sharply to the terrorists and ask them to stop."

"He doesn't have a permit," Tobe said.

"If he robs a bank, I'll be directly responsible," I said. "In the meantime, I don't want him kidnapped again in the middle of the night—permit or no permit."

She tilted her head, considering it. Then she said, "I didn't see any of this," and wandered into the kitchen.

I rummaged around in my desk drawer and pulled out a twenty-dollar bill and a ten. "For the cab," I said. "And tomorrow, figure out what was in your wallet—credit cards, driver's license—and make the appropriate phone calls."

"I can identify the guys whose pictures were on my ten-dollar bills."

"Don't push your luck, K.O.," I said.

When he left, I went into the kitchen. Tobe was opening and closing cabinets.

"Making an inspection?" I said.

"If I were, you'd flunk. Why's there nothing here besides tea and crackers? If you ever got snowed in, you'd starve to death."

"In October, I buy thirty cans of tuna and lots of macaroni and cheese, just in case I can't get out the door for a month or so."

"I won't worry about you, then," she said, and went back into the living room to sit on the sofa.

"What do you make of all this, Tobe?"

"It's hard being a cop when I'm naked," she said, "but I'll do my best. The kid has an old car, and he doesn't look like he'd carry a fortune in cash, so the kidnap wasn't a robbery. It was specific— and as far as I know, so was the death threat."

"Were they trying to scare him?"

"Scare him for what? So he could phone his rich daddy for a million bucks in small bills? No—they think he knows something, and they wanted to make him quiet before he told anyone."

I sat down next to her, discreetly arranging my bathrobe around my knees—which, now that I think about it, was pointless by then. "He's been open with me about the people he's talked to, so he probably doesn't know anything." I considered this. "But maybe somebody *thinks* he does."

"As long as he's safe, it'll wait until morning." She stood up and headed for the bedroom. "I have to be out of here by seven at the latest."

I stood up, too. "You look good in my shirt, Tobe."

"I grabbed the first thing I saw in the closet."

"That's an expensive shirt."

"Sorry about that," she said over her shoulder, giving me a breathtaking look. "You can have it back now." She began undoing the buttons as she went back into the bedroom.

I waited no longer than three seconds before I followed her in.

CHAPTER TWENTY-THREE

K.O.

By the time K.O. got back to his apartment in Mentor, it was nearly four a.m. He needed coffee, but he couldn't face the thought of drinking instant and didn't feel like getting back in his car to look for a McDonald's drive-through that was open all night.

He called the three credit card companies, though he would have to wait for regular business hours to tell the Bureau of Motor Vehicles that his wallet and driver's license were stolen.

He was angry someone had stomped on his phone, but it was probably the worst thing to happen to him all night. If he hadn't made the supreme effort to escape from his captors, he would now be thirty feet under the surface of Lake Erie with a bag of rocks tied to his ankles.

What he wondered most was: *Who* was behind the kidnapping and murder plot in the first place? He'd done nothing wrong to anyone—at least not recently—and agreed with Tobe that somebody thinks he knows something that he really doesn't.

He wadded up his torn shirt and put it in the trash, and after his shower he donned jeans, a black T-shirt, and a lightweight black jacket, left his apartment early, and stopped at Panera for some too-fattening bear claws—he hadn't eaten anything since lunch the previous day—washed down with several cups of coffee.

He arrived in the Flats at 9:30; Milan was in the office ahead of him, and the first thing K.O. did was to return his 9mm Glock.

"I didn't rob a bank with it," he said.

"Make sure you tell that to Detective Blaine."

"I'll let you tell her for me." He sat down in his own special corner; it was still new enough to him that he always took the time to look out the window at the river. Then he told Milan what he'd gone over again and again in his mind the previous night and early morning.

"You can't think of what anyone told you that'd get you killed?"

"I didn't learn anything except that Seena Bergman was a hooker, which doesn't sound like a secret to me. She had lots of clients."

"Not clients, exactly," Milan said. "She was actually an employee, paid to be available for anyone important who wanted kinky sex."

"And she *was* killed." K.O. played with the pens in the oversized coffee mug on his desk. "That fits."

"Except she didn't tell you anything shocking."

"Not that I know of."

Milan checked his watch. "You're due at cop HQ soon. Ever worked with a police sketch artist before?"

"Never even met one—just seen them on TV."

"Those are actors."

K.O. nodded. "But we're all actors, aren't we? Trying to be what people think we are, or what we should be?"

"Most of us aren't good enough actors. We do what we do to make money—but we don't steal it. And we try not hurting anyone. Just do your best with the sketch artist—and tell him not to make the kidnappers look like Brad Pitt."

K.O. stood up and started toward the door. "Look like Brad Pitt?" he said. "I've got a big oil painting of *that*."

His drive across the river took him about ten minutes through heavy downtown traffic. The Third District police headquarters on Payne Avenue—once referred to as the Rock Pile—was a colonial building resembling the home of some not-very-important government agency in Washington, D.C. K.O. parked across the street—he already knew visitors weren't supposed to park where the cops do.

He gave the desk sergeant his name; when he mentioned he

was to see Detective Blaine, the sergeant looked puzzled, fumbling through some papers to discover there really was such a person as Detective Blaine. Then he sent K.O. up to the second floor.

Tobe's desk faced that of Bob Matusen, who looked up and nodded.

"Uh—good morning, Detective," K.O. said to Tobe.

She battled a smile. "Good morning to you, Mr. O'Bannion—again."

"You want me to sit down with a police sketch artist?"

"Right. We want to find those guys—and who sent them."

"I don't know how good my descriptions will be."

"Don't worry; our sketch guy is as good as one can get." She leaned back in her swivel chair. "You really beat up two big guys all by yourself?"

"One big guy—and one mean little guy."

"A mean little guy with a switchblade. Frankly, you don't look that tough."

"I've got a secret weapon," K.O. said. "When anyone pisses me off, I turn into the Incredible Hulk."

"Turn green, do you?"

"Get me mad enough, Detective, and you'll find out."

Tobe noticed he didn't meet her eyes that often, and that he was shifting from one foot to the other. "Do I make you uncomfortable?"

"No, ma'am."

"Don't 'ma'am' me; I'm not your science teacher. Are you upset about last night?"

"Being kidnapped?"

"No, *not* your kidnapping, if you get my drift."

His cheeks reddened.

"Grow up, okay? You bothered us last night. So what?"

K.O. looked helplessly at Bob Matusen, busy studying some report on his desk despite being only six feet away from them.

"I'm forty-four years old, and—this may shock you—but I'm not a virgin," she said, and then laughed. "I'm just giving you a bad time, which doesn't excuse you from barging into the middle of—of my night."

"Should I apologize?"

"Too late now." She looked at the ceiling for divine guidance, then sighed. "Skip it. I'll call the sketch guy." She tapped out an inside number on her phone and sent K.O. up to the third floor.

The artist introduced himself as Xavier Redondo, very young, tanned and Hispanic-looking, wearing tan Dockers and a blue-and-orange-flowered Hawaiian shirt, which was fast becoming a Cleveland trend. On his bare feet were leather sandals. His tiny office, once a broom closet, seemed more like a starving artist's studio than a place where cops spend their days.

K.O. sat next to him at a drafting table as he prepared his sketch pad and made sure his pencils were all sharpened. "Are you actually a police officer?" K.O. asked.

"Nope. I just work here. What makes you ask—the loud shirt or the sandals?"

"Both."

"It's summer, and I like wiggling my toes." He did so.

"Looks comfy."

"You were just curious, huh?"

"I'm curious about everything."

"Me, too," Redondo said. "That's why I can't wait to see what I'm gonna draw."

"Are you going to draw a picture of me, too?"

"Sometimes I get paid to do caricatures of people."

K.O. grinned. "I'm thinking about giving it to my girlfriend."

"Maybe—if there's time. So, you know some bad guys, huh?"

"Just by sight—not by name."

"If you knew their names," Redondo said, "you wouldn't need me drawing pictures. Which one do we start with?"

"How 'bout the guy with the nose like an axe?"

"The guy with a nose like an axe." Redondo shook his head as he carefully selected a pencil. "This sounds like it's gonna be fun."

Ninety minutes later, K.O. was back at Tobe Blaine's desk with several copies of Xavier Redondo's latest works. He peeled two off the top and handed them to her.

"Here you go," he said.

She examined both sketches closely. "Are these close to accurate?"

"I guess so. I think—especially the one guy—he doesn't look much like this anymore. I messed him up a little."

Blaine's eyebrows arched. "You like messing up people's faces?"

"I don't like to," K.O. said. "But you gotta do what you gotta do."

"John Wayne. Why didn't you have Xavier draw him like he looks now?"

"I didn't take that good a look at him after I dislocated his jaw. I think his chin is now somewhere on the side of his face."

"We'll use our imaginations," Tobe said. Then she pointed to another piece of sketch paper folded carefully under K.O.'s arm. "What's that sketch?"

"Oh—it's nothing."

"You wouldn't carry it around if it were nothing." She chuckled. "I'll flash my buzzer and demand you show it to me."

Reluctantly, K.O. passed to Detective Blaine a caricature of himself. She studied it. "You're better looking in person. This is a typical police sketch; Redondo did you like he did these other two guys. It makes you look like a criminal, too."

Bob Matusen craned his head to see the sketch. "Yeah—you look just like Jeffrey Dahmer. You know, the cannibal—"

Annoyed, K.O. snapped, "I don't eat people, okay?"

"Easy does it," Tobe said. "No insult intended. What are you going to do with the sketch?"

Sullen: "I *was* going to give it to my girlfriend. Now I won't."

"Go to Walmart and have them take a picture of the two of you together. That'll be way more romantic."

K.O. rolled his eyes. "I never thought anything romantic ever happened in Walmart."

"Start a trend," Tobe said.

Both detectives stiffened their spines as their supervisor, Lieutenant McHargue, stepped out of her office and came down the narrow aisle in the squad room. She noticed K.O. and stopped.

"I heard all about your kidnapping, Mr. O'Bannion," she said. "You don't look any the worse for wear. Everything okay?"

"I'm fine."

"Detective Blaine here told me all about it." McHargue perched on the edge of Tobe's desk. "I guess you really *are* tough, fighting your way out of that mess."

"I leap tall buildings at a single bound, too."

"Why didn't you just shoot them?"

"I did," K.O. said, shooting at McHargue with his finger and making a BANG noise at the back of his throat, "like this—but I must've missed them."

McHargue wasn't amused. "Your boss asked about you getting a carry-concealed permit. We'll have to see about that. Your record sounds like you can be violent."

"That's why the army liked me so much, they sent me to Iraq."

McHargue folded her arms across her chest. "This is different from Iraq. Cleveland isn't a combat zone."

"And not much sand, either."

Tobe broke in, hoping to ease the tension. "He worked with Xavier Redondo and came up with sketches of the guys, Lieutenant."

Florence McHargue considered pushing her conversation with K.O. even further. Then she changed her mind. "Okay—let's see 'em."

She reached over and took the top one from Tobe's desk. "Christ," she said. "This looks like O'Bannion."

"It *is* me, Lieutenant," K.O. said. "I asked the sketch artist to do me, too. I hope that was okay."

"Lovely! Do we sell funnel cakes and salt water taffy upstairs, too?"

Tobe said, "The sketch probably took Redondo three minutes."

"Sure—and that dead hooker out by the zoo is now three minutes deader."

"I'll talk to Redondo," Tobe said.

"Maybe *I* should talk to him."

"I wish you wouldn't."

McHargue's eyes got smaller and meaner. "Why?"

Tobe tried inflating her lungs without McHargue noticing her. At length she said, "Because he's scared to death of you."

A moment of silence—some might it call a pregnant pause. Then: "Interesting. Is everybody else scared of me, too?"

"Almost."

McHargue looked from Tobe to Matusen and then back again. "How about you, Blaine? Are you afraid of me?"

"You're my immediate superior," Tobe said. "I respect you. From what I've seen so far, you seem to be a damn good cop, and I respect you for that, too. Do you scare me?" She chuckled. "Not even close, Lieutenant."

Matusen's eyes bugged open, not believing what he'd just heard. Lieutenant McHargue, however, looked pleased. Smug, admittedly, but pleased.

"Finally! A cop around here with balls! Welcome to the Cleveland P.D., Detective Blaine."

Tobe didn't rise from her chair but snapped off a salute, anyway.

McHargue said, "Okay, now let's see the sketches we paid for."

Tobe gave her the first sketch, and K.O. said, "That was the big dumb one."

"How big?"

"We didn't measure ourselves back-to-back. Maybe four inches taller than me."

"And what did you do to him?"

"I told him I was very annoyed with him."

McHargue sighed. "Another smart-ass around here!"

"I didn't take notes. I hit him a few times and he went down."

"The other guy, too?"

"I hit him a few more times than the first one—and I think I fucked up his kneecap, too." He quickly looked at Tobe. "Sorry, didn't mean to use that word in here."

"This is a police station," McHargue rumbled, "not the First Baptist Church. The second guy was bigger than you, too?"

"About the same size. Older."

The lieutenant asked Tobe, "You got a drawing of that one?"

"Here you go."

McHargue stared at the sketch of the man K.O. thought of as Hatchet-nose for almost a minute, her brows lowered, her mouth tight, chewing on the inside of her lower lip. "I'll be a sonofabitch!" she said. Then she stood up and turned to Tobe Blaine. "Get Jacovich on the phone," she ordered. "Now!"

CHAPTER TWENTY-FOUR

MILAN

I wrote myself a note to take home my Glock that K.O. had borrowed from me, and replace it in my coat closet. Then I called Bert Loftus's office but got Pam Marek instead, and after she hinted she'd just *love* to hoist another beer or two with me, she told me Bert had not come in that morning, although he called and said he was taking the entire day off.

Sometimes I wish I could take a day off, too—but it never seems to work out that way.

I finished up a few bills and checked my e-mail. I don't get many personal e-mails anymore; everyone is on Facebook and Twitter, and they can contact their friends and acquaintances where everyone else in the world can see. I wish for the lifestyle of eons ago when people used the telephone to actually make a call and not bang out a text.

Well, *somebody* made a phone call to me that morning.

"Mr. Jacovich?" The voice sounded older, and shaky. Not the aged, confused kind of shaky, but the scared-to-death kind of shaky. "This is Bill Gorney."

"Yes sir, how can I help you?"

"Uh—I'm the CEO of Cuyahoga Cement. You know—the cement and blacktop and concrete all over Cleveland's roads and sidewalks? Well, that's me. That's us, I mean. My company."

"Yes?" I reached for a pen.

"I'm—uh—the federal government is going to put me on trial sometime after the first of the year, you know? It's part of all the shit about Bert Loftus."

I decided not to use the pen after all. "I'm under contract to

Bert Loftus," I said, "so I can't help you, other than to recommend another security specialist—"

"*No*, damn it! I need to talk to you."

"We're talking."

"Not over the phone, for God's sake!"

I decided to invite him over for later, after I'd had lunch. "Can you be in my office at two o'clock, or two-thirty?"

"No, not at your office—and not mine, either. I might be followed."

"Sir, if you've already been indicted, I don't think the FBI is trailing you around town."

"It's got nothing to do with the FBI! This is—different."

More hysteria from a new source. Was *everyone* in Cleveland scared out of their socks? "What then, Mr. Gorney?"

"Do you know where Veterans Memorial Plaza is?"

I rubbed my forehead with my fingertips; Mr. Gorney was giving me another headache. "I've lived here all my life—I know where almost everything is. What time do you want to meet?"

"Right away. I'll be by the fountain. I'm wearing a tan suit."

Just past noon. Well—there went my lunch hour. "Fifteen minutes," I said.

I was down the stairs and halfway out the door when I heard my phone ring; this time it was my cell phone, and I realized I'd left it on the desk. I paused momentarily; I'd have to run back upstairs and fumble with my ring of keys to unlock my door again. By the time I'd finally answer the phone, the caller would have hung up anyway.

Screw it, I thought. Get Bill Gorney out of the way first.

My drive took twelve minutes, and my search for a parking spot in the vast garage beneath the plaza took another ten. By the time I emerged once more into the sunlight, Gorney was impatiently pacing back and forth before the Fountain of Eternal Life—a 46-foot-high sculpture honoring the killed or missing war veterans of Greater Cleveland, dating from the Spanish-American War to Baghdad, with names of the fallen in Afghanistan yet to come. I assumed it was Mr. Gorney, anyway, in a tan summer suit with his tie pulled down past the two opened buttons of his shirt. When he saw and apparently recognized me, I knew it by the way he tentatively approached me and stuck out a cautious hand, offering no intro.

"I'm scared shitless," he said by way of greeting. "I gotta tell somebody, and you're as good as the next person."

"As I told you, I can't work for you."

"I don't care! I could be dead by six o'clock tonight!"

"Let's sit down." We moved to the edge of the fountain and sat on the ledge surrounding it. I put on my sunglasses. I hate wearing sunglasses—most Cleveland guys do—but when the sun is right in your face, you need some sort of protection. "Okay, Mr. Gorney—who's threatened you?"

He looked around to make sure no one could overhear him, even though the person nearest to us was a middle-aged woman approximately thirty yards away and strolling briskly in the other direction. "You know I'll get convicted for all the shit I did for Bert Loftus, right?"

"Everyone's innocent until proven guilty. Even you."

"I *am* guilty—and I'll cop to it at the beginning of the trial. I paid for a hell of a lot of Loftus's crap. I set up trips for us to Las Vegas, luxury suites for the both of us, I paid for every morsel he ever put in his mouth, I gave him five bills just to gamble with—he lost it all, by the way. And I set him up with top-dollar hookers—a thousand bucks a pop in Vegas. He was really into broads, and he was okay if they were pros as long as somebody else paid for it."

I just nodded. What could one say?

"I took him to Miami a couple a times, too. Gambling down there—Miami. Dog tracks, again the best five-star hotels, again the expensive whores." He shook his head. "They were cheaper in Miami than in Vegas, but not by much."

"Vegas, Miami—is that it?"

"Hell, no! Bought our way to the Super Bowl in New Orleans, too—the two of us. Thirty-yard-line seats, up close. And parties out the kazoo the whole week before."

"No more about hookers," I said. "I haven't had lunch yet."

"Now," Gorney said, holding up a hand, "Loftus was never my best friend. Hell, no! You might not call it a bribe, but that's exactly what it was. I wanted city contracts for concrete and cement and gravel. And Loftus likes being entertained—royally. So he got what he wanted and I got what I wanted. It worked out great for us both."

"Has it?"

"Where do you think I got all the money to spend on Loftus? You'd faint dead away if you saw my company's books—the real ones, anyway. I made millions. *Millions.*"

"I get all this. But who's going to kill you? And why tell me?"

"You don't think all my business came from Loftus, do you? I mean from him *alone!* Loftus is *owned.*" Gorney raised his hand and pointed to the sky, almost the same pose as the statue in the fountain's center, reaching heavenward to escape the flames of war. "He walks around like a big shot, but he can't blow his nose in this town without asking permission."

"Permission from the mayor?"

Gorney blew a breath between his lips to indicate how ridiculous my question was.

"Who, then?"

"You know who owns Loftus and takes a big cut of everything everyone gets? Who went with us to Vegas and to the Super Bowl? Who owns all those buildings—and that dominatrix hooker that got blown away the other night? And now who's afraid I'll talk and Loftus'll talk and a hell of a lot of other people will talk, too—enough to rub all of us off the fucking face of the earth?"

He looked fearfully around again and whispered, "Any of these people walkin' around here might have one of those things you can put in your ear and hear a pigeon fart from half a mile away. They could be listening to us right now."

"They aren't listening to me—they're listening to you. Now, who do you suppose might've hired them to do that?"

One last frightened look at the pedestrians who seemed to be ignoring us, busy with their own lives and own lunch hours—and then Gorney told me.

K.O. and Tobe Blaine were waiting when I returned to my office—hungry. K.O. was disturbed. Tobe was madder than hell.

"I tried calling you an hour ago," she accused.

"I left my phone here."

She was sitting at my desk, and she held my phone up for me to see. "No shit, Sherlock."

"I was in a hurry. I had an unexpected meeting."

"You care why I called you in the first place?"

"Of course I care."

"K.O. here helped the sketch artist draw the two guys who kept him prisoner last night."

"He said he was going to."

K.O. muttered, "Talking about me again like I'm not here, huh?"

"Sorry," I said. "So what about the sketches?"

"McHargue took a look at them and flipped," Tobe said. "She recognized one of them right away."

"It was Hatchet-nose," K.O. said. "The guy with the knife."

"What's his name?"

"McHargue doesn't know," Tobe said, "but she knows who he is—the hired driver and bodyguard for Jim Hundley."

"Zowie."

"She's ringing up Hundley's office to find out his name. When we get our hands on him, we'll nail the other one, too."

"The Big Dumb Guy," K.O. explained.

"B.D.G. for short," I offered.

"K.O.'s brand spanking new in the business," Tobe said. "He didn't know these two punks, didn't have anything to do with them, didn't have anything to do with the county prosecutor, either. So why did these guys in Jim Hundley's office pluck him off the street to ferry him out into Lake Erie and use him as an anchor?"

"Wait, Detective Blaine," K.O. said. "I may have a connection for you. A few days back, I invited a woman to lunch—a woman who'd been out to dinner with Bert Loftus the night he claimed someone ran him off the road. I didn't tell her much about who I was or who I worked for, and I didn't get that good a chance to pump her for information before she got up and left me sitting in Café Sausalito."

"Where's Café Sausalito?" Tobe said.

"In the Galleria," I told her.

"So—during our short lunch, she told me where she worked, a law firm upstairs—Meacham, Bestwick and Wardwell. So I called, found out that she works directly for Curt Wardwell—and that Wardwell is the prosecutor's private attorney."

"What's her name, Mr. O'Bannion?"

"Deluke. Dolores Deluke."

He spelled the last name and Tobe scrawled it in her notebook. "Did you tell her on the phone who you were?"

K.O. shook his head. "I told her my name at lunch but never mentioned Hundley, never mentioned I worked for Milan. She knows I'm on Facebook—I friended her on that, but there's nothing in my profile about what I do or where I live. When I finally got connected to Wardwell's office, I recognized her voice so I hung up without saying a word."

Tobe's cell phone buzzed, and she flipped it open, turned her back to K.O. and me, and recited her last name. She listened, then said, "Keep at it, okay?" and hung up without waiting for a reply. Then she swiveled around to look at me again. "Matusen. He's trying to reach Jim Hundley, to ask him about these two gangstas, but so far no soap. He's tried home, cell phone, the County Administration Building, the Whiskey Island marina office, even the Sunset Grille bar—which doesn't open until five o'clock. Wherever he is, Hundley's hiding from us."

"If Hundley is invisible," I said, "his lawyer isn't." I looked at K.O. "What was his name again?"

"Curt Wardwell. Their office is in that building where the Galleria is."

"Erieview Tower," I explained to Tobe. "Do you want to call him?"

"Lawyers always manage to be otherwise engaged when the police call. We should drive over and talk to him in person."

"We? You actually want me to go with you?"

"I'd think you'd be busting a gut to accompany me."

"I am," I said. "I'll even drive you."

She shook her head. "This is an official police visit—so unless you have a two-way radio in your car, and both an unregistered pistol and a sawed-off shotgun under your front seat, we'll go in *my* car."

She got up, but K.O. didn't. I said, "Don't you want to come?"

"Dolores Deluke works in Wardwell's office; she'd recognize me in a New York minute if I tagged along," he said, "and that will screw things up. I'll stay here and answer the phone."

That pleased me. K.O. was starting to think like a cop—even a wannabe private cop.

As we went down the stairs, Tobe said to me, "You really think Hundley's lawyer will know the name of his driver and bodyguard?"

"On that level, a lawyer even knows the color of his client's underwear."

We didn't say anything until we reached her car and got in. As she fired up the ignition, she said, "I should've been a lawyer."

"Why?"

"Because," she said without a smile, "I know what color *your* underwear is." And we roared out of my parking lot.

The lobby of Meacham, Bestwick and Wardwell's law offices was only slightly smaller than a soccer field. The stunning receptionist, who was probably dressed more expensively than most of the lawyers, said that Curt Wardwell was "in a meeting," the standard lie told in large corporations that no one really believes. Tobe Blaine didn't believe it either, and leaned on the receptionist pretty hard while waving her gold badge until a call was made announcing us. After a moment another woman, dressed not nearly as nicely, appeared and led us down a corridor so long you couldn't shout to a person at the other end.

When she ushered us into Curt Wardwell's office, he barely smiled and said, "Thank you, Dolores," and she nearly bowed as she backed out. So, I thought, that's Dolores Deluke.

Curt Wardwell was pushing sixty, but his salon tan, his hundred-buck silver-tipped hairstyle, his trim racquetball-playing body, and his gold tie that probably cost more than my car made him look considerably younger.

"I'll help if I can," Wardwell said to us. He hadn't bothered putting down his pen to shake hands. "But I'm wondering why you didn't call first."

"Because if police officers only got to ask questions and make arrests by calling and making an appointment," Tobe Blaine said, "Bonnie and Clyde would still be running around sticking their guns up people's asses and robbing banks—and your clients would be losing money. Does that answer your question, counselor?"

That got Wardwell to put down his pen. He sat back in his leather throne and crossed his hands over his stomach—but I don't think he learned that from a Buddha statue. "Go ahead."

"Thank you," Tobe said with overdone sincerity and not meaning it. She took Redondo's folded sketches from her notebook. "Do you recognize either of these two men?"

The attorney only glanced at the sketches; he'd have taken more time checking the javelin scores in some obscure sports newspaper. "No," he said.

"Look again."

"Excuse me?"

"It took me about twenty minutes to get here, Mr. Wardwell, and another five just waiting for the elevator downstairs. It'll take me another half hour to get back to my office. So you owe me more than two seconds to look at those sketches and decide."

Tobe Blaine worked very well. I doubt anyone would mess with her even if she didn't carry a gun. She moved the sketches about half an inch closer to him. "Try again. Harder."

Wardwell's angry face now looked like a bust of one of those extremely pissed off Roman emperors, but he leaned forward and this time studied the sketches more carefully. Then he pushed one of them away, the sketch of Big Dumb Guy. "I have no idea who this is."

"And the other one?"

He frowned, stroking his chin like a wise elder. "He does look kind of familiar, but I can't—"

"Could it be the driver of Prosecutor Hundley's car? His bodyguard?"

The muscles at the corners of Wardwell's jawbone jumped and wiggled. "Could be. I've only seen him a few times, so my memory plays tricks with me—but it could be."

"What's his name?"

"I don't know—Dan, maybe? Is it Dan?"

"You tell me."

"It's—Dan."

"Dan. Goody, you've really narrowed it down for me—to about ten thousand people in Cleveland named Dan." She printed "DAN" in her notebook in big elementary school letters, her tongue peeking out the side of her mouth—annoying Wardwell even more.

"How the hell would I know his last name? He's just a county worker—an employee, and somebody else's employee, too."

"Like you," Tobe said.

"What?"

"*Dan* is just an employee who works for the county prosecutor—you said so. Well, so are you. You work for Jim Hundley, just like Dan. The only difference is, you're in a higher pay grade."

"You're very rude, Officer Blaine."

"That's *Detective Sergeant* Blaine—and you ain't seen nothin' yet. You're Hundley's personal attorney; you know every nickel he's spent in this town on every drink, every meal, every bimbo. And you're insulting my intelligence telling me you don't know the name of the man who's his driver? *That's* rude, counselor."

"I swear, I don't remember the sonofabitch's name! What do you want me to do?"

"Look it up."

Finally, Wardwell became frightened. His head actually quivered, like a man suffering from a palsy. He couldn't recall the last time anyone told him what to do. Finally, though, he took out his BlackBerry, played with it for awhile, and then said, "Daniel Vetter." Sigh. "Daniel J. Vetter. Is that good enough for you—*Detective Sergeant* Blaine?"

Tobe looked as if she were thinking about it. Then she said, "Good enough—for the time being. Thanks for your time, counselor."

We both stood to leave. Then Wardwell said, "Hold on."

We turned back to him.

"Jacovich, is it? Milan Jacovich?" he said to me.

"That's right."

"Private eye. I've heard about you."

I didn't know whether or not to thank him.

"You come in here with a police officer, she asks all the questions, and you don't open your mouth, right? Don't you have questions of your own?" His lip curled in a sneer; he was desperate to win at least one point. "Or are you just here for entertainment?"

"Not at all, sir," I said. "My ultimate life's ambition is to become a female African American police detective sergeant like Blaine here. That's why I watch her so carefully—so I learn to do what she does."

Walking out of Wardwell's office, Tobe rolled her eyes at me, dripping sarcasm. "That last remark of yours—just precious."

"Cute as a button," I said. Then I stopped her in front of Dolores Deluke's desk. "Do we have time to talk to Ms. Deluke here?"

"Do we?"

"Stay with me." I turned to Deluke. "Detective Blaine and I want a few words with you, okay?"

The woman's eyes were as wide and frightened as those of a rabbit who sees a speeding semi rumbling toward her on the highway. She put a hand to her throat, tried to swallow.

"Not here," I said. "Is there a conference room or somewhere we can talk privately?"

"I don't . . ." she croaked. "I'm just a secretary here."

"There's no such thing," Tobe said, "as *just* a secretary. Lead the way, Ms. Deluke."

The woman, wearing a straight skirt and a gray blouse, boring stockings, and flats she might have bought at Walmart, led us down another corridor, peering timidly into all the rooms. She looked more lost than we were. Eventually we settled into a large conference room. Sixteen executive chairs lined a long, humongously expensive table; we occupied only three of them. If I felt diminished in that room, standing six three and weighing about 230, I couldn't imagine how Dolores Deluke must have felt as she huddled in one of those oversized chairs.

"Just for the record," Tobe said, flipping open her notebook, "you are the executive assistant of Mr. Wardwell. Is that correct? How long have you worked here?"

"About four years," Deluke said.

"All that time for Mr. Wardwell?"

She nodded.

I took over. "Ms. Deluke—a few weeks back you had dinner

with City Councilman Bert Loftus, didn't you? Out in Chardon?"

Her timing was off; she waited a few seconds too long before answering. "Yes," she almost whispered.

"That was a date?"

"No, not at all."

"Platonic?"

She blushed. "Business. Mr. Loftus wanted to talk business."

"Ms. Deluke," I said as gently as I could, "I don't mean this as dismissive—but if he wanted to talk business, why didn't he ask his attorney to dinner instead of you? Your boss, Mr. Wardwell?"

"I don't know. I didn't ask. He's a very important man in Cleveland, so I didn't ask why. But he told me he wasn't hitting on me or anything—that he wanted to talk about business."

"Did this business have something to do with the county prosecutor?"

She squirmed. "I guess. He asked questions about Mr. Hundley."

Tobe and I exchanged a look. I said, "What kind of questions?"

"I shouldn't be talking about this."

"You're not a lawyer—there's no attorney-client privilege here. Besides, Loftus isn't your boss's client. So . . ."

Deluke's shoulders sagged and she dropped her chin to her chest. It was her moment of surrender. "Councilman Loftus was asking all about Hundley's properties. I don't know why."

"What properties?"

She shrugged. "All sorts of stuff. Real estate Hundley owns or controls—like buildings in Cleveland or in the suburbs. Businesses—stuff like that. And I swear to God, half the time I didn't know what Loftus was talking about."

"Doesn't all that business stuff that comes through your boss's office cross your desk first?"

"Well—yes, sure," Dolores Deluke said. "But most of the time I don't even read it. I open the mail, put stuff in different piles, and then take it in to him after lunch."

"And phone calls? You answer all Wardwell's calls?"

She hesitated, then nodded.

"People call about Hundley's properties and businesses?"

"Sometimes."

"Did Wardwell ever get calls from people like, say, Reverend Whitby?"

She nodded.

"Jeff or Vicki Ogrin?"

Just a blink that time.

"How about Sergei Chemerkin? Judge Pollard? Bill Gorney?"

"I guess they've called. I always write it down."

"Buster Santagata?"

"I think his first name isn't Buster. Something else . . ."

Tobe said to me, "Where the hell did you come up with those names? The White Pages?" She turned back to Dolores Deluke. "How about Seena Bergman? Does she ring a bell?"

"Seena?" Deluke said.

"That's the first name."

"Oh—well, yes ma'am, she does call every once in a while."

Does call. I refrained from saying *Wow!* "Detective, do you have more questions for Ms. Deluke?"

She shook her head. "No, but I want a list of those calls—from the past month or so. I'll send someone by to pick them up. Is that all right, Ms. Deluke?"

Now the young woman's hands were shaking. "I'm not supposed to do that."

"I asked you whether that was all right, but I was being polite. That was a courtesy. Now it isn't. I'm investigating a homicide, and I want that list by five o'clock. Do we understand each other?"

Poor Dolores Deluke, caught between the police and her own boss. I worried whether she'd lose her job—what she was telling us, or more specifically telling Tobe Blaine, was way over the line. But a woman was dead, another man's life seemed at stake, and K.O. had nearly been murdered.

I waited until we were back in the car. Then I said, "I appreciate your running interference for me, Tobe, but that part of it— the part about who called Hundley—that was about my case, not yours. More specifically, about K.O."

"It's how it started," she said, "until Seena Bergman's name was mentioned. She's a murder victim, Milan—that *is* my case."

"Our two cases are connected."

"I'm not at all surprised," she said.

CHAPTER TWENTY-FIVE

MILAN

Tobe Blaine dropped me off in my office parking lot and toot-led away with a casual wave. Upstairs, K.O. was studying something on his computer, and when I walked in he was anxious to share it with me.

"How come," he said, turning the laptop around so I could read the monitor, "those people everybody calls the Ogres live in a shithouse apartment, and Jeff Ogrin is actually on Medicaid, but they own a whole bunch of apartment buildings on the west side? How can they do that, Milan?"

"If they were on Medi*care*, they might be screwed; that's federal. Medi*caid*, though, that's run by the state—which means they might get some sort of cover from a very important local someone."

"Loftus, you think?"

"Loftus is a city councilman; I don't think he has that much juice in Columbus. Now, Jim Hundley—that's another story. He wants to be governor. Come on, we have to go talk to our client again."

"Loftus? Oh, boy!"

"I'll tell you about my day on the way. A lot has to do with you."

"Great," K.O. said. "And it's not even my birthday."

We headed for the door. "When *is* your birthday anyway?"

"I forget."

"Nobody forgets their own birthday. Is it a secret?"

"If you actually give me a birthday present, I'll tell you."

"And until then?"

"Pound sand," K.O. said.

Driving west on Edgewater Boulevard, we watched sailboats scudding across the lake, white dots against the different shades of blue—sky and water. It was such a good, warm summer day that even boat owners—people with money—were taking the day off to go sailing.

Jana Loftus answered the door. She looked at K.O. first and offered a reluctant smile. "Hello again. Is this your father?"

"He's my younger brother," K.O. said.

I identified myself, gave her one of my cards, and said we wanted to speak with her husband.

"Terrific timing," she said. "He's actually home. Come in."

She led us to a pleasant family room overlooking the lake, offered us iced tea neither of us wanted, and went upstairs to tell Bert he had visitors. We sat together on the sofa; the coffee table didn't look as if anyone had ever put their feet up on it.

"She's a nice woman," K.O. said. "I kind of feel sorry for her."

"Why's that?"

"Because her husband is a Class A asshole."

"That's our client you're talking about," I reminded him. "Our cross to bear."

Our cross to bear picked that moment to appear. I was used to seeing Bert Loftus in thousand-dollar suits and bow ties; at home he wore faded light blue Dockers, open-toed sandals, and a blue Cleveland Indians T-shirt with a huge likeness of the team's mascot, Chief Wahoo, on the chest. Native Americans protest every year about the bright red racist caricature, but it doesn't seem to bother Cleveland baseball fans. It sure didn't bother Loftus.

"The phones have been going crazy at the office," he said, sitting down across from us, "so I decided to stay home."

"Who's been calling?"

He made a wide gesture with both hands, indicating the entire world. "Everybody who wants something from me, as usual." He looked from me to K.O. "You guys want something from me, too."

"Just corroboration," I said.

"Of what?"

"Of what I've heard about you—and your relationship with Jim Hundley."

His summer tan turned as white as a piece of paper. "Hundley and I—we're in the same business."

"Politics."

"Yes, sure."

"Then how come all the people who call you for favors—the Ogrins and Sergei Chemerkin and Bill Gorney, to name just a few—how come they regularly call the county prosecutor, too?"

"How would *I* know who they call?" Loftus said.

"You're not really the power in this city, are you?" K.O. said.

Loftus drew himself up into his most arrogant pose, slightly ridiculous with that big red Indian cartoon leering from the middle of his chest. "I'm damn well the power," he snapped.

"You think so, Bert—but you're not much more than a puppet. The County Prosecutor pulls the strings," I said.

That shut him up. He stared straight ahead, trying to keep from dissolving into tears or panic.

"You have a nice little nest egg, Bert. We knew that anyway, from the bribes."

"Favors!" he said nervously. "Not bribes! Friends doing favors for me, and me doing favors for them. I'm innocent, Milan—and K.K."

"Please, Councilman, get it right. K.*O*. Like knock-out. Like a punch in the mouth. And if the feds really thought you were innocent, you wouldn't be going to trial."

"I'm . . ."

"Bert," I said, "Seena Bergman called Prosecutor Hundley all the time—or called his lawyer."

He shook his head violently. "I don't know who she called. Maybe Hundley was another one of her clients. Or Curt Wardwell."

"I don't know about Wardwell," I said, "but Jim Hundley has all the gorgeous young floozies in town eating out of his hand. I've seen it, Bert. Hundley doesn't have your particular—tastes."

"Then why did Seena call *him* all the time?" He asked but knew the answer all along.

"He's her employer," I said. "He owns that building she lived in—or co-owns it—and loaned her out to all his buddies who enjoy sexual kinks. Just like you."

"Christ on a crutch!" Loftus bellowed, then looked around to make sure Jana wasn't listening. Then he whispered, "How did you find out—about Jim Hundley?"

"We found out plenty," K.O. said.

"But we want to hear the rest of it—from you," I added.

He gave it one more valiant try. "I told you, Milan—I can't discuss that."

"Too late, Bert. Someone's been trying to kill you. Someone kidnapped K.O. and tried to kill him, too. And somebody strangled Seena Bergman and threw her dead body out in the Metropark, like garbage. So unless you tell us everything now—and I mean *everything*—we'll walk away, and then the chances are really terrific you're going to wake up dead some morning."

All the air went out of him slowly; he crumpled like a gigantic balloon springing a leak in the Macy's parade. He sat with his forearms on his thighs, head down, shaking back and forth as if he might make us go away. At length: "I need a drink."

He stood and disappeared into the depths of the house. "If that fuckwad were honest with us from the beginning . . . ," K.O. said.

"It wouldn't have changed a thing. None of us realized how serious it was before, so I didn't lean on him. Now, we've got to hear the whole story."

"With music," K.O. said.

Bert Loftus came back in carrying a large water glass, and I didn't have to guess to know it contained a *very* healthy portion of vodka. Nobody would make a confession like Bert did while drinking water.

"I told my wife to go upstairs and stay there," he said softly. "I hope to Christ she doesn't hear me; then I'd be in deep shit!"

He didn't sit in the chair opposite us, but came very close and sat on the coffee table, close enough that I could smell his breath. I was as discreet as possible when I opened my notebook and clicked open my pen, ready to write down whatever he might say.

Councilman Bert Loftus took a big gulp, almost a quarter of the vodka, then put down the glass, sighed sadly once, and began his story, speaking barely above a whisper.

*　　*　　*

"All politicians are on the take—one way or another. It's why we become politicians in the first place—so we can put a little aside for a rainy day. I'm not saying I don't care about the city or its people, because I do. Look at my record; I've been a damn good councilman, especially for my own district. You got a humongo pot hole in front of your house? Contact me and I'll get it taken care of—because I call the guy supplying the concrete and the labor, and he'll get out there in a flash and make your street look as good as new. Who cares if he schmoozed me a little so I made sure he got that contract in the first place? 'Cause if I didn't take care of him—if we hired some yo-yo that I got no control over who might fix your street or might not for another two weeks, then you'll be up my ass bitching I'm a lousy councilman.

"Sure I skimmed a little cream off the top. I always do. So put a gun in my mouth—that's how I get my job done. You get what you want, the guy who does the work gets what he wants, and I get what I want. But—and I hope to God everybody's gonna understand this—I'm just a middle man. Somebody bigger than I am, more powerful, really calls the shots. I'm comfortable financially—but I'm nowhere near rich, because when I get it off the top, he gets it off my top. And not just me, either. Damn near everybody who works a city or county job that makes more than maybe forty grand a year, they put aside a little extra, just like I do—and it winds up in his pocket, or in some bank account a thousand miles from here.

"I'm not talking about the mayor! The mayor's a pussy—scared of his own shadow. He hardly sticks his head out of his office. He's scared that if he so much as farts in public, he'll have to run to the bishop, confess his fart, and do a shitload of Hail Marys and Our Fathers to make him feel better. So, it's not the mayor, not by a long shot.

"Jim Hundley is the County Prosecutor. In other places like Chicago or Los Angeles they call them the district attorney. In Cuyahoga County, Hundley is all about giving—when he feels like it—and about taking, which is all the time. A powerful guy? Are you kidding? Jim Hundley is the Big Kahuna.

"We have to keep him smiling—but he has to keep us smiling, too. That's why he sets up things for us, so we keep smiling. He makes sure we get the invitations, the trips, the free football tickets and stuff. And—well, yeah, Seena Bergman, too. She made me smile. So what? I'm a human being, I've got needs and desires and fantasies. There's a hell of a lot of men—really successful, powerful, important in business and politics—who get off with a strict woman, a dominatrix, who literally takes control of everything. It might've been fun at home, but if I even mentioned something like that to my wife, much less suggested it, she'd shoot me dead where I stand. All she knows is the missionary position. I never was with a woman like Seena before, a really controlling take-charge woman—but I always thought about it, fantasized about it until Hundley introduced me to her. God, I'm getting a woody just remembering it.

"Don't kid yourself, I wasn't in love with her or anything close to it. But I was damn grateful to Hundley for putting that all together—for me, and for some others whose names you'd know if I told you, who run this whole city.

"There are other top-drawer hookers who live in the same building, younger ones than Seena, who cater to men that might have more normal kinks than me. Not that everything isn't normal, you know. Everything is normal as long as it's mutually agreed on between two condescending adults."

I wanted desperately to make a note of that last remark because I wouldn't want to forget it: Two *condescending* adults. What a great mental picture that makes.

"Hundley is part-owner of that building," Loftus continued, "or his wife is. She's part of a blind company, along with Jeff and Vicki Ogrin and even Reverend Whitby and a few others. They're slipping me cash and gifts and things they earn partly from that goddamn building!

"Hundley isn't into kinky sex himself. I know he likes young women, he goes out with a different one every night. But he ran the whole sex deal out of that building, and paid for it, because he liked complete control over all of us—everybody with a decent job at the city or county. Heads of departments, managers, budget directors—damn near everything except cops and firefighters and EMS people. Hundley has bigger plans than any of that. He wants to be governor of Ohio, and he makes no bones about it.

He's young, not even fifty, and guess what job he'll want after being governor. That means all of us who trot along after him and pay him off and take his shit will be scuffling around his feet waiting for him to throw us even better jobs in Washington.

"But here's the trouble, and he never knew it was coming. Seena made videotapes of all her—appointments. Secret videotapes; I had no idea I'd be in them. I found out by accident. After one of our—sessions about a month ago, she went into the bathroom, and while I was getting dressed, I saw a little red light on the dresser across from her bed that I never noticed before. When I looked closer, it was a vidcam—and I was some kind of goddamn star!

"All I wanted was to get the hell out of there, get my head together, and figure out what to do about it. After about a week I called for another appointment with her—not for anything sexy. I told her I knew about the camera and asked her if she was going to blackmail me with those tapes. She laughed—said they were for blackmail, but not for me. I guess she had tapes of everybody, not just me, and she planned on using them for a big payoff—big! She planned to get Jim Hundley by the short hairs. I don't know whether she wanted money or some big deal job besides being a resident hooker and dominatrix—but she made me promise I wouldn't tell anyone about those tapes, especially Hundley.

"I guess, though, that she finally did tell him. She'd run as far as she could with it, and it was time to cash in. Don't know what she wanted, exactly—but he must have been royally pissed off.

"When I went to see her the other night—the night somebody shot at me—it was a good-bye. She'd be moving onward and upward. She was in her forties—tired of turning tricks, even for the big bucks.

"I think Hundley was furious with me, too, because I warned him I was going to name names at my trial—everyone's names! A lot of the names that were on that list I gave you, Milan, the ones that I—did favors for. I know I'm going to prison—but the more I spill my guts out to the feds, the lighter my sentence. And that'll mean longer sentences and worse trials for all of—my friends.

"So somebody on that list might be trying to kill me. I can't ask the cops for protection—they'll laugh in my face. I sure as hell can't ask Jim Hundley. And the mayor of Cleveland won't even take my calls. So, that's why I hired you boys—to protect me.

"Jesus Christ—I hope I don't get murdered in prison."

By the time Loftus had finished talking, the vodka was gone, his words slurred and stumbling, and he was broken, confused, defeated. He sat on the edge of the coffee table, his shoulders and head hanging almost to his thighs.

K.O. nodded at me. We both stood, and I reached down and put a hand on Bert's shoulder; his Chief Wahoo T-shirt was damp with sweat. Maybe tears, too.

"We'll be in touch," I said. He didn't answer, just shrugged my hand off his shoulder. We headed into the atrium, pointing toward the front door, when Jana Loftus came down from upstairs.

"Excuse me," she said from midstairwell, and then again, louder, *"Excuse me!"*

We stopped and she came up to us. "I'm sorry—I didn't get your name, Mr. . . . ?"

"Jacovich."

She closed her eyes for two seconds, then said, "And I'm afraid I've forgotten your name, too, young man—from yesterday."

"O'Bannion. Kevin O'Bannion."

"Jacovich and O'Bannion. Is that a law firm?"

"Security specialists. We're temporarily working for your husband."

"Ah—yes, young Mr. O'Bannion here told me that. I hope you and Bert had a nice conversation." She stood close to us but looked down at her feet and chewed nervously on the inside of her cheek. Then she said, "Will you be able to keep Bert from going to jail?"

It was a question I didn't want to answer, but she left me no choice. "I—don't think so, Ms. Loftus."

It hit her hard. She didn't cry, though, or even tear up a little, gritting her teeth tightly shut so she wouldn't. Finally her shoulders relaxed and she sighed. "I didn't think so, either," she said. Then she turned quietly and walked back up the stairs, holding on to the handrail.

K.O. and I let ourselves out.

CHAPTER TWENTY-SIX

K.O.

After leaving the Loftus home, Milan and K.O. went back to the Third District—the Rock Pile—where Detectives Blaine and Matusen were still working away. Even though it had turned dark, high-level detectives were never nine-to-fivers. Milan often said most really bad people are easier to find and arrest at night.

K.O. didn't say much but let Milan do most of the talking, quoting from his notebook jottings, reporting as accurately as he could what Loftus had said. When he was about halfway through, Blaine interrupted him.

"Why don't you share all this interesting stuff with the FBI?"

"The FBI and I don't get along."

Blaine laughed. "You're on bad terms with the whole bureau?"

"I work for Loftus. Why would I wave him under the nose of the government? He'll probably do that himself—hoping they won't put him away for the rest of his life."

"As far as Hundley's concerned," K.O. said, "if anybody decides to expose him—like Loftus will probably do—his career is over. No more skimming off the top, no governorship, no president of the United States from Ohio."

"So?"

"So maybe he's deciding to shut them up."

Tobe Blaine processed that. "Like trying to kill Bert Loftus?"

Milan nodded. "Or like *actually* killing Seena Bergman— which is your case, and that's why I'm telling you."

K.O. said, "I don't want to be pushy—but let's not forget that last night two guys kidnapped me so they could kill me, too—and one of them was Hundley's bodyguard."

She nodded. "Daniel J. Vetter. We're looking for him."

"Did you ask Hundley's office if he's working today?"

Blaine's eyes turned to slits. "How dumb do you think this department is, K.O.?"

"Sorry—but they wanted me dead yesterday, and they're probably not in love with me today, either. So it *is* my ass."

"We'll try to keep your ass from harm; maybe you can frame it." She opened her desk drawer and took out a plastic bag containing the knife K.O. had taken from his attacker the night before. "This is a cheap knife. You can buy one exactly like it at just about any pawn shop or flea market in America. There are my fingerprints on it—thank you for tossing it to me—and there are yours, and probably a hundred other people's—all smudged. It's worthless." She pushed it toward K.O. "You want it as a souvenir?"

"The bastard hanging upside down from a tree limb—that's the souvenir I want," K.O. said.

Bob Matusen shifted in his chair, undecided whether to act upset and nervous, or to make everyone think he wasn't paying attention. Milan looked at him without joy and then said "I hate to interrupt this conversation, Tobe—sorry, *Detective Blaine*—but there's lots more to tell you."

"I can barely wait. Continue your report, please."

Milan finished telling them about the so-called confession of Bert Loftus, and Blaine made a steeple with her fingers. "From what Loftus says, it might actually be Jim Hundley taking shots at him."

K.O. said, "I think he was even more scared of Seena Bergman. Loftus can get him in trouble at his trial—but Seena could've washed Hundley right over the side."

Tobe Blaine drummed on the edge of her desk as if she were playing the opening of Beethoven's "Für Elise" on the piano. Then she said to Matusen, "Bob, let's drop by Hundley's office and chat with him."

Matusen jumped as if he'd been shot. He stared for a moment too long at K.O. and then said, "Uh—you better do it yourself, Blaine. I have—stuff to take care of."

There was an awkward silence in the room, as if someone had passed gas. Finally Blaine spoke quietly: "Do you have a problem talking to Hundley?"

Matusen's hands fluttered around his mouth. "He's the county prosecutor! You mess around with him, he can make one phone call—*one phone call!*—and he'll have your job on a platter." He finally realized what his hands were doing and clasped them in front of him like a first-grader. "I'm thirty-one months away from retirement. I don't want to be on Jim Hundley's bad side."

Blaine pressed her lips together until they almost disappeared. Then she said, "Fine. I'll do it myself."

"We'll come with you," Milan said.

"Like hell you will. If and when I find Hundley, I don't want an entire army behind me. If it's about murder, or attempted murder—then it *is* my case, Milan—and the department's. It's not yours."

"What am I supposed to do, then?"

"Go home. Take K.O. with you. I'll call if I turn up anything."

"Go home?"

"Go home, get drunk, watch a movie, or catch up on your sleep—but you can't come with me." She avoided looking at anyone else in the room, but her words were biting. "Or you and Matusen find something to do together." She stood and moved toward the stairwell that would take her to the main floor and eventually to the police parking lot. "As for me—I'm working."

Milan and K.O. left shortly thereafter. K.O. waved good-bye to Matusen, but Milan did not. When they got downstairs, K.O. said, "Are you pissed at that other detective, Milan?"

"Bob Matusen? No—just disappointed. A police officer doesn't tiptoe around trying not to offend important people just because he's close to retiring." He shrugged. "I'll talk to him again. Sometime."

"Where are we going now?"

"*You* are going home."

"Why?"

"Maybe," Milan said, "because you haven't seen Carli for a few days. It'll do you good."

"Why can't I come with you?"

"You don't know where I'm going. How do you know you want to come with me?"

"You're not going to be with Tobe Blaine because she's working—trying, I guess, to find Hundley. So where *are* you going?"

"I'll try finding Hundley, too—just in different places."

"So why is it again I can't come with you?"

"Because," Milan said, "you're not licensed to carry a weapon."

K.O. didn't go very far. He pulled into a parking lot on East 30th and Payne in an all-Chinese shopping plaza, Asian Village, a few blocks east of Cleveland P.D.'s Third District, and made a call on the new cell phone Milan bought for him earlier that day. Jake Foote wouldn't be in his office that late, so K.O. dialed him at home.

When he told Foote what information he wanted, the Lake County cop was eager to comply. "That stuff is usually only available on police computer systems—but most of us who don't pound a beat worked out a way to have online software at home. Hang on a sec."

K.O.'s wait was closer to five minutes than a sec. Well-dressed Chinese customers leaving the restaurant inside the plaza stared at him, but he ignored them. He usually ignored strange looks, anyway.

Finally Foote came back on the line. "Daniel J. Vetter? Is that the one you want?"

"That's him."

"Bad boy—he's got some sheet. Burglary. Assault and battery. Attempted rape. More A and B. Shall I go on?"

"I get the idea."

"What do you want him for?"

"To inquire about his health," K.O. said. "He got hurt last night and I wanted to check up on him."

"Oh? How'd he get hurt last night?"

"I kicked the crap out of him."

Jake Foote sighed. "You won't get into more trouble, will you? I can't save your ass again. You're a grown-up. No more juvie for you."

"I won't hit him anymore, Jake. I want to be his friend."

A pause. Then: "K.O., you're a lying sack of shit."

"Some Iraqis called me that, too."

Jake Foote chuckled. Then he read off Daniel J. Vetter's last known address—on the near west side of Cleveland.

It took K.O. fifteen minutes to get there. In the short time he'd been employed by Milan Security, he was beginning to learn the city. This enclave, southeast of downtown, was called Tremont— an old neighborhood with aging housing stock cheek-by-jowl with top-of-the-line restaurants owned by celebrity chefs, an interesting offbeat bookstore, and a population of young up-and-comers neighboring with families who've inhabited those houses for nearly a century. Carli had mentioned once that she'd one day want to move to Tremont, but at the time he'd had no idea where it was or why she longed to live there.

As he approached the brownstone converted into small and dusty apartments, K.O. thought that he would certainly try discouraging Carli from living in a place like this one. The entire building, brick-faced and covered with fading paint, looked as if it had endured forever, bowing down to the years and the many people who've climbed its worn, sagging stairs leading up to the dusty porch. Nailed to the wall were eight rusting, dented mailboxes installed decades before anyone ever heard the names of Al Pacino, Jimmy Carter, or Reggie Jackson.

He examined the mailboxes until he found D VETTER scrawled on a strip of surgical tape. As he climbed the inside stairs to the second floor, K.O. wondered if Vetter had acquired another knife to replace the one he took from him.

His knock was answered by a woman wearing cut-off jeans and a long-sleeved black T-shirt. Few people wore long-sleeved shirts at home in the Cleveland summertime, which caused K.O. to take a closer look at her. She was closer to forty than thirty, had dull and lifeless eyes, and her dank hair needed a comb-out. K.O. could easily spot an addict when he saw one.

"What!" the woman almost snarled.

"I'm looking for Dan Vetter. Is he here?"

"No," she said, and began to close the door. K.O. put out a hand to stop it from slamming in his face.

"Are you his girlfriend?"

"Uh—yeah."

"Where can I find him?"

She had to think about that for a while before trying—unsuccessfully—to toss her hair out of her face. "Hospital."

"Which hospital?"

The question knit her brows. Finally she said, "Metro."

"Metro. Thanks," K.O. said before the door closed. As he made his way down the stairs, he mentally counted how many words she'd actually spoken to him. There were five—*not* counting "Uh."

Metro Health, off West 25th Street, is a huge hospital, although it could easily be swallowed whole by the Cleveland Clinic campus. K.O. wandered for half an hour before discovering where Daniel Vetter was staked out. It was officially past visiting hours, but in a hospital that huge, nobody paid attention to who might be walking down the hall. A heaviness pressed against his chest as he recalled that twenty-four hours earlier the man behind that door had planned to kill him.

He took a deep breath and walked in.

The bed closest to the door was occupied by an elderly black man. K.O. couldn't discern why he was hospitalized or what was wrong with him, as his eyes were half-closed. He moaned softly with every breath.

In the bed by the window was Daniel J. Vetter—formerly known as Hatchet-nose. His arm was in a cast from elbow to fingertips. His leg, also encased in plaster, was elevated and hanging eighteen inches above the bed, as surgery had been performed that morning to move his kneecap from the side of his leg to where it belonged. Beneath the lightweight blanket and his hospital-issued gown, his smashed ribs were taped.

When he saw K.O. in the doorway, whatever color left in his face fled and his eyes bulged. "Oh, shit!" he said quietly, and the words came out slushy through his few remaining teeth.

"Don't panic," K.O. said, "I won't hurt you again. Relax."

"Look at me, for crysakes!" Vetter almost blubbered. "Relax is about the only goddamn thing I can do in here."

K.O. sauntered over to him. "Vetter? It's nice to finally know your name. Daniel J. Vetter. What does the J stand for? Jag-off?"

Vetter tried to say "Fuck you," but it's hard to say the *f* without any front teeth.

"Not so good with talk anymore, are you?" He moved closer. "It's late and I'm tired. If I have to stand here too long, I'm going to sit down on the bed—and bounce. Imagine how much that'll hurt. Whaddya think?"

"Oh, God," Vetter whispered. Maybe he really was trying to contact God. K.O. had seen men up close before he killed them in Afghanistan, but he couldn't recall anyone as terrified as Vetter.

"You were going to take me out in the middle of Lake Erie and drown me—as you were kind enough to let me know. Since that wasn't working, you came at me with a knife—and ripped my shirt, you sonofabitch. That was a nice shirt, too."

"It—wasn't personal."

"If not personal, why did you want me dead?"

"A job—it was just a job." Vetter closed his eyes, hoping when he opened them again, K.O. would be gone.

No such luck.

"You're a hired killer?"

Vetter used his only available hand to wipe the slobber spittle from his lips. "I got a regular job, just like everybody else."

"A regular job, huh? For who?"

Vetter's eyes were wet, as though he were about to cry. "Don't ask me, man."

"Don't ask me *not* to—man."

And now those eyes widened in terror. "Don't hurt me! I'll call a nurse." His hand scrabbled around looking for the call button.

"My hurting you is nothing compared to what the cops will do to you," K.O. warned, snatching the button from Vetter's reach. "Do yourself a favor: Tell me what I want to know before you'll *have* to tell it to the cops. If you do, I'll try to put in a good word for you." He tried not to smile at his own completely ridiculous lie.

Vetter was almost too frightened to speak until K.O. came

closer to him and looked almost hungrily at his leg in traction. "Who ordered you to kill me, Vetter?"

No answer, and a stubborn chin.

"Tell me," K.O. said, "because just one good kick at that knee in traction and they'll hear you screaming somewhere in Pennsylvania."

"Please," Vetter begged. "Please."

"Name." He glanced at the plastered leg again. "*Name!*"

The injured man closed his eyes and stifled a sob. Then he said, "Hundley. The prosecutor." Bitterly spitting it out, again trying unsuccessfully to say the F-word. "'uckin' Jim *Hundley.*"

CHAPTER TWENTY-SEVEN

MILAN

Was it Sherlock Holmes who first said "The jig is up?" That meant that the villain has been identified. Things were coming together quickly for the police, and County Prosecutor Jim Hundley must have known it was only a matter of time before he'd be on the wrong side of the bars.

Tobe Blaine was going to land on him with both feet, but I doubted he'd be at his office. Apparently the guy had millions stashed away in the Cayman Islands, or Switzerland, or some other place nobody else knew about. He wouldn't stick around and face the consequences. I wouldn't either, if I were him.

I wanted to alert Tobe as to where Hundley might have gone to ground. She wasn't answering her cell phone—and if the police waited until morning, Jim Hundley, with money and method for travel, would be no more than a bad Cleveland memory.

I stopped in my office, took a few moments to strap on my holster and check my 9 mm to make sure it was loaded, and then found my way back to Whiskey Island.

Once you get off the Route 2 freeway westbound, the road to Whiskey Island is long, narrow, and very dark at night, and I bounced along, hanging on to the steering wheel like a bronco rider clutches the reins. In summertime, Whiskey Island jumps until way past midnight, and I'm amazed anyone who'd had a few drinks could drive this stretch of road on their way home without careening into a wall or a tree.

I found a parking place. The Sunset Grille seemed relatively crowded, and music floated out over the harbor. I didn't think, though, that Jim Hundley would be at the bar this time, drinking happily and groping young women.

I doubted Hundley had any friends in Cuyahoga County so devoted they would allow him to crouch in the shadows of their home until his troubles disappeared; it was too late for that—Hundley himself would disappear first. Besides, he'd already screwed most of his so-called pals. So my mind eliminated all *im*possibilities, leaving me, like Sherlock Holmes, with the only possible place to look.

I couldn't begin to count the number of boats moored along the endless piers that jutted out into Lake Erie, beyond which the bright blue breakwater was illuminated by a bright moon, and which welcomed at least a thousand gulls who apparently spent their time there when the sun went down. Jim Hundley had a large boat, much bigger than most of the others, and after I searched for ten minutes, it was little trouble for me to spot it, moored way out on one of the piers, probably as far from the crowded restaurant as it could get. I didn't have a flashlight with me but didn't need one to read the name on the boat's hull: *The Good Guy.*

The recreational trawler was approximately sixty feet long, costing well into the middle six figures—no decimal points. A Portuguese bridge, or walkway, wound around the foredeck, and there was an elegant-looking raised pilothouse. No wonder vessels like this were referred to as trawler yachts.

You have to be much more than comfortably well-off financially to own a yacht.

Inside, the cabin looked like a living room, including a bar. A spacious galley was off to one side. A sleeping area, aft, was enough for six or eight, except that Jim Hundley's boat had been reconfigured so that one king-sized bed fit in stately luxury.

Hundley was aboard, all right, but didn't look as if he were readying for slumber. Two large suitcases were in the main cabin, and two even larger ones out on the deck, and he was busy, quickly moving papers and files from another, smaller traveling case into a wall safe built into the bulkhead. As I watched, he'd stop frequently and take a pull from a tall drink he'd mixed that sat on one of the tables, and the way he drank told me this one was not his first. He was getting things ship-shape (no pun intended) so he could take the boat out somewhere. Whether anyone was sharp enough to pilot a boat after a few bountiful drinks, I had no idea.

It was 10:30 p.m., an unseemly hour for a boat ride—especially alone.

I swung myself onto the deck, bending slightly as I entered the cabin. Hundley was so badly startled, he dropped a sheaf of papers.

"Jesus," he said. "Milan Jacovich." Flustered, he bent to scoop the scattered documents together. "How'd you know which boat was mine?"

"By the same strange power that allows me to cloud men's minds so they cannot see me."

"Huh?"

"From an old radio show."

"I don't remember old radio shows. What do you want here?"

I chose not to answer. "Looks like you're going on a trip."

"How's it your business?"

"My business is finding out who's trying to kill my client—that would be Councilman Loftus—*and* my assistant."

Hundley reached for his drink. "We've been through all that. What are you doing on my boat?"

"You told me you knew nothing about Loftus's business dealings that got him arrested—that the county is your job but the city isn't. You're in trouble, and you damn well know it. Is that why you're aboard in the middle of the night with suitcases?"

His lips nearly disappeared. "Why should I tell you that? Why should I *talk* to you? Get off my boat."

"I know a little about boats myself, but naturally I could never afford a big, elegant trawler like this. It has a pretty large fuel capacity, doesn't it? Half a tank will get you out in Lake Erie and on to Canada in no time. Or maybe from one Great Lake to another until you wind up at the top end of Michigan or Minnesota."

"Shut up, Jacovich."

"There must be a pretty big engine room below, too—you can go damn near anywhere you want. Leaving town before the FBI comes knocking on *your* door?"

His eyes were blinking too rapidly, and he tried wetting his lips. "I'm the prosecuting attorney!" he almost shouted. "Nobody fucks with me! Nobody'd *dare*—or I'll crush 'em like a cockroach!"

I tried not to show how satisfied I was that Jim Hundley was close to losing it. "You're going to crush the Federal Bureau of Investigation? Don't make me laugh, Jim."

"Don't call me Jim, dammit, you don't know me that well." He waved a threatening finger at me. "I told the FBI what I told you—that I don't know a damn thing about Loftus and his outright stealing."

"Nobody believes that. You've skimmed off the top of Bert's bribes and kickbacks from the start—and everyone else's, too. You think just because you're the county prosecutor, nobody can touch you? Is that why you're sailing away in the middle of the night?"

"You've said enough!" Hundley snarled.

"I'm just getting started. Your wife owns everything—the house, your businesses, the whole nine yards. Are you leaving her holding the bag when it's just a matter of time before the feds find out that Pequod Managers is in her name but is really your own private holding company? And that Pequod owns half this town—which means that *you* do. You'll have a hell of a time explaining all that."

His angry eyes were like bullet holes in his face. He reached into a drawer in the table where he'd set his drink, and I found myself staring down the barrel of a Smith & Wesson. "The conversation is over. For you, everything is over."

"Always armed?"

"Sure," he said. "I put a lot of people in prison that are mad as hell at me." He gestured at me. "I can see you're carrying heat. Take it out slowly—two fingers—and drop it. Gently, now."

Miffed, I did as I was ordered. "The innocent ones you prosecuted are probably even madder—just so your conviction record looks good."

He actually sniffed at me. "My record is damn near spotless," he bragged. "Kick that weapon over here."

I nudged my Glock several feet toward Hundley. "Will your record take you to the governor's mansion?"

"I thought so," he said, "until people started squeezing me. I had to take care of them first."

"And *then* run for governor."

"That would've been a beginning."

"Governor, senator—and then the White House?"

He shrugged, but his gun didn't waver. "The White House is bigger and nicer than the house I'm in now."

"You tried to 'take care of' Bert Loftus."

"When he gets on the stand, he'll throw me under the bus without even blinking." Hundley shook his head as if to rattle loose his thoughts. "It got—complicated."

"I'll bet it did," I said. "So you'll shoot me and tell the police you thought I was a burglar?"

"Not until I get you so far out in Lake Erie that the fish will eat you before you float back and wash up on the beach in Edgewater Park." He motioned with the gun. "Lean against the bulkhead with both hands—and if you move an inch, I'll blow away your spine."

That was creative, I thought. Jim Hundley wasn't nearly the tough guy he thought he was. "Sit down!" he ordered. "On the floor."

I didn't think boat people call it "floor," but I sat down anyway, feeling the constant gentle rocking beneath me. I wondered if he'd tie me up, or whether he had handcuffs. A cop knows all too well how to apply handcuffs, even on a struggling perp, but I doubt Jim Hundley'd ever even used a pair, and I couldn't imagine him holding his weapon aimed at me while he fumbled with cuffs, or even a rope. Neither lawyers nor politicians have much expertise immobilizing criminals.

Or those who think *they* are criminals.

"Comfortable," I said, feeling the carpet rough through my pants. "Aren't you going to offer me a drink?"

"Shut up."

"I don't think so. You won't shoot me here. There's a hundred people getting shitfaced in the Sunset Grille, and they'll hear the shot. Or should I just wait here while you go buy a silencer at a gun shop at eleven o'clock at night?"

"You think you're so smart," Hundley said, "but you're not smart at all. You're dumb—a big dumb Polack."

"Big dumb Slovenian," I corrected him. "At least get your facts straight."

"Well, here's a fact: You're gonna wake up in the morning looking at the sun through thirty feet of water."

I thought of the few people I'd ever seen, besides cops, who *didn't* look ridiculous waving a gun and spouting tough-guy sarcasm out of the side of their mouth. John Wayne. Robert Mitchum. Eastwood. Bogart. Cagney. Jim Hundley was not on that list.

"Are you going to kill me yourself?" I said. "You can't have your punks do it for you, because one's in the hospital and I don't know where the other one is—unless John Whatsisname the Third is your paid executioner?"

That made Hundley mad all over again. "You leave John out of this! He's got nothing to do with anything. He's my executive assistant and that's all. Damn you anyway, Jacovich!" He drained his drink and reached for a bottle to pour himself another—Johnnie Walker Blue Label. Not Red Label—that's for peasants, I guess—and not Black Label for top-shelf drinkers. *Blue* Label, I suppose, shouts out how important, rich, and powerful you are. Never tried it, but I imagine it's pretty good whiskey. This time he drank it neat.

"If you get out of the country, will you leave your wife here to face criminal charges?"

"Don't you worry about her."

"What about Pequod Managers? Who owns that company with Mrs. Hundley?"

"Lotta people." He swallowed Blue Label, and wasn't smiling nearly enough to appreciate it.

"Reverend Whitby, for instance? Or the Ogres?"

"Who?"

"Sorry, the Ogrins. Jeff and Vicki."

Suspicious, bristling. "What do you know about the Ogrins?"

"Just asking."

"Don't waste your breath. You don't have many of them left."

He scowled, frowned, and mumbled a syllable I couldn't quite get.

"What's that, Jim?"

"Nothing."

"Last request—humor me. What did you just say?"

"I said *cunt!*" he bellowed, swaying slightly.

That got my attention. "Are you referring to your wife?"

"No. To that goddamn whore. Seena." He leaned on the first syllable, like a preadolescent feeling a new filthy word on his tongue for the first time.

"Why is she a whore and a cunt, Jim?"

"'Cause she had me by the balls and she knew it." He burped around his next swallow. "And she waggled her mouth to that kid working for you."

The hair on my forearms stood up straight. "She told you about him? The—kid?"

"Bitch!" he said. He was exhausting obscene epithets for women; he might start inventing new ones.

"How did you know about my assistant?"

"I know *everything*—and if I don't know it, I make it my business to find out." He sidled over and stood directly over me, pointing the gun at my face. "You think I'm some fucking no-body? Don't you know who I am? Don't you know I got more goddamn clout in this county than the mayor and the governor and the two U.S. senators combined? Anybody messes with me, they're history. *History!*"

And he kicked me hard in the ribs.

Not really as bad as it sounds; he wore deck shoes, not boots, and the kick didn't do much damage. Besides, he was a lousy kicker. If he'd tried out for kicking field goals, the Browns wouldn't keep him around for even one day. And he grew drunker by the minute.

Still, the kick hurt, and I grunted from the impact.

I took a few seconds to catch my breath. Then I said, "Is that what happened to Seena Bergman? Is that why she's 'history'?"

"She was blackmailing me!" He looked sad and sullen. "She had all those tapes of a lotta people I helped who—like gettin' kinky sometimes. She set up a camera in her bedroom, f' God's sake! It'd ruin them—and wreck me even worse. She wanted a million bucks for those tapes. *A million bucks!* I couldn' let that happen."

"So you killed her."

"I never touched her, never fucked her, never killed her."

"Who did kill her, then? Your bodyguard—Dan Vetter?"

"Shut your mouth." Another deep gulp.

"I always knew you were more crooked than the Cuyahoga River—but I didn't think you'd be a murderer."

Now his mouth twisted into rage, and he drew back his foot for another kick—but I didn't give him the chance. I butted him in the crotch with my head. The first thing he dropped was his drink—a waste of great whiskey. When I launched myself up at him, crashing my shoulder into his stomach, he dropped the gun, too.

But then I made a mistake; I bent back down to pick up the weapon, and he brought the side of his hand down hard on the back of my neck and laid me flat again. I went down, Fourth of July fireworks exploded behind my eyes, and I pushed myself up onto all fours and shook my head to clear the big black dot in the center of my vision.

Goddammit! I thought. Was this another concussion in the making? That was why I'd hired K.O. in the first place—so I wouldn't get hit in the head anymore.

It took me a few seconds to get my bearings. I heard Hundley's footsteps. He was running now—running away from me. Bad idea. I took hold of the table and dragged myself to my feet, picked up my own Glock, and started after him.

The fresh air made me think more clearly. He was heading up the dock toward shore, going from side to side in a spiffed, serpentine effort not to fall into the harbor. I had no idea where he was going, but when he hit dry land he turned and headed in a westerly direction, away from the restaurant, away from the partying crowd. Still dizzy, I went after him on the dock—hoping I wouldn't get wet.

Or get killed.

My weapon felt comfortable in my hand as I pounded after him. I visited the shooting range at least once a month to stay in practice, but I didn't want to shoot Hundley. I wanted the local police and the federal authorities to take care of him.

Ahead of us, looming against the night sky, were two large buildings, bigger than many warehouses but with wide open doors, and Hundley raced for the nearest one as if his life depended on it. Maybe it did.

With one quick look back over his shoulder at me, he ducked inside, into the blackness.

The last time I played football was in college at Kent State—and even then, not much running was required from an offensive guard. So I was gasping for breath, with a pain in my ribs from exertion when I arrived at the building—perhaps forty-five seconds behind him.

I stopped at the entry, peering into the dark, realizing I was silhouetted against the sky, which glowed from the light of the moon partly covered by clouds. I counted myself lucky, as the county prosecutor didn't have a gun anymore. In his semidrunken condition, Jim Hundley couldn't hit water if he fell out of a boat. Still, I had no idea what I was walking into. I took a few steps inside and let my eyes grow accustomed to the dark.

As I discovered much later, when I asked someone, I was inside what's called a dry stack building. All around me on either side were large racks extending four flights up, in which boats can be stored during the winter when an owner would be insane to allow his vessel to sit in Lake Erie while it froze and thawed and froze again, or if he or she would be out of town or out of commission for a while and needed their water-going property taken care of. Forklifts lifted these large boats up to their assigned berths. In the dark I noticed no forklifts around and assumed they were parked elsewhere.

This was summertime, though, and more than half the racks were empty—many boats, like *The Good Guy*, were docked out in the water, or were off on a trip somewhere. None of them was nearly as large as Hundley's trawler. What piqued my curiosity, though, was why he'd raced in here in the first place.

I stayed very quiet for a moment and listened. I had no flashlight, so I hoped to *hear* where Hundley might be hiding. I didn't hear much—distant music from the Sunset Grille, gentle sloshing of the water in the nighttime breeze about thirty feet from where I stood, and the occasional sound of cars whizzing by on the nearby freeway.

I didn't know if there were doors at the rear of the building for anyone to escape. I began moving slowly around one side of the building. The boats dry-stacked there, so close to me, seemed like ghost ships. I wondered what secrets each concealed.

I heard something—someone—moving around in the dark.

"Hundley!"

No answer, but the noise stopped for a moment. Then it began again, coming from toward the rear of the building. I moved back there, trying to stay in the shadows. "Don't be a damn fool. Turn yourself in to the police—maybe you can work something out."

"Work something out?" His voice was almost soprano, probably from sheer terror, and he sounded as if he'd climbed higher, up to one of the racks off the ground. "So I'll only get twenty years in prison instead of a death sentence? Fuck you!"

"You can't stay in here forever," I said, having moved below where I thought he was. "Come on down before you hurt yourself."

More noise; he was climbing higher. I stuck the Glock back in my waistband where I could get to it quickly if I had to. There was no point in holding it, as I couldn't see to shoot. "You're wasting your time; I'm not climbing up there after you."

No answer. I wouldn't leave him, or he'd be waterborne and halfway to Canada in his boat before the sun came up.

I called out again: "Jim?"

More noise; the racks, made of structural steel and held together by strong galvanized nuts and bolts, groaned a bit. If they supported boats weighing well over two tons, they could survive a middle-aged man in deck shoes climbing all over them.

"Jim, come down," I practically shouted. "Use your head!"

Hundley did not come down. *Something* did. His aim wasn't that good—close enough that it made my right arm useless, as a large chest sailed down on top of me. Later I found out it was full of sheets and towels, but it was damn heavy, and falling at least forty feet as it did, it numbed the upper right side of my body.

Now I wouldn't be able to use the Glock, even if I wanted to. I almost sank to my knees from the pain, even as I sent up a thank-you prayer that the damn thing had not struck me on the head, which, I believe, was Jim Hundley's plan.

I ducked again as I sensed rather than saw something else falling down on me—another chest, a cooler for holding cans of beer and pop. This one was empty; still, I was glad it missed me.

Hundley was looting somebody else's boat up there in the dark. "Hundley, I'm coming up to get you. And when I do, you're going to be so damn sorry!"

A stupid decision, naturally—I wouldn't be able to see where I was climbing, what I could step on, what I could grab to leverage me up. But for a change, luck was with me, as the entire dry stack building blazed with light—a bright glare, as if from a powerful spotlight. I turned toward the entrance, only seeing vague shadows in front of the light. Shading my eyes with my left hand, I recognized the voice at once.

"Hundley! Cleveland Police! Come down from there—you're under arrest!" Tobe Blaine barked.

I turned around and looked above me. Hundley was balanced hanging outside the rail of a cruiser up on the fourth level. The blast of high-powered light in his eyes after spending some time in the dark confused him, blinded him. He waved his arms in front of him as if to brush the light away, staggered a few steps, and pitched over the rail of the deck—landing about seven feet away from me. I found out the next morning that the fall broke his back, shoulder, and elbow when he hit the concrete floor.

He was lucky at that; it's a damn good thing he didn't land on his head.

CHAPTER TWENTY-EIGHT

MILAN

What the hell were you doing chasing the county prosecutor in the first place?" Lieutenant Florence McHargue demanded. "He's a homicide suspect—and that means it's a police case! You private investigators are supposed to stay the hell away!"

It was two mornings later. Jim Hundley had been arraigned the day before and was refused release on his own recognizance—i.e., no bail—so he was cooling his heels off in a hospital room at Metro with two armed cops guarding the door all day and all night. We were sitting in the squad room on the third floor of the Rock Pile—McHargue, Tobe Blaine, Bob Matusen, K.O., and me.

I'd gone to see Special Agent Jeffrey Kitzberger twenty-four hours earlier, despite his being one of the last people in the world with whom I wished to spend another hour, and told him all I'd learned about everybody on the margins of Berton K. Loftus's strange, crooked world. Now the bureau was preparing arrest paperwork for even more crooks who'd played dirty ball with the city councilman and the county prosecutor. The lawbreakers were falling faster than the Dow Jones on a bad day.

Some digging by FBI underlings revealed that Lexia Hundley was in the process of selling her shares of Pequod Managers to, of all people, Jeff and Vicki Ogrin, who owned 30 percent of it already, so she wasn't the innocent bystander she claimed to be. She planned to buy a one-way plane ticket for somewhere like Costa Rica, a country that has no extradition treaty with the

United States, to live with her husband in more or less stinking-rich obscurity.

That plan won't fly, either.

Sunlight streamed through the window. The squad room was on the east side of the building, and on good weather days (Cleveland doesn't have all that many of them) the whole place looked bright and almost cheery, if one doesn't count the panic and the fear and the nasty things that went on here all too often. As usual, things were happening around us even on a pleasant summer morning, but the other detectives paid little attention to our meeting. It was none of their business—unless McHargue told them it was.

"He was *my* suspect who tried getting rid of my client," I said, shifting around in my chair because my right shoulder was tightly taped, courtesy of the Emergency Room at the Cleveland Clinic, and my arm was in a sling. "And he'd tried to wipe out K.O. as well. That's why I went to find him. Detective Sergeant Blaine was looking for him, too—but I knew about his big seaworthy trawler." I looked at Tobe. "Right, Detective?"

"I didn't know what kind of boat he owned," she said. "You told me he hung out at the Sunset Grille, so I was checking it out. I noticed *your* car parked. I thought you were in the Sunset, too, until I saw Hundley running for dear life down the docks like he was on fire, with you on his heels. I guessed there was more to that than something about Bert Loftus, especially when you both disappeared into that dry stack building. My gut told me to call for back-up, and it was my luck—and yours, too, Jacovich—that the squad cars showed up within three minutes, with really powerful flashlights."

McHargue was giving me a look reserved for something that had died several days ago in her basement. I jumped in. "I wasn't going to shoot him, in case anybody's wondering."

"Nobody's wondering," she said. "I have a problem with you going after him in the first place. You have no right to chase down and arrest *attempted* murderers, either."

"In Jacovich's defense," Tobe Blaine said, "no one would sit still for O'Bannion being kidnapped and marked for elimination."

"What I want to know," K.O. said, "is why me? They nailed me in the parking lot of Milan's office." He ducked his head to hide a grin.

"Maybe," McHargue mused, "Hundley made Seena tell him all about you before he had her killed."

I said, "A security camera in the vestibule downstairs in Seena's building took your picture—what time you arrived, what time you left. It was all on tape."

"Yeah, but how did Hundley watch that tape?"

"Uh . . ."

McHargue almost never pays any attention to Detective Bob Matusen, which is why he rarely speaks in the office—or out of it, for that matter. His "uh," coming after an uncomfortable silence, made all of us turn and look at him.

"Listen, don't get mad at me, but . . ."

"But *what?*" McHargue has that scary way of narrowing her eyes when she's angry, and with them now she drilled Bob Matusen.

"Well—Jim Hundley's office called me—his private assistant, I mean. I forget—I think he has three names."

"John Michael Belmont," I supplied. "The Third."

"Anyway, he said that Hundley was demanding to see the security tapes for the last three days. So . . ."

That even got McHargue up on her feet. "You *gave* them to Jim Hundley?"

"Well—he *is* the county prosecutor! I didn't want him getting all bent outta shape about me. Up until he fell out of the sky the other night at Whiskey Island, he was a tough, vengeful guy. So—"

"You let those tapes out of police custody and gave them to someone just because he *asked* for them? Matusen, you dumb *fuck!*"

I've known and dealt with Florence McHargue for fifteen years, most of which she spent disliking me. She'd lost her temper before—but I never for a moment thought she might draw her weapon and blow someone away. Now she looked like an enraged bull about to charge a matador who'd just dropped his sword and cape.

"But," Matusen said, and I won't describe how badly he stuttered over that one syllable, "he's the county prosecutor!"

"County is right," McHargue said, dropping her voice to a near-whisper—more intimidating than when she yelled. "You don't work for Cuyahoga *County*, Matusen. You work for the city of Cleveland—and you don't jump and shit your pants whenever a county D.A. snaps his fingers." The whisper grew, matured, and rolled into a serious clap of thunder. "*And you don't give away evidence!*"

"I only—loaned it to him, Lieutenant."

"Like a lawnmower? Jesus Christ! Well, did you get it back?"

Matusen would probably have exchanged this moment for a root canal or a colonoscopy; I would have, too. "Uh—not yet, no."

Florence McHargue's fists were knotted at her sides. Her whole complexion had turned several shades darker; if anyone had sketched her at that moment, they'd have drawn smoke coming out of her ears. The rest of us—Tobe, K.O., and I—didn't dare move. Finally she leveled one red-tipped finger at Bob Matusen. "My office. Now!" Then she spun on her heel and walked away.

Matusen looked like he was about to cry. "Jesus, guys, I didn't know I was doing anything wrong."

He realized we could do nothing to help him. His chin almost resting on his chest, he rose and followed the lieutenant into her office, and quietly—perhaps too quietly—closed the door.

"Wow," K.O. breathed.

"Sometimes," I said, "Bob's porch light isn't working."

Nobody looked at anybody else for a while. Then Tobe said, "Okay—I'm the new kid on the block. What'll happen to him? A royal ass-chewing?"

"A royal ass-chewing is when it's snowing outside and you say good morning to the lieutenant. This—it doesn't look good."

"I don't suppose we can do anything about it."

"I hope McHargue scares up a scrap of leniency in her heart. Bob has less than three years until he puts in his papers; if she takes his badge and gun, there goes his pension. He'll be lost."

"Tough," Tobe said.

"You don't sound sad, Detective," K.O. said.

"Everybody steps in shit sometimes; cops should be more careful."

K.O. remained sullen. "Jim Hundley was sort of a cop—and he left shitty footprints wherever he went."

"I don't think he started that way," I said. "He got elected—convinced he'd do good things for this county. He *did* some good things. But when you get that big, that important—maybe the most powerful person in this state—your pocket fills up with money and power before you know it. When you start using that power, running everybody else and skimming the top off *their* corruption—and they're all crooks, too—then the whole system looks broken.

"That's why the feds took over—or Cleveland would turn into a totally corrupt city, and nobody'll want to live here anymore. I'd hate seeing that happen. So think good thoughts about Matusen. He'll come out of McHargue's office different from when he walked in."

"Let's not be here when it happens," Tobe said, standing up. "Are my two best buds going to have lunch with me? Dutch, of course—I can't look like a cop taking bribes."

"From the hot dog stand on the corner?" I suggested.

She shook her head. "I want to sit down and eat for a change."

K.O. said, "I'm going to take a raincheck—if that's okay."

"Okay with me," I said. "Where are you off to?"

His cheeks turned more pink than usual. "It's Carli's day off, so I thought I'd run up and have lunch with her."

"Day off?" Tobe said. "You should take the whole day off, too."

K.O. looked startled, but glanced at me with hope.

"You were supposed to be with Carli the other evening and got yourself kidnapped instead," I said. "I guess I owe you a day off."

"Thanks, boss," he said.

"And don't call me 'boss.'"

"Oh. Sorry. Thanks, your Imperial Emperorship. Better?"

"Go away, K.O.," I said.

He did. Tobe and I waited a few more minutes, but no one exited from Florence McHargue's office. It was, as they used to say in those corny westerns when the Apaches were about to attack, *too quiet.* She and Bob Matusen weren't arguing in there; Bob isn't an argumentative kind of guy. He never fit my criteria for being a police officer at all, not in the homicide division. He was a follower, a worker, a meat-and-potatoes guy who wrote good reports. But he was nowhere near being a good hard cop—and in the unwritten job description, that's the number-one requirement.

Tobe, on the other hand—from the moment I met her, I didn't think of her primarily as a police detective at all. But she *was* tough and proved it when she knew enough to find and apprehend Jim Hundley. When we were having lunch that day at John Q's, a great old steakhouse right on Public Square, I did what I should have done at the time: thanked her for being there in the dry stack building on Whiskey Island.

"That's how I make a living," she said, shrugging it off. "Catching bad people who are killers—and keeping people like you from shooting them."

"I was just doing my job, too—trying to stop Hundley from trying to murder Bert Loftus."

Tobe tried not to smile. "Hundley thought he was invincible, like Superman—and for a lot of years I guess he was. The other night, though, he learned a hard lesson: for all his so-called superpowers, he can't fly."

She delicately carved into her steak. "They'll probably charge him with Seena Bergman's murder, too. If Hundley didn't cough up whatever she wanted, she'd have hung him higher than any of the others."

I was eating pasta—there was no way I could have cut a steak with one hand—my left one, at that. "It must have been heavy-duty blackmail to make the county prosecutor strangle her to death and dump her in the park."

"Not personally, of course—he left it up to Daniel Vetter and the other guy—his name was Fred Bondurant, who we arrested yesterday morning. We got *his* name from Vetter, who's all of a sudden not so leathery anymore, all banged up in the hospital and scared to death, and he sang like Whitney Houston. He'll keep on singing until Jim Hundley's wearing an orange jumpsuit. That's how it turned out, but they weren't pros. They'd just do anything Hundley told them to."

"From my end of it—or I should say *our* end, because K.O. was right in there with me—everybody in this town seems to do whatever somebody else asks them to. There's such a long list of politicians and guys who got screwed by them that federal trials will be going on for a decade." I reached for my iced tea. "I'm glad I'm out of it now—unless somebody else tries to rub out Bert Loftus."

"If they do, you're in no condition to handle it," she said. "Not with one hand."

"That's temporary. What about those other guys who were on one side or another of the bribery scandal? What happens to them?" I said.

"I don't care," Tobe said, "whether they go live in a deep, dark dungeon, or all go to some luxury resort in the Caribbean."

"Still," I said, "I'm interested in how they all end up."

"Read it in the papers—like I do."

I nodded, and neither of us said anything for a while.

"I guess," I finally said, "that we probably won't be crossing paths—in our jobs."

Tobe said, "Not in our jobs, no."

"And the rest of it? I mean, with us . . ."

"Whatever happens with us, Milan, it's a mutual decision. You won't sit around waiting for me to make up my mind, and I won't be sitting around, either."

"That's good, then."

"It's good that it is what it is. When it's something else—or *if* it's something else—we'll discuss it."

"You've always dated cops before."

"Yeah, and you fit in there someplace. You *were* a cop, which counts for something. And you're still kind of a cop now."

"Kind of a cop?"

"You don't follow all the rules, or sign in and out every day—but you don't have to deal with Florence McHargue, either."

"I don't have to salute," I said, "or stand at attention, or even shine my shoes unless I feel like it."

"You don't shine your shoes enough, if you want to know the truth."

"In the old days there was a shoe shine parlor on every other block. Now you have to shine them yourself."

"And another thing . . ."

"Oh-oh," I said.

"Because of my hyperosmia—you remember what that is, don't you? My *über* sense of smell? Well, whatever you're putting in your hair gives me a headache."

"I just keep it from blowing around making me look like a maniac escaping from a barber shop."

"Figure out something else. You smell like a French brothel."

"Been in lots of French whorehouses, have you?"

Her eyebrows climbed for her hairline and her eyes sparkled. "How badly do you want to find out?" she said.

So our cases ended at pretty much the same time, with the same culprit involved—former Cuyahoga County prosecutor James B. Hundley. They didn't really nail him for murder in the first degree, or aggravated murder, in the killing of Seena Bergman—but they got him for Murder Two. Despite the desperate gyrations of his lawyer, Curt Wardwell, and the defense attorneys from Wardwell's law firm, he couldn't get off the hook. He also got ten years for each of his bribery convictions, to be served concurrently with his murder conviction. As soon as he's released from the hospital for treatment of his broken back and other broken bones, he'll be heading for prison.

He'll be an old man when he gets out, assuming he doesn't die inside—and that's a big assumption. Hard-bitten cons aren't fond of police officers who've been thrown in there with them, and they particularly dislike district attorneys.

Daniel J. Vetter and Fred Bondurant were easily convicted of murder, too. Vetter got fifty years, uneligible for parole for at least thirty-five of those years. Bondurant got twenty-five to life.

My client went on trial, too, but not for murder. There's no law forcing someone to testify in his own defense, but Berton K. Loftus insisted on getting up there and singing arias from operas no one ever heard of, all pointing out how naughty were the people who had bribed him and whose bribes were skimmed off the top by Hundley. There were twenty-three other names on his bad-boy list that K.O. and I never got the chance to investigate, but Loftus took them all over the side with him. They were later tried and convicted, including Sergei Chemerkin, Donald Kaltenborn, Bill Gorney, Buster Santagata, Reverend Clarence Whitby, Jeff and Vicki Ogrin, and even Lexia Hundley, who was probably less guilty than the rest of them but had cheerfully signed her name to everything her husband illegally owned. She was given a three-year suspended sentence, but she had to report to a parole officer once every two weeks, and did so from a cheap apartment on Lake Avenue because the law took away the Hundley home and cars.

Lieutenant Florence McHargue made it her business to see Detective Bob Matusen demoted to patrolman until his retirement; he was assigned to Buckeye Road, once the Hungarian center of Cleveland but now heavily African American, where he drives a much younger partner around in a patrol car and breaks up fistfights or issues speeding tickets to unruly drivers. I never see him anymore.

All this was many months after both Tobe Blaine and I had closed our cases and gone on to other things. But I still think about it all the time, wondering if the new clowns who've been named to replace the old clowns now in jail are actually going to behave like real people, or remain the clowns that they are.

Here's what astonishes me the most: When Bert Loftus hired me, he'd already been indicted, and the general assumption around town was that he'd go inside for about a decade before he'd see the light of day again. But after he named names and pointed fingers at all the people who aided and abetted his so-called sinful pursuits, and they had the book thrown at them—maximum sentences in most cases—Bert himself was punished by twenty-seven months in a federal lock-up in neighboring West Virginia.

Repeat: twenty-seven *months!*

K.O. has settled into his job with me. We still butt heads once in a while, as we are 180-degree opposites in a lot of ways, and because I'm the one who signs his paychecks, I usually win the arguments.

Usually. Not always.

I still hear, off and on, from my old pain-in-the-behind nemesis, Special Agent Jeffrey Kitzberger, Federal Bureau of Investigation. Not that we're friends all of a sudden; far from it. But I did point him in the direction of several people illegally involved with Berton K. Loftus, and he—or his FBI associates there on Lakeside Avenue in downtown Cleveland—pursued and brought them to trial.

And that's what brought one of the most unforgettable phone calls of my life.

It came with a brisk midmorning ring, about four months after the arrest of Jim Hundley, and when I heard Kitzberger's voice my heart sank into my stomach. I didn't want to deal with him anymore.

His hello sounded cheery—and for the first time he didn't identify himself by his lofty position, as he always had before. He just said, "Hi—it's Jeff Kitzberger," and it took me a few seconds to remember who it was without the "Special Agent" in front of it.

"Hope I'm not bothering you," he said.

Of course he was bothering me; he always does. I chose not to tell him so. "How are you?" I said instead.

"I want to let you know how we're progressing—thanks in part to you."

"Okay."

"The latest is that last night the FBI arrested Jeff and Vicki Ogrin for all sorts of illegal goings-on, financially, regarding Jim Hundley, his wife Lexia, Pequod Managers, and your boy, Bert Loftus."

I was only mildly impressed; as usual, the FBI had dragged its collective feet in amassing enough evidence against the Ogrins to initiate an arrest. A four-month wait wasn't very long at all.

"He's not my boy," I said. "He *was* my client, but case closed."

"So when we got them to a holding cell, we made an interesting discovery."

"What's that, Special Agent Kitzberger?" I enjoyed reminding him he hadn't used his title yet.

"Well—they aren't really husband and wife."

"They aren't?"

"No," he said, and I couldn't believe how delighted he sounded, "they're not."

I took a guess. "Brother and sister? That would explain some things, I guess."

"Incorrect. Wanna try again?"

"I give up. Does that mean I get lovely parting gifts?"

"Ready, Mr. Jacovich? Are you sitting down?"

"I am sitting down, Special Agent Kitzberger."

He sucked in a large breath and then expelled it along with his answer. "Try sister and sister."

Pause.

Pause.

Another pause. I was indeed glad I was sitting down.

"What?"

"I'm sure you heard me the first time. Jeff Ogrin," Kitzberger announced, "was born *Jessica* Ogrin. Vicki's older sister. She—or he, depending on your choice of reference—is a pre-op transsexual. That means," he explained—as if he had to, "that she gulps down enough testosterone every day to float a battleship, but as yet she doesn't have a wiener."

And he started to laugh. I never realized Kitzberger even *knew* how to laugh, but his thoughtless yocks were over something that wasn't funny at all. He was bigoted about almost everything—including *me*.

"Can you imagine a big hippo like that really being a girl? Jesus!"

His cruelty was boiling over the top, annoying me worse than he ever had before. "I've got a question for you, Special Agent Kitzberger," I said.

"Shoot." He was still chuckling.

"When Jeffrey Ogrin gets convicted," I said, "to which prison will they send him?"

And that got the sonofabitch to stop laughing.

Life is never dull in Cleveland.

ACKNOWLEDGEMENTS

Thanks for Dr. Jonathan Sears and Dr. Richard Millstein of the Cleveland Clinic Cole Eye Institute, who made sure I could see well enough to write this book.

Thanks to Dale Finley, who filled me in on local politics and who is a terrific lunch partner.

Thanks for my Whiskey Island expert, Mary Bodnar, for taking me on the tour.

Thanks to Dr. Milan Yakovich and Diana Yakovich Montagino.

And thanks, as ever, to Holly Albin, who makes me a better writer and a better human being.